Forty Years of India-Korea Relations and Looking Ahead

Published by
ACADEMIC FOUNDATION
in association with

INDIAN COUNCIL FOR RESEARCH
ON INTERNATIONAL ECONOMIC
RELATIONS (ICRIER),
NEW DELHI

Forty Years of India-Korea Relations and Looking Ahead

Editors

RAJAT KATHURIA and SANJANA JOSHI

ACADEMIC FOUNDATION
NEW DELHI

www.academicfoundation.com

First published in 2014
by

ACADEMIC FOUNDATION
4772-73 / 23 Bharat Ram Road, (23 Ansari Road),
Darya Ganj, New Delhi - 110 002 (India).
Phones : 23245001 / 02 / 03 / 04.
Fax : +91-11-23245005.
E-mail : books@academicfoundation.com
www.academicfoundation.com

in association with the
Indian Council for Research on International Economic Relations (ICRIER),
New Delhi.

Cataloging in Publication Data--DK
Courtesy: D.K. Agencies (P) Ltd. <docinfo@dkagencies.com>

India-Korea Dialogue (12th : 2014 : New Delhi, India)
Forty years of India-Korea relations and looking ahead / editors, Rajat Kathuria and Sanjana Joshi.
p. cm.
ISBN 9789332701243

1. India--Relations--Korea--Congresses. 2. Korea--Relations--India--Congresses. I. Kathuria, Rajat. II. Joshi, Sanjana. III. Title.

DDC 327.540519 23

Typeset by Italics India, New Delhi.

Printed and bound by The Book Mint, New Delhi.
www.thebookmint.in

Contents

About the Editors/Contributors

Editors:

Rajat Kathuria is Director and Chief Executive, Indian Council of Research on International Economic Relations (ICRIER). He has over 20 years experience in teaching and 10 years experience in economic policy, besides research interests on a range of issues relating to regulation and competition policy. He worked with Telecom Regulatory Authority of India (TRAI) during its first eight years (1998-2006) and gained hands on experience with telecom regulation in an environment changing rapidly towards competition. His role entailed analysis of economic issues relating to telecom tariff policy, tariff rebalancing, interconnection charges and licensing policy, and his research eventually formed the basis of tariff and interconnection orders applicable to the industry. He is currently on leave from the International Management Institute (IMI), New Delhi, where he teaches Managerial Economics and International Trade. He has published in international and national journals, besides in popular magazines and newspapers. He has an undergraduate degree in Economics from St. Stephens College, a Master's from Delhi School of Economics and a PhD degree from the University of Maryland, College Park.

Sanjana Joshi is a Senior Consultant with ICRIER. She has been working on East Asia from an Indian perspective for several years, and was Japan Foundation Research Fellow affiliated with the University of Tokyo (August 2000 to July 2001). Her published work includes *Changing Japan: Opportunities and Challenges for India* (2008) in addition to various articles and papers in several journals and newspapers. She has an MPhil in International Relations from Jawaharlal Nehru University, New Delhi.

Contributors:

Choong Yong Ahn is currently the Foreign Investment Ombudsman and responsible for resolving grievances raised by foreign investors in Korea and also Distinguished Professor of Economics at Chung-Ang University. He is former Chairman of the Presidential Regulatory Reform Committee (2010-2012). While on sabbatical from Chung-Ang University, he also served as the President of the Korea Institute for International Economic Policy (2002-2005); Chair of the APEC Economic Committee; Chair of Board, Choheung Bank; consultant to the World Bank; UNIDO Chief Technical Advisor to the Economic Planning Unit of Malaysia to design Malaysia's industrial master plan; and served as President of several academic societies in Korea including the Korea International Economics Association, Korean Association of Trade and Industry Studies, and the Korea Econometric Society. Since receiving his PhD from Ohio State University, he has published many articles in prestigious international journals.

Divya Chaudhry is currently pursuing her Masters in Economics from Ambedkar University, Delhi, and holds a Bachelor's degree in Economics from the University of Delhi. She has been a consistent recipient of academic scholarships at the post-graduation level and secured meritorious positions during graduation. Her research interest is in key development sectors such as education, health and nutrition.

Choongjae Cho is a research fellow and head of South Asia team at Korea Institute for International Economic Policy (KIEP). Prior to joining KIEP, he was a researcher at Daewoo Economic Research Institute and Lotte Economic Research Institute. He also worked for The Seoul Economic Daily as a reporter. He is an expert on Indian Economy and the economic cooperation between Korea and India. He holds a PhD in Economics from Hankuk University of Foreign Studies.

Jung-il Choi is former Ambassador of Korea to India. He joined the Ministry of Foreign Affairs in September 1975 and during his distinguished career, has served as Ambassador to the Federal

Republic of Germany, Chief of Protocol MOFAT, Director-General Treaties Bureau, Aide to the Minister of Foreign Affairs, and Trade and Deputy Director-General North American Affairs Bureau. He graduated from the Department of International Relations, Seoul National University, and later he studied at the Royal Institute of International Affairs (RIIA), London.

Ram Upendra Das is Senior Fellow at the Research and Information System for Developing Countries (RIS), New Delhi. In his research career of over 20 years, he has conducted and supervised a number of studies for various institutions including the ADB, Commonwealth Secretariat, ILO, EXIM Bank of India, SAARC Secretariat, UNDP, UNESCAP and the World Bank. He has also contributed to various studies, including the inter-governmental Joint Study Groups (JSGs), and international negotiating processes on behalf of the Government of India with countries and groupings such as Sri Lanka, Pakistan, Nepal, Maldives, SAARC, Thailand, ASEAN, Singapore, GCC, Indonesia, Malaysia, Australia and New Zealand. He was a member of the Track II Study Group of the CEPEA under the East Asia Summit process. He contributed to drafting of the SAFTA Treaty and SAARC Agreement on Trade in Services for the SAARC Secretariat. His most recent books include *Perspectives on Rules of Origin* (2011) and *Regional Trade and Economic Integration* (2012). He obtained his PhD and MPhil degrees in Economics from the Jawaharlal Nehru University, New Delhi.

Kim Do-Young majored in Chinese language and literature along with English literature at Korea University, Seoul. He completed his MA and PhD in English Literature at Jawaharlal Nehru University, New Delhi. His work has served as backbone for Korean language education in India. He has established Korean BA and MA programmes at Jawaharlal Nehru University and part time, full time, MA, MPhil Korean programmes at the University of Delhi. He has published a variety of Korean language education material in India including *International Korean Grammar* (2010), *Bharati Korean Basic, Intermediate, Advanced* (2009), *Korean-English Students' Dictionary in Romanized & Hindi Pronunciation* (2013) and *English-Korean Students Dictionary* (2009). In recognition of his devotion towards Korean language development, he has been awarded with the Korean National Award for Culture by the Korean Government.

Changho Kwag got his PhD degree in economics at The University of Texas at Austin, USA, in 1991. He worked as a research fellow in the Investment and Finance Research Institute from 1991 to 1994. In 1994, he joined the POSCO Research Institute (POSRI) as a research fellow. He worked for the Korean government as counsellor for the Prime Minister of the Republic of Korea in the year 2000, and also advised the Korea Fair Trade Commission from 2001 to 2003. From 2005 to 2009, he worked for POSRI Delhi Office as chief representative and studied Indian steel and iron ore markets, FDI environment and how to improve bilateral relationship between India and Korea. Now, as Managing Director of POSRI, he is conducting in-depth research on the global steel industry, FDI environments in some major countries like China and India. He is also deeply involved in mapping POSCO Global Strategy. He has published several papers in renowned international journals and each year participates as speaker in about four to five international conferences on steel and steel making raw materials.

Daewoo Lee is working at POSRI Steel Research Center as a Senior Principal Researcher. He graduated from Korea University in Business Administration and received a master's degree at KAIST (Korea Advanced Institute of Science and Technology). His main research area has been the steel industry of China and India. He has worked at POSRI Delhi Office from 2007 to 2011 as a representative.

C. Raja Mohan is a Distinguished Fellow at the Observer Research Foundation, New Delhi, where he is leading the Strategic Studies Initiative. He is also a foreign affairs columnist for *The Indian Express*, a Visiting Research Professor at the Institute of South Asian Studies, Singapore and a Non-Resident Senior Associate at the Carnegie Endowment for International Peace, Washington, DC. He is currently a member of India's National Security Advisory Board and has served there earlier during 1998-2000 and 2004-

2006. Earlier, he was a Professor of South Asian Studies at the JNU, New Delhi and the Nanyang Technological University, Singapore. He was the Henry Alfred Kissinger Chair in Foreign Policy and International Relations at the Library of Congress, Washington, DC, during 2009-10. Dr Mohan served as the Diplomatic Editor and the Washington Correspondent of *The Hindu* and the Strategic Affairs Editor of *The Indian Express*. His area of expertise includes India's foreign and defence policies, asian security, arms control and disarmament, and the impact of rising powers on the global order.

Ali Mehdi is a Consultant at ICRIER, New Delhi. He pursued MA and PhD on Indian public health policy at the Albert-Ludwigs-Universität Freiburg (Germany) with a full fellowship under the Excellence Initiative of the German government. His master's thesis was recently published by Springer, Heidelberg. Before his sabbatical from ICRIER to pursue his PhD, he co-authored ICRIER working paper on *Impact of Preventive Health Care on Indian Industry and Economy*, whose research findings were covered in more than 70 major newspapers across the world, and taken up for consideration by India's Ministry of Health and Family Welfare as well as global health care giants like GE Healthcare and CIGNA International. He also co-authored ICRIER working paper on *Health Care Delivery and Stakeholders' Satisfaction under Social Health Insurance Schemes in India*. He has also written journal articles and columns, presented papers at international conferences on issues relating to Indian health policy.

Neetika Kaushal Nagpal is a postgraduate in Economics and Finance from the University of Warwick, UK. She has more than four years of experience in economic policy research. Her areas of interest include tax policy, tax administration, international trade and investments. She is currently engaged in a Ministry of Finance project on estimating cost of compliance of direct taxes in India. Her other assignments include a study on cross-country comparison on India's General Anti-Avoidance Rules (GAAR). She is also co-editing a book on *Global Economic Cooperation: Views* *from G20 Countries* with Rajat Kathuria. Her publications include journal papers, book chapters, working papers and media articles.

Changhee Park is Associate Professor of Military Strategy Department at Korea National Defense University in Seoul. He received his MA in National Security Affairs from the Naval Postgraduate School in Monterey, CA and PhD from Korea University in Seoul. He was a member of Executive Course #04-1 at the Asia-Pacific Center for Security Studies at Honolulu, Hawaii. His research area is China's military affairs, war and strategy, and national security affairs. Some of his writings include: *On Military Strategy* (in Korean); *Why China Attacks: Geostrategic Vulnerability and its Military Intervention* (in English); *Enhanced Sino-Russian Relations and its Implications for Security of Korea* (in English); and *China's Military Strategy in the 21st Century* (in Korean), among others.

Vyjayanti Raghavan is Professor and Chairperson of the Centre for Korean Studies at the School of Language, Literature & Culture Studies, Jawaharlal Nehru University, New Delhi. Some of her recent publications are *Korean Wave in India: Present Status and Future Prospects* (co-authored, 2012); *Comparative Security Dynamics in Northeast Asia and South Asia* (co-authored, 2010); "China's Rise and the Korean Peninsula" in Srikanth Kondapalli and Emi Mifune (eds.), *China and its Neighbours* (2010); *India and Korea through the Ages: Historical, Religious and Cultural Perspectives* (ed., 2009); *A Text Book on Korean Culture* (co-authored, 2008) and "Security in Northeast Asia: Alternative Scenarios" in Chandra Chari (ed.), *War, Peace and World Hegemony in the Twenty-first Century* (2007). She has been a Visiting Scholar at Yonsei University, ROK, and a Senior Research Fellow at the Academy of Korean Studies. She is the Co-President of the Association of Korean Language Educators in India and has been on the Board of Studies of Banaras Hindu University, Chairman of the Pacific-Asia Conference on Korean Studies for a year and a member of its Executive Committee for a number of years. She has a Master's degree in Korean History from Seoul National University and a PhD from the Department of Disarmament, School of International Studies, Jawaharlal Nehru University.

Saon Ray is a Senior Fellow at ICRIER. Her areas of interest include international trade, industrial economics, microeconomics, and applied econometrics. Her teaching experience includes microeconomics at Jawaharlal Nehru University and international trade, globalisation, competition policy and economics of regulation at TERI University. She has worked in the area of trade policy, technology transfer, foreign direct investment, efficiency and productivity issues, behaviour of firms, energy, and climate change related issues. She has worked on projects on free trade agreements and trade creation effects, the textile industry, India's ethanol blending policy feedstock, upgradation of firms in the garments industry in India, and demand and availability of feedstock for the petrochemical industry. She is currently engaged in projects that examine the impact of American investment in India; link between climate change adaptation and competitiveness of cities; implications of commodity transaction taxes and evaluating India's participation in global value chains. She has publications in various national and international journals as well as in edited books. She has a PhD in Economics from Jawaharlal Nehru University on the role of intellectual property rights in transferring technology to developing countries.

Nisha Taneja is Professor at the ICRIER, New Delhi. Her broad areas of interest include regional trade, transport, industrial economics and institutional economics. She has worked extensively on South Asia. Some of her research work has been on trade and transport facilitation, non-tariff barriers, and informal trade in South Asia. She has also worked extensively on various aspects of India-Pakistan trade, Indo-Nepal trade and India-Sri Lanka trade, India-Korea and India-Japan trade. Her work is a key contributor to the SAFTA negotiations and to the ongoing negotiations on Indo-Pakistan trade. She has served on committees set up by the Government of India. She received her PhD in Economics from Jawaharlal Nehru University, New Delhi.

Skand Tayal is a Visiting Professor at the Department of East Asian Studies, University of Delhi. He joined the Indian Foreign Service in 1976 and served in Indian Missions in Sofia, Warsaw, Geneva and Moscow. He was India's Consul General in Johannesburg and Houston, and Ambassador of India to Uzbekistan. In 2008, he was posted as Ambassador of India to the Republic of Korea. He has wide experience in both bilateral and multilateral diplomacy and has been a frequent speaker on contemporary affairs. He has a postgraduate degree from Indian Institute of Technology, Kanpur.

Message

It gives me great pleasure to contribute a congratulatory message to the commemorative volume *Forty Years of India-Korea Relations and Looking Ahead*. It is a formidable task to attempt an examination of the ever-evolving engagement and interaction between two of Asia's major cultural, political and economic entities, and I congratulate the various contributors and all those associated with the production of the book.

The ancient cultural and historical links between India and Korea have been reinforced in modern times on various fronts. In the past century, as two young nations, India and Republic of Korea (ROK), have played an important role in each others' advancement through steadfast mutual support and understanding. Based on the friendship established early in our existence as nations, and the subsequent establishment of diplomatic relations in 1973, our ties have grown from strength to strength.

This is especially true of the new century which has witnessed prolific growth in our exchanges. Economic engagement has often been seen as the bedrock of our partnership in recent years. It is significant to note that while our economic and trade relations have indeed provided an important and vibrant platform for interaction, our ties in the political, security and cultural spheres have gained unparalleled momentum. The establishment of Strategic Partnership in 2010 is indicative of the importance both countries attach to our ever-expanding cooperation. With the steady flow of bilateral visits over the past decades, expanding dialogue mechanisms in a number of areas and thriving trade and people to people relations, the stage has been set for an unprecedented growth in our bilateral ties.

It is thus a meaningful undertaking at an important juncture to attempt an examination of our interaction in the past 40 years, as well as the unique possibilities and promises that the future holds for our countries. The book gives an overview of the various aspects of our interaction including its past, present and future. I am happy to note that it draws the viewpoints of a cross-section of experts.

I once again offer my congratulations to all who have been associated with this historic project, and conclude with the firm belief that this book will make significant contribution to existing literature on the subject and speak to diverse audiences including all those who have an interest in the India-ROK relationship.

—Salman Khurshid
External Affairs Minister
Government of India

Message

I offer my sincere congratulations on the publication of *Forty Years of India-Korea Relations and Looking Ahead,* a commemorative volume celebrating the 40th anniversary of the establishment of diplomatic relations between Korea and India. I think it is very meaningful to reflect on the development of Korea-India relations and present a vision for the future at this point in our history.

Since Korea and India established diplomatic relations on December 10, 1973, the bilateral cooperation has flourished in a wide range of areas spanning the political, economic, cultural and social fields. In its initial phase, the bilateral trade recorded a mere 15 million dollars and there was virtually no bilateral investment. Today, our annual two-way trade stands at 20 billion dollars, while bilateral investment has reached 5 billion dollars. Such thriving economic relations led to the conclusion of the Comprehensive Economic Partnership Agreement in 2010, serving as the basis for the further expansion of Korea-India economic cooperation.

Furthermore, people-to-people exchanges increased significantly, with more than 150,000 Koreans and Indians travelling between the two countries annually. As a result, there is now a deeper sense of awareness, understanding and appreciation of each other's cultures and societies.

Korea and India have fostered strong political and security relations beyond economic and cultural relations. Friendship between the leaders of our two countries have been further strengthened through exchange of visits. In addition, Korea and India have put in place various mechanisms for dialogue between the two countries and also engage in close consultations and coordination in various regional and multilateral fora with a view to developing a common policy response on security and strategic issues of mutual concern such as counter-terrorism, piracy, non-proliferation of weapons of mass destruction, and energy security.

This continued nurturing of thriving ties led to the milestone agreement to establish a strategic partnership in 2010, with the aim of deepening and expanding bilateral cooperation in a wide range of areas including politics and security.

Korea and India are now embarking on a new journey toward the next four decades. With the tremendous achievements of our two countries over the last four decades as a firm basis, we will seek to further deepen our cooperation and work together to rise to the challenge of the various global issues we face, thereby contributing to the ushering in of a new era of happiness of the international community as well as of our two countries' peoples.

Given the current geopolitical and geoeconomic dynamics of international relations, there is still tremendous potential for the further deepening of cooperation between Korea and India. I am confident that the shared values of democracy and the market economy will serve as a basis for our two countries to play a proactive role in shaping the global agenda for peace, prosperity and security.

Forty Years of Korea-India Relations and Looking Ahead sets out a powerful articulation of ideas by scholars and experts from the two countries on the past, present and future of the bilateral relations. The scholarly contributions in the volume cover a wide array of areas encompassing political, security, economic, education and cultural aspects of Korea-India bilateral relations in the past, and also set out important tasks for the future development of our strategic relations.

It is my firm belief that this volume will serve as a valuable guidance for enhancing understanding of Korea-India relations among readers. In closing, I would like to thank all the contributors for their efforts in making this valuable project possible.

—Yun Byung-se
Minister of Foreign Affairs
Republic of Korea

Acknowledgements

ICRIER has a long standing vibrant research and dialogue engagement with the Republic of Korea. The most notable is the Annual India-Korea Dialogue organised by ICRIER and the Seoul Forum on International Relations (SFIA) alternatively in New Delhi and Seoul. The 12th India-Korea Dialogue was held at New Delhi on October 24-25, 2014. The papers presented at the 9th dialogue have been brought out as a book by ICRIER, while the papers presented at the 10th dialogue have been brought out as a book by SFIA.

This book is a continuation of ICRIER's endeavour to foster mutual understanding through dialogue among scholars, industry representatives and policy-practitioners on contemporary issues relating to Indo-Korean relations.

We acknowledge the generous support received from the Embassy of Republic of Korea at New Delhi and the Ministry of External Affairs, Government of India, for the publication of this book and convey our deep appreciation of the same.

Introduction

Rajat Kathuria and Sanjana Joshi

The financial crisis of 2008 that grew into a full blown economic crisis triggered what has come to be termed as the 'new interventionism' around the world. The US pumped billions of dollars into banks and auto companies as part of a revival package that saw the government take 'strategic decisions about strategic industries.' Similar aggressive industrial policies were developed in Japan, United Kingdom, China, France, Germany and South Korea (herein after referred to as Korea).

These actions are not new. Intervention to improve functioning of markets has been a time tested instrument employed around the world with varying degrees of success. For example, industrial policy that targeted manufacturing played a crucial role in Japan, Korea and more recently, in China to boost exports, promote domestic jobs and lift GDP growth. A key element is devising appropriate ways in which the state can supplement for market failure and facilitate structural change. But it is also possible that state intervention could be counterproductive. Therefore, states that possess a well-informed, effective bureaucracy embedded in the realities and needs of local industry are more likely to succeed.

Both in India and in Korea the recent decline in growth momentum has obliged a search for new sources of growth, including a stronger role for government and policy. A more reform minded India and a Korea having entered the ranks of the Organisation for Economic Co-operation and Development (OECD) are well placed to reap rewards of an economic partnership that arguably is a text book case for the Ricardian doctrine of comparative advantage. The Comprehensive Economic Partnership Agreement (CEPA) of 2010 between the two countries however needs nurturing, and the extent to which this can be done will crucially depend on the political and international situation, including significantly the role of China in the region.

There are, however, several reasons for optimism. Bilateral trade between India and Korea is more than US$ 18 billion, and Korea's cumulative investment in India exceeds US$ 2 billion. Numerous high-level exchanges have taken place across several dimensions such as culture, education, labour and tourism, and these bode well for the future. Korean companies such as Samsung, Hyundai and LG are household names in India that have 'localised' significantly to lay the foundation for robust economic and political relations ahead. The recent visit of Korean President Park Geun-hye to India in January 2014 reflects the weight placed on the relationship by both countries.

The present volume is a compilation of papers commissioned by ICRIER to mark the 40th anniversary of the establishment of diplomatic relations between India and Korea. The endeavour has been to review the evolution of India-Korea relations as well as highlight the opportunities and challenges in the coming years. We hope that the volume will be an enriching addition to the existing literature on India-Korea relations.

Since the formal establishment of diplomatic ties between India and the Republic of Korea in 1973, the two countries have made significant progress and are today strategic partners. In the words of Ambassador Vishnu Prakash: "The relationship is firmly anchored in a commonality of mutual interests and outlook." However, as Ambassador Lee Joon-gyu points out, "Korea and India began to factor in each other in their economic and strategic calculus only recently and the vast potential of our strategic partnership still remains untapped."

Chapter one by Jung-il Choi presents an overview of the past, present and future relations between India and Korea. He points out that the rich experience of relationship building and accomplishments prove how much the two countries have achieved over the years. However, according to him, the two countries possess much more potential and should direct their energies to achieving this. The complementary economic structure promises a great deal of mutual benefit and the strategic locations of the two countries mean a formulation of powerful partnership that can project peace and stability throughout Asia. How such strategic partnership will unfold in years to come will critically depend on discussions and consultations at various governmental levels, as much as private and commercial sector cooperation.

Chapter two by Skand Tayal traces the journey of India-Korea relations to the advent of Buddhism in Korea highlighting the fact that the first direct and long-lasting contact between the two distant lands had a spiritual and intellectual basis. In recent times, the two countries have shared a similar history of colonisation, struggle for freedom and painful geographical partition. However, for a long time, political relations remained frosty in the context of the Cold War and diplomatic relations were established only in 1973. According to him, India and Korea today once again share a similar world view and it would be in the long-term interests of both these democracies to work towards a multi-polar Asia.

Chapter three by Changhee Park analyses Korea-India security relations and their future direction. He argues that the security relations between the two countries should develop further into a strategic partnership. According to him, there exist clear limits in enhancing the strategic linkage due to different strategic aims, security issues, and perceptions on China and Japan. Nevertheless, there is much room for Korea and India to strengthen their strategic ties, and enough reason why they should do so. The changing global power dynamics shaped by the rise of China and exhausted America provide middle powers Korea and India the opportunity to play a more active role in regional peace and stability. The enhancing Korea-India strategic cooperation will contribute to a 'healthy balance of power' in Asia. What the two countries need to work on is the big picture of basic principles, strategic aims and linkage of issues, and also more practical way of interaction.

The fourth chapter by C. Raja Mohan examines the changing geopolitics of Asia and consequentially discusses the imperatives for enduring and strategic cooperation between India and Korea. According to him unlike in the past, when Asia was a mere theatre of confrontation for Western powers, today the regional actors have considerable capacity to shape the strategic outcomes. That is true especially of India and Korea. The changed nature of their domestic capabilities, the absence of any clash of national interests, the growing comfort among the political elites of the two countries, and the larger circumstances in Asia make it possible and very necessary for a stronger strategic partnership between India and Korea. Greater security cooperation among the two middle powers of Asia, without prejudicing their pre-existing special relationships, will contribute to regional stability and reduce the vulnerabilities arising from twists and turns in great power politics.

Chapter five by Choong Yong Ahn provides an overview of the evolution of Korea's unique economic development in terms of industrial and trade policies over time as they have adjusted to changing market environments at home and abroad. He then goes on to explain some practical lessons and policy implications for India-Korea economic cooperation. Overall, the main message of this paper is that Korea's policy instruments designed for trade expansion and industrial development toward a matured advanced economy have been automatic, transparent and moving toward an open trade regime step by step. With regard to India-Korea economic cooperation given the outward-looking and liberalising economic orientation, economic diversity, and factor endowments inherent in India and Korea, the two countries are likely to benefit from each other by maximising the potential benefit of the CEPA. Also as global economic gravity shifts to Asia, the mutual cooperation of two like-minded countries, India and Korea, can serve as an important step toward the early completion of the Regional Comprehensive Economic Partnership (RCEP) and eventually the Asia-Pacific economic community.

The sixth chapter by Rajat Kathuria highlights the key role of institutions in Korea's successful transformation from a domestic economy based on agriculture to a leading world industrial power. According to him, part of the reason that economic reforms were much more efficient in Korea is due to their sound governance mechanisms. By contrast, institutional capacity and implementation has been weak in India. While India can certainly learn from Korea's experience, it must devise policy solutions that are appropriate to its unique context. This means creating appropriate institutions that are accountable and transparent; it means devising policy initiatives that clearly spell out long-term goals and above all, it means focused implementation. Only then will India be able to replicate the success of countries such as Korea that showed that transitioning from a low-income to high-income country is possible in a single generation.

Chapter seven by Choongjae Cho examines the steps that should be undertaken to further enhance bilateral economic cooperation between India and Korea. He compares India-Korea economic relations with India's economic relations with Japan, Singapore and China in terms of trade, foreign direct investment (FDI) and free trade agreement (FTA). The objective is to derive lessons for strengthening the economic partnership between India and Korea. He points out that Korea's performance in economic cooperation with India is poorer as compared to that of Japan, Singapore and China, and that if economic cooperation does not result in significant accomplishments for both countries, their relationship will weaken.

The eighth chapter by Ram Upendra Das analyses the implications of the CEPA for India-Korea trade in goods and services. This is done by analysing the bilateral macro profile of trade in its varied dimensions, followed by an analysis of tariff liberalisation commitments by both countries and the rules of origin formulation in the CEPA. He points out that the India-Korea CEPA has covered vast ground in terms of tariff liberalisation and rules of origin formulation, in a manner that is contrary to popular expectations of low trade coverage and complexities in Indian rules of origin. In trade in services too, the CEPA provides a good base to be built upon further through mutual recognition agreement (MRAs) and more effective market access in sectors and modes of mutual export interests.

Chapter nine by Changho Kwag and Daewoo Lee points out that the CEPA agreement symbolises an ever improving relationship between Korea and India. The paper analyses the impact of the agreement on the bilateral FDI relationship. The authors' first finding is that after the CEPA bilateral investments have shown increasing trends; however, a quantitative analysis using bilateral investment intensity suggests that the agreement has had a negligible effect on bilateral FDI flows. This implies that some follow-up measures must be taken to boost bilateral investment. Secondly, general performances of Korea and India in drawing FDI are below the global average, implying that the two governments should make efforts to draw more FDI. The paper concludes with policy recommendations for both countries.

The objective of Chapter ten by Saon Ray, Nisha Taneja and Neetika Kaushal Nagpal is to identify the potential areas for harnessing services trade between India and Korea. The paper discusses existing trade, future trade complementarities and market access barriers in four sectors of mutual interest: information technology (IT), transportation, construction and audio-visual services. The analysis shows that there are strong complementarities in services sectors such as IT, transportation, construction and audio-visual services which can be accentuated by further liberalising trade and movement of natural persons. The authors feel that by deepening cooperation in areas of mutual interest and taking measures to provide more effective market access by removing substantial barriers to bilateral trade in services, both countries can benefit by gaining a competitive advantage in the global supply chain.

Chapter eleven by Kim Do-Young traces the development of Korean studies in India. According to him as the Korea-India relationship intensifies, there has been an unprecedented increase in the demand for scholars specialising in the field of Korean studies. There has been marked development in this regard but there are certain issues that have to be addressed to improve quality. These include more research activity in area studies, improvement in the course content, increase in fellowships to Indian students to study in Korea and greater number of native Korean faculty.

Chapter twelve by Ali Mehdi and Divya Chaudhry presents the findings and analysis of the motivational factors and the varied experiences of Indian students in Korea based on an online survey that they conducted last year. The survey responses show that there are a number of cultural issues that negatively affect the experience of Indian students in Korea. These include language, limited intercultural understanding between teachers and students, limited exchange between Indian and Korean students and society, and limited personal time and leisure. The authors conclude with a set of recommendations that could be considered by relevant Korean policy makers and institutions to enhance educational exchange and the experience of international, especially Indian, students in Korea.

The final chapter by Vyjayanti Raghavan suggests that cultural factors have also played a significant role in the slowdown of FDI inflows from Korea to India in recent years. The first part of the paper highlights the larger cultural differences that Koreans encounter in India which start at the level of difference in language and extend to behavioural dissimilarity, human nature and work ethics. She then goes on to identify some core non-verbal cultural concepts of a Korean society which would be useful for Indians to imbibe while interacting with Koreans. With the help of a survey conducted online, the author also describes the cultural differences experienced by Indians in Korean firms.

The India-Korea strategic partnership is still a work in progress. India is an emerging global player, while Korea, having created economic ascendancy, is ready to play a meaningful role in global affairs. It is hard to imagine any pair of countries that are geographically so far apart and with varied and distinct national characteristics, to have succeeded in cementing such a close partnership over a short span of time. What began as a minimum level of interchange and relationship has transformed into a strategic partnership with high expectations for the future. As we celebrate 40 years of the establishment of diplomatic relations, we look at the future with optimism to build a long-lasting friendship that could even transcend national level relations and provide an archetype of a mutually beneficial relationship contributing to global peace and prosperity. How such a strategic partnership will unfold in years to come will critically depend on cooperation and commitment between the various levels of government and between the private sector and academia, among others. The scope and potential for cooperation is substantial for both the countries to rejuvenate efforts to build on the strong foundation that has been established in the last 40 years.

1 Overview of Korea-India Relations

Past, Present and Future

Jung-il Choi

Introduction

Entering the 21st century, Korea and India established a strong and robust cooperative relationship. After a rapid growth for almost half a century, Korea transformed itself into an economic powerhouse of north-east Asia. India also experienced rapid economic development starting from the 1990s, and by 2000, established itself as a new contender in an increasingly polarised global arena. It was in such an atmosphere that Korea and India reached new heights in formulating a relationship.

The facts and figures depicting the relationship between Korea and India are quite extraordinary. Bilateral trade stands at almost US$ 20 billion, contrasting significantly with a figure of US$ 15 million recorded back in 1973. Two-way foreign direct investment (FDI) stands at US$ 4 billion, contributing greatly to the economic growth of Korea and India. Politically, Korea and India established strategic partnership relations in 2010 and numerous exchanges of high-level government officials are continuing in all areas. Ministerial level exchanges are frequent, such as in the areas of foreign affairs, defence, finance, commerce, education and culture. Cooperation on issues such as maritime security, freedom of navigation, maintaining a stable balance of power, and putting in place an open and inclusive regional security architecture are amongst the many items that Korea and India are actively engaged in.

As the two countries celebrate the 40th anniversary of the establishment of diplomatic relations, the rich experience of relationship building and accomplishments prove how much the two countries have achieved over the years. But Korea and India possess much more potential. Their complementary economic structures hold the promise of more cooperation to their mutual benefit. Politically, the strategic locations of the two countries mean the formulation of a powerful nexus in Asia that can project peace and stability throughout Asia. Other relations in the cultural and social fields also promise fruitful development, based on robust people-to-people interchange. How such cooperation will unfold between the two countries as the 21st century progresses will be interesting to observe and predicting its direction, a useful endeavour.

Perspectives on the Analysis of Korea-India Relations

Relations between Korea and India could be viewed from different perspectives. From the historical viewpoint, the relations can be traced back almost two millennia. The legendary Queen Ho of the ancient city of Ayodhya in India visited the southern part of the Korean peninsula and later became Queen to King Suro of the Gaya Kingdom in Korea. The early age relations flowered through the spread of Buddhism from India to Korea, where Buddhist monks from Korea and India visited one another as part of religious interchange. From a modern political viewpoint, the interactions between the two could be viewed from the perspective of global politics, philosophical influence of great thinkers of India on Korea during the era of imperialism and in the post-independence period through the string of events that constituted the aftermath of World War II and the ensuing Cold War between the United States (US) and the Soviet Union. A final perspective could come from the economic standpoint.

The economic viewpoint is also an offspring of the working of global politics manifested in the form of international trade. The General Agreement on Tariff and Trade (GATT) of 1947 ushered in a limited form of free trade, mainly because of the formation of the Communist trade bloc. In this way, international trade could be viewed as having been dependent on the political landscape of the Cold War, a period during which Korea and India played a somewhat limited role in the global economy and in trade. This certainly changed as the Soviet Union disintegrated in the early 1990s and with it, the international economy globally integrated under the new World Trade Organization (WTO) regime of 1994. Korea-India's relations, in the form of economic exchange, deepened significantly with these developments, and with it, new ways of interactions between the two countries emerged.

As Korea-India relations entered the 21st century, diverse forms of interactions emerged. Primarily fuelled through economic relations, other areas of exchange such as art, education, tourism and media entertainment began to develop. It is noteworthy that such expansion of areas of exchange could also be viewed from the perspective of the overall trend of globalisation and the advance of information technology (IT) and transportation, significantly reducing the cost of information exchange and human-to-human interaction. Korea-India relations, viewed from such a perspective, could be analysed as being dependent on world politics and its ramifications, which took shape in the form of globalisation.

Historically, India takes credit for being one of the significant players in the global arena. Its unique position as the cradle of major religions, including Hinduism and Buddhism, is well recognised. The Non-Aligned Movement, espoused by the first Indian Prime Minister Jawaharlal Nehru, presented a third factor in the bipolar world crafted by the US and the Soviet Union. But then again, on the economic front, Korea's strategy of engaging in industrialisation based on export rather than following the then popular import-substitution strategy became a dominant development model to be followed later by most developing countries.

Looking at Korea-India relations from a global perspective, it is interesting to note that bilateral relations were influenced by global events, but not entirely governed by them; rather, in some ways, it shaped them as well. On the question as to where the relations between Korea and India should be heading, these viewpoints could present a workable schematic framework.

Some Notes and Implications of Pre-modern Era Interactions

Legend has it that Queen Ho of the Indian city of Ayodhya visited Korea and subsequently became the Queen to King Suro, the founder of Gaya Kingdom in the southern part of the Korean Peninsula. It is probably based on visits of Indian ship-merchants looking for trade routes and business opportunity in Asia, following the coastal sea lane from Eastern

India to Southeast Asia and northward from Indochina all the way up to Korea and Japan. Southeast Asians, Koreans and Japanese were more or less familiar with Indian traders and Middle Eastern seafarers who ventured into far-east Asia. Gaya was a well-known maritime trading kingdom, its booming international business based on triangular trade connecting the Japanese, Korean and Chinese sea coasts. With the main export item being high quality iron products, Gaya was a strong contender for influence in the Korean Peninsula alongside other bigger adversaries such as Baekjae and Shilla Kingdoms of the Korean Peninsula. The legend of Queen Ho, as chronicled in Samgukyusa, one of the oldest historic texts in Korea, lends credence to its international trading presence.

The records of interaction among Buddhist monks are well chronicled in Korean and Chinese historical texts. During the heydays of Buddhism in India in the era of Gupta Empire, prominent Buddhist monks are said to have visited the Korean Peninsula and preached Buddhism. Ado, Bimarachikche, Nonggata and Bultasengga are some of the names recorded in historic scripts, who are said to have visited ancient kingdoms in the Korean Peninsula and helped spread Buddhism. It is interesting to note that as Buddhism was accepted as the primary religion in all Korean kingdoms, the visits of Korean monks to India increased. The facts that Indian names such as Ananyabalma, Janasampada, Sarvajanadeva and Parampujya were given to Korean monks, that several visited Northern India and even studied at Malinda monastery are well recorded, giving a glimpse of the extent of people-to-people exchange during the period, despite the difficulty of transportation and the sheer distance that separated the two countries.

It is worth noting that the Gupta era marked the golden period of Buddhism as a world religion. It was the governing religion and influenced art and philosophy in most of Asia. The Chinese, Korean and Japanese kingdoms and dynasties all accepted Buddhism as an official state religion as did Southeast Asian kingdoms. The religion led to the development of Buddhist architecture, designs, frescos, and related arts that still remain to this day and are the major philosophical lynchpins that link Asian countries with a common identity. At the centre of developments was India, which projected such a powerful religious and philosophical impact on Asia including Korea; Korea naturally looked to India for enhanced understanding of Buddhism and with it, for commercial interests as well. It is also interesting that unlike the projection of other world religions such as Christianity and Islam that went side-by-side with military and territorial expansion, the spread of Buddhism was anchored more on pure religious tenets, perhaps combined with an artistic and philosophical influence, but never used by Indians for territorial expansion. Buddhism was certainly used by local converts as a new and superior form of religion to overtake other neighbouring contenders for supremacy, but rarely did Indian missionaries form an alliance and attempt to dictate Indian influence under the cover of Buddhism.

Korea's Economic Projection and the Formation of Modern Era Relations

Relations between Korea and India in the modern era, especially after the independence of the two countries, cannot be viewed without keeping in mind the context of the global environment during the Cold War. When the two superpowers were vying for global supremacy, Korea and India took singularly different paths. Whereas Korea relied on the support of the US and other western countries to undertake the task of nation building following the devastating Korean War, India chose to spearhead the Non-aligned Movement under the leadership of Prime Minister Nehru, first maintaining equidistance from both the US and the Soviet Union but later tilting toward the Soviet Union after entering into the Indo-Soviet Friendship Agreement in 1971. The interactions between Korea and India during the period were minimal, to say the least, even after the establishment of diplomatic relations in 1973. It should be understood that Korea was in no position to actively engage in bilateral relations with other countries. Its economic resources were minimal, barely enough to ignite a spark of economic growth. At the same time, Korea was faced with the economically and militarily superior North Korea, constantly threatening the South's very survival. At this time, Korean diplomacy was centred on maintaining a continued alliance with the US, gaining favourable views of the South against the North in multilateral fora such as the United Nations (UN), and seeking economic support from other western countries. With India maintaining equidistance both from the South and the North, and given the limited diplomatic resources that South Korea had, the relations between the two countries were severely restricted.

It is interesting to observe that at present, the relations between Korea and India are centred on economic relations. But the origin of such relations could be traced back to much earlier times. While the positioning of Korea as an ally of the US and India's independent stance not siding with either the US or the Soviet Union led to limited bilateral interactions, a sort of a breakthrough was initiated by Korea's extraordinary economic growth, described as the Miracle of Han River, which catapulted Korea into the ranks of a developed economy in a matter of just 30 years. The economic development strategy of Korea, based on an export-oriented economy, was not new at that time, its success having already been demonstrated by Korea's neighbouring state, Japan. By the 1970s, Japanese products overwhelmingly dominated the global market with its superior price competitiveness and product quality. Korea imitated its strategy. But this is where the similarity ends. Japan had already achieved industrialisation in the early 1900s, and only needed to recuperate from the aftermath of World War II, with its highly trained and disciplined manpower and infrastructure hardware left more or less intact without significant destruction. Korea, on the other hand, lacked any of Japan's industrial hardware or manpower foundation, and with the near total destruction of the entire Korean Peninsula due to the Korean War, the recourse to an export-oriented strategy for economic growth, by all reckoning, was a bold and decisive step in the direction of rapid industrialisation.

The bold decision of the Korean government to adopt an export-oriented economic development strategy must be viewed in the context of the governing economic principle at the time. Not independent from the historical legacy of just having escaped the clutches of colonialism, any move of newly independent states to approach the western market was viewed with much suspicion. Despite the formation of the GATT regime in 1947, the usual norms for the new states were to close its market, raise a high-tariff wall, and engage in substituting goods from developed countries with indigenous production, the so-called import-substitution strategy. FDI from developed western countries was viewed with great suspicion, as 'imperialist capital' disguised to penetrate the market of developing countries and to reduce them to a 'neo-colonial' state. Having suffered gun-boat diplomacy, where opening of port and trade was a standard way of spearheading colonial expansion, such weary views on foreign trade and investment could be well understood, as India also followed a similar path. Nevertheless, the Korean government, under the leadership of the late President Park Chung-hee, resorted to an export-oriented economic development strategy, marshalling its meagre financial resources into building factories and plants aimed at producing export ware destined for developed countries markets. This proved to be the starting point of a model success story for economic development in the 20th century, which was duly followed by countless other countries, including China, which demonstrated another giant economic leap.

Korea's export-oriented economic policy, despite its intrinsic belief in more liberal trade and the Ricardian theory of comparative advantage, was based on the straight forward reasoning of earning hard currency by selling goods, by whatever means available. As the then popular song of Saemaeul Undong chanting "Jal Sal A Bose (Let us all be well-off)" depicts, Korea was desperate to escape prolonged and chronic poverty, and viewed exports as the most sensible method to attain the stage of "Jal Sal A Bose." Such dogged trudging along the path of economic growth would ultimately find its way even into India, as its bilateral trade volume took off starting from the 1970s; along with it, political relations also started to warm up. In its relations with India, Korea did not intend to use the export-oriented development strategy to bypass and overlook the non-aligned stance of India. But the result was, nevertheless, the same. Korea was able to foster a close relationship with India through bilateral trade, something Korea would never have accomplished while maintaining its alliance with the US. And this economically driven relationship was destined to evolve into a new dimension as India adopted a more liberal economic stance following the trend of economic globalisation in the 1990s.

Touching on the economic trade figures of the 1970s, two-way trade between Korea and India amounted to a mere US$ 15 million, US$ 3 million worth of export, from Korea to India in 1973. This trade figure increased exponentially to US$ 170 million in 1979 (see Table 1.1), more than a 10-fold increase, in a matter of six years. The export volume from India touched US$ 87 million, an almost 30 times increase. As for political exchanges, there were limited interactions during this period. The Minister of External Affairs Swaran Singh visited Korea in 1974 followed by Minister A.B. Vajpayee in 1978. On the Korean side, the Minister of Foreign Affairs,

Yongshik Kim, visited India in 1972 followed by Dongjo Kim in 1974. There were a few Members of Parliament of both the countries paying reciprocal visits, but the extent of high-level visits, let alone working level visits, were limited and certainly did not match the extraordinary growth and development demonstrated on the economic front.

Table 1.1

Korea's Trade with India, 1973-1979

(million dollars, %)

Year	*Export*	*Rate of Increase*	*Import*	*Rate of Increase*
1973	3	-72.3	12	173.1
1974	5	79.1	22	88.2
1975	7	43.7	39	76.6
1976	11	73.1	34	-13.0
1977	21	79.3	23	-31.8
1978	78	227.8	39	69.9
1979	87	11.9	83	111.4

Source: Korea International Trade Association.

New Phase of Economic Relations in the 1990s

The export-oriented strategy proved to be a winning formula throughout the 1980s and went on high gear with the end of the Cold War and the conclusion of the Uruguay Round in 1994. The level playing field in international trade and the reduction in tariff barriers meant that a country with international competitiveness would be the winner in the field of international trade. Korea became one such winner, having honed its trading skills for the past three decades and continued onward with its immense trading capabilities. A newly liberalised Chinese economy helped Korean trading drive even further. India was not an exception to this newly established international trade order and Korean goods found the Indian market a lucrative one. Korea enjoyed a trade surplus of approximately US$ 200 million per year throughout the 1980s, and the figure increased further in the 1990s. Korea's global presence as Asia's trading powerhouse and a newly industrialised country raised its status and profile significantly; it did not go unnoticed by Indian foreign policy makers.

Korea's export-oriented strategy was followed by yet another bold economic move. Whereas the export-oriented strategy was formulated by the Korean government, the outward flow of capital in the form of FDI was initiated by Korean companies. It is especially noteworthy that FDI to India began as early as in 1982. As labour costs in Korea rose, Korean companies looked to other countries including India for cheaper labour, and embarked on joint collaboration in such areas as auto parts, TV components and other mid-stream supply chains. By 1990, major companies from Korea—Samsung, Hyundai, LG—began to establish minor production facilities in various cities of India. For a country that posted a per capita GDP of around US$ 3000 in the 1980s, the outward FDI, still viewed with suspicion as 'capitalist intrusion,' then undertaken by more advanced Korean companies was considered a novel initiative. In the context of relations with Korea, the foundation for more robust political relations would not have been possible only with increased trade alone.

The presence of numerous Korean companies doing good business with significant localisation in India raised awareness regarding Korea amongst Indians as a country worth studying at least for its economic development experience, if not as a rising Asian country with which good relations should be maintained. Korea's clean slate as a country that suffered under colonial rule in the 20th century with no trace of any imperialist imprint also altered the perception of FDI in India, where any extensive FDI undertaken by companies of Western developed countries would have been viewed with more suspicion.

In bilateral trade, only goods are transported between the two countries with minimal people-to-people interaction. FDI is different from simple trade, requiring substantial understanding of a recipient country by foreign investors on all aspects from its politics to economy to social issues to legal framework, and such other relevant information in order to make the investment a successful one. Especially in the form of green field investment, the presence of factories and plants built by foreign investors and subsequent employment of local labourers, followed by actual marketing and selling of the products in the local market inevitably lead to a closer understanding between the two countries through private entities. The understanding is also dependent on how harmonious such business undertakings are between the foreign investors and the local employees, and between foreign investors and consumers.

Trade volume between the two countries stood at more than US$ 2 billion and total inflow of FDI from Korea to India hit US$ 200 million by the mid-1990s. Political relations began to warm up between Korea and India, and led to the blossoming of high-level interactions between officials, going all the way up to summit-level exchanges. The first-ever visit to Korea by an Indian Prime Minister, Mr Narasimha Rao, took place in 1993. The visit was reciprocated by the Korean President Kim Young-sam in 1996 and by Prime Minister Kim Jong-pil in 1999.

Economic relations were the primary driving force for the deepening of the political relationship, but there were several other factors in play as well. Korea, by the early 1990s, had begun to use its economic resources and confidence to be more proactive in international relations. The buk bang weigyo or 'nord politik,' under President Roh Tae-woo, embarked on establishing diplomatic relations with the newly democratised countries in the Communist camp. Following the establishment of diplomatic relations with China, Russia and other eastern European countries, Korean diplomacy gained new confidence and looked proactively towards building closer relations with other countries with which it had limited contact, primarily due to the Cold War stand-off. Korea's economic strength provided the necessary resources for such a diplomatic endeavour.

India also gradually distanced itself from the non-aligned movement, and began to seek space in the new global landscape after the collapse of the Soviet Union. "Look East" became the new buzzword of Indian diplomacy as it looked toward Asia for closer ties. The Association of Southeast Asian Nations (ASEAN), with its increased economic presence, became the centre of India's new diplomatic initiative. But China's increasing influence in the region also alarmed India, which viewed the area as a traditionally pro-Indian region, not only due to its proximity, but also due to long-standing historic and cultural relations. India enlarged the scope of its "Look East Policy" by including mainland China, the Korean Peninsula, and Japan as well. India's increasing involvement in regional fora such as Asia Regional Forum (ARF), East Asia Summit (EAS) and Asia-Europe Meeting (ASEM) also demonstrated India's increasing willingness to create a more robust bond with Asian countries, but again, the main focus was on ASEAN countries. This was aptly demonstrated by a series of high-level meetings. In the early 1990s, India held summit meetings with Thailand, Vietnam, Malaysia, Singapore and Indonesia.

It should be noted that both Korea's and India's diplomatic endeavours in this period toward one another were not of a primary character, but rather a peripheral one. Korea's diplomatic engagement and direct interest remained with building new relations with East-bloc countries, especially with China and Russia. India's "Look East Policy" also maintained primary interest in forging closer relations with ASEAN countries. Seen from this perspective, both countries were inclined to probe the potential of the other in terms of forging closer relations and in terms of the usefulness and resulting benefit from closer relations in an increasingly volatile international environment. The two countries found the new international environment challenging and began working towards building a new security framework in the backdrop of the power vacuum created by the disintegration of the Soviet Union, first by securing more stable relations with their immediate neighbours and, once such relations had been achieved, looking further to the next tier of neighbouring countries.

Viewed in this way, the economic ties between Korea and India had placed the countries ready to engage in closer interaction, but economic ties had to wait their turn until more pressing and immediate concerns with neighbouring states were addressed. Prime Minister Rao's visit to Korea in 1993 and President Kim's visit to India in 1996 were a litmus test of the potential of their future relations. Such exchanges continued for another two decades until a strategic partnership was finally reached.

Forging of a Strategic Partnership and Beyond

Korea and India agreed to establish a strategic partnership in 2010, during President Lee Myung-bak's visit to India. By 2010, bilateral trade volume was US$ 17 billion and Korea's cumulative investment in India stood at more than US$ 2 billion. Numerous high-level exchanges were made and other areas such as culture, education, labour and tourism witnessed increased cooperation. A Comprehensive Economic Partnership Agreement (CEPA) was also agreed upon in 2010, setting an important foundation for economic cooperation. Korea, now a global powerhouse with the 15th largest GDP and the 8th largest trade volume, was well poised to look for a country that could provide added security and economic benefit. India was a natural candidate for such a strategic partnership in southern Asia. Again, economic considerations were at the top of the list—India's billion-strong market provided Korea with trade and investment opportunities when the rest of the world was becoming increasingly saturated and competitive. It is also worthwhile to note that India's support of any endeavour by Korea was much sought after during the Cold War era when India often sided with North Korea in many multilateral fora. Securing more solid support and cooperation from India probably satisfied South Korea as having finally captured a much sought-after Indian verdict on who had the upper hand on the Korean Peninsula.

India's choice of selecting Korea as a strategic partner involved more mixed considerations. Korea's economic resources, especially in the form of capital and technology, were beneficial to India's economic growth and development. But increasingly, China's rising power was another factor in selecting Korea as a strategic partner. Korea's middle-power status was a favourable factor in its politico-economic considerations. India's wariness about the possibility of foreign capital overtaking India's domestic market was still strong, despite the opening up of its economy through the last two decades. This continued to be the case even though foreign companies were supplying Indian consumers with affordable and highly competitive goods and services, increasing general welfare. Korea enjoys relative freedom in this respect and it partly explains the reason behind the huge success of Korean electronics, automobile and other goods in the Indian market, apart, of course, from the fact that Korean products do enjoy global competitiveness.

The Joint Statement signed during the occasion of President Lee Myung-bak's visit in 2010 outlined a broad and ambitious roadmap of the direction that the strategic partnership envisaged. The statement outlined expansion in various areas of bilateral relations including defence, trade, science and technology, information and communication technology, education, and culture. The CEPA was recognised as the bedrock of a new comprehensive partnership, which had the capacity to promote regional growth and to contribute to prosperity and economic development in Asia.

In the political and security cooperation area, it was agreed that summit and working-level diplomatic meets would be held on a regular basis; it was also agreed that the two countries would cooperate in the manufacture of military equipment. Agreements on strengthening cooperation in IT, peaceful use of outer space and nuclear energy were the main items for cooperation in the science and technology domain. Cooperation in the international arena was also included, with the two countries having agreed on close co-ordination in the EAS, ARF, Asian Cooperation Dialogue (ACD), and ASEM processes, common commitment on nuclear disarmament and the non-proliferation of weapons of mass destruction and recognition of the legitimate and long-term interests of both countries in peace and prosperity in the Asia-Pacific region. While many items were enumerated, the main focus of the cooperation again centred on economic issues, clearly demonstrating that the nature of ties between Korea and India revolved around economic issues.

The strategic partnership between Korea and India, as has been the case in almost all their bilateral relations in the past, must be viewed in conjunction with global affairs, in order to gain some understanding of and insight into how the partnership will play out in the future. Considering that much of the two countries' bilateral relations centred on economic affairs, the world economic situation will play a significant part in determining how the strategic partnership will materialise in the economic field.

The weakening of the global economy through a series of financial shocks has already provided some snapshots of what is in store. In this case, one scenario depicts India undertaking more aggressive economic reform and liberalisation to cope with the international economic situation. Under this scenario, Korea would become a welcome partner. As it has done in the past, Korea will provide capital and technology to boost India's economic potential and fuel its continued growth. Korea will enjoy a more business-friendly atmosphere and make use of India's huge domestic market and labour force. All the co-operative areas enumerated in the Joint Statement will come into play.

An alternate picture may have a detrimental effect. This would be similar to the pre-1990s era, when India would cringe from international economic fluctuations by isolating itself from the global economy. This would mean that much of the foreign capital inflows would be curtailed and foreign companies' business in India would be severely restricted. Korea would not be an exception. With much of economic cooperation cooling down, bilateral relations between Korea and India would also be restrained.

Which direction Indian economic policymakers will choose will depend on the domestic political as well as international situations. But the China factor will not assume an insignificant portion. Economic rivalry between India and China does not stay within the framework of the international economic realm alone. It translates into supremacy in Asia as reflected in military spending and other resources directly affecting various means of projecting influence. Continuing its relentless economic growth, China has already far surpassed India economically, and the discrepancy in military presence is growing as China charges on with the modernisation of the People's Liberation Army and other military arms. India will face domestic pressure to safeguard its economy from external ups and downs, but at the cost of forgoing economic growth and at the risk of falling further behind China. India risks the annual growth rate of a meagre three to four per cent, while China still has enough momentum to move along at seven per cent. India will be increasingly under pressure to accelerate its reform and liberalisation agenda.

From the Korean side, it should be noted that for the past 50 years, every administration belonging to all political spectrums has upheld the export-oriented economic policy and outward looking stance in economic activity. The difficult international economic atmosphere will only strengthen such a stance, given that Korea's economic size cannot provide enough market for all its companies and producers if it were to limit its foreign exposure. The question is whether Korea will choose India as a priority destination for trade and investment.

Korea successfully implemented its outward-looking economic policy, but this was not done equally across-the-board. Some choices were involved in selecting primary trade and investment destinations. Of emerging markets in the 1990s, China, India and Vietnam were the main destinations. Market sizes were the primary attractions in the case of China and India, while Vietnam also conferred advantageous economic conditions that were suitable for the then labour-intensive, light industries of Korea. Similarities between India and China are many, but the extent to which Korean companies ventured into China and India differs significantly. This began to take place after China's entry into the WTO in 2002 and with it, transparency and rule of law in business and commercial activities were strengthened. Whatever China's shortcomings, this single event boosted China into an internationally acceptable level of business environment and with it, China was able to attract not only giant multinational companies that could withstand the until-then unfavourable business conditions in China, but also small and medium-sized companies from all over the globe, including from Korea.

Table 1.2

FDI into India

(billion dollars)

2006-07 FY	2007-08 FY	2008-09 FY	2009-10 FY	2010-11 FY	2011-12 FY
22.8	34.8	37.8	37.7	30.3	46.8

Source: Indian Ministry of Commerce and Industry.

Whether India walks the same path will govern the future of Korean companies doing business in India. Until then, big Korean companies will command a presence in India. Samsung, Hyundai, LG and others will be the primary players. Those lesser known companies will more or less work in India in conjunction with other bigger Korean companies as first and second tier suppliers. Most of Korea's US$ 2 billion of accumulated FDIs to India are from such multinationals.

India, starting from the new economic policy back in the early 1990s, has come a long way in fostering a business friendly environment, of which many companies in the world took advantage. If the economic element is to be a decisive factor for Korea-India relations, then Korea should continue to invest in India. The big companies' investment is already there. Any increase in the investment of big companies will have to come from increased returns and profitability from previous investments. In the automobile and electronics market, the potential is still there, as an increasing number of middle-class Indians demand such products. But more robust economic relations require not only investment by big multinational companies, but small and medium-sized companies as well.

This will require reform at a level similar to that which China underwent through its accession to the WTO.

Another way to boost bilateral trade and investment is to create common goods and facilitate commercial activities between the two countries. This can take the form of an agreement in the field of aviation, maritime shipping, tax, tariff, labour, immigration, government procurement, education and other government services that can lay a favourable institutional infrastructure. Another way is to explore public sector collaboration that can spur private sector cooperation. The Joint Statement mentions IT, space and nuclear energy. But other areas such as renewable energy, commercial aviation, ports and railways all hold great promise and potential that could lead to greater private sector involvement.

Trade is an important economic linkage between the two countries but more than trade, it is bilateral investment. Like with trade, if Korean investment into India continues, and reaches a critical level, Korea will view India in a different light. This is because after this critical mass of investment, Korea will need to take numerous measures to safeguard its investment. This will come in all forms, such as legal instruments, closer political ties and other measures that will make sure that Korean investment is safe. India will also need to factor in the value of Korean investment, taking into account the generation of jobs, products and other welfare measures that benefit India. If such a level is reached, then bilateral relations of Korea and India will enter an entirely new dimension.

If the economic dimension of the relationship between Korea and India is determined proactively by Korea with its drive for continued outward expansion, and passively by India with its continued liberalisation and reform of its economic structure, the political dimension will be more evenly matched by reciprocal and balanced interests between the two countries. What prompted India to engage in the Look East Policy will become more prominent. As the 21st century progresses, the unipolar world that initially shaped the world will increasingly become multi-polar. China will continue its economic growth, gaining ever more clout in global affairs. Other players such as India will also demand more power-sharing, which could lead to an unstable and unpredictable international landscape. Selecting and maintaining good relations with strategic partners will be a key to successfully navigating such uncertain waters in the future. From a geographic perspective, Korea and India will go ahead and select power-contenders from different regions of the world, and as a strategic partner, India and Korea are attractive partners. India is a regional hegemon in South Asia. Korea is new economic powerhouse in Northeast Asia. Korea's proximity to China gives India an extra reason to have Korea as a strategic partner.

The partnership will manifest in many forms. The most likely will be in the form of international collaboration on new global issues. Unlike in the past, when most global issues revolved around issues pertaining to political stand-offs, the issues of the 21st century are more diverse and affect the international community in more complex ways, requiring collective participation to resolve them. A single hegemonic country cannot single-handedly solve them. The resolution will have to be multilateral and require close cooperation, exchange of ideas and the building of consensus. It is in such an environment that Korea and India are increasingly asserting leadership on international issues. This is natural, given the fact that India was always vocal on global issues, while Korea strives to become a more respected and responsible member of the international community. Environmental issues are one of them, ranging from green growth, alternate energy, nuclear development, climate change, arctic development and numerous others.

There are plenty of other issues where the usual path-setters in the past are increasingly constrained by their national interests. It is in these areas that Korea and India can assert new agendas and initiatives. Non-traditional security issues are also areas that promise greater collaboration. Disaster relief, humanitarian assistance, regional cooperation in combating piracy, and search and rescue operation are some of the areas where Korea and India are already collaborating. Korea, like all other Asian countries, has an immense stake in maintaining stable maritime shipping line from the Gulf states, and around the Indian sub-continent, and onto Southeast Asia. Most of Korea's oil and natural gas are shipped through this route, as is a sizeable volume of maritime trading. Continuous engagement of India by Korea on maritime issues is of great importance to both countries.

Conclusion

The Korea-India strategic partnership is still a work in progress. At the end of the Cold War, both countries faced a new international environment and sought to proactively take initiatives. India has always been a global player, while Korea, now having the economic resources, looks for new ways to engage the world and to take a meaningful role in global affairs. As the world gets increasingly polarised, Korea and India are a good match to face challenges and work together to proactively resolve them.

Korea and India have proven to be great partners over the past 40 years. What began as a minimum level of interchange and relationship evolved into a strategic partnership aiming for even greater peace and prosperity. In the context of both Korea and India, it is hard to find two countries, which are as far apart geographically and have different national characteristics, succeed in having forged such a close partnership. Celebrating the 40th year since the establishment of diplomatic relations, Korea and India are well positioned to cooperate closely to build a long-lasting friendship that could even transcend national level relations and provide a fine example of a mutually beneficial relationship that could contribute to global peace and prosperity.

How such a strategic partnership will unfold in years to come will critically depend on discussions and consultations at various levels of governmental, private and commercial sector cooperation. Whatever the results, there certainly will not be a shortage of issues and areas of cooperation that will help forge strong relations between Korea and India.

2 Looking Back at 40 Years of India-Korea Relations and Future Perspectives

Skand Tayal

Introduction

The Indian subcontinent and the Korean Peninsula are home to two ancient and highly developed civilisations dating back to the dawn of history. Millennia of creative endeavour by artists, intellectuals and artisans have enriched the two cultures and the peoples of peninsular 'Bharat' and 'Koryo' were among the most evolved societies of the ancient and medieval world.

The first direct and long-lasting contact between the two distant lands was spiritual and intellectual. The vast land mass of China between the Indian and Korean peninsulas was the bridge for two-way exchange of thoughts, philosophies and Buddhist theology. Records establish that a monk, Marananta, from the then North-West India preached extensively in the Southern part of the Korean Peninsula in the ancient Paekche Kingdom in the 4th century.

After the advent of Buddhism in Korea, Korean monks journeyed to the universities and monasteries of India since the 6th century. Taebom and Hyecho are perhaps the most well-known Koreans in this tradition. This exchange of students, scholars, monks and seekers lasted till the 14th century when monk Dhyanabhadra came to Korea in the year 1326 and visited many monasteries over a period of two years. This rich and important link was snapped with the decline of Buddhism in India.

Intellectuals and freedom fighters of the two countries again became conscious of India and Korea from the third decade of the 20th century. The two countries were experiencing the scourge of colonisation and looked towards each other for inspiration to gain freedom and independence. India's nationalist leader with an international outlook, Jawaharlal Nehru, wrote appreciatively of the Korean struggle for independence, particularly the March 1919 movement. Korean thinkers and particularly the popular newspaper *Dong-a-Ilbo* discussed Mahatma Gandhi's strategy of non-cooperation.

The cement to this intellectual bond between Korea and India was provided by Gurudev Rabindranath Tagore, who had a large number of Koreans among his audience during his several journeys to Japan. Deeply troubled by the plight of the Koreans under the heavy-handed Japanese rule, Tagore penned the famous lines in 1929 which became a source of inspiration and optimism in Korea:

> In the Golden Age of Asia
> Korea was one of its lamp bearers.
> That lamp awaits to be lighted once again
> for the illumination of the East.

The Korean nation as a whole offered a touching tribute to this great poet and philosopher by installing a bust of Tagore in the bustling area Daehangno in central Seoul in May 2011.

Evolution of Bilateral Relations

The end of the Second World War ushered in a new world. Korea witnessed the end of colonisation with the defeat of Japan in 1945 but fell under Trusteeship because of big power machinations. India won freedom in 1947 and the two countries share the same date of independence—15 August. But both the countries had to bear the pain of partition, Korea on ideological grounds as a victim of East-West rivalry and India on religious grounds. Pre-occupied with their respective existential struggles, India and the Republic of Korea (ROK) did not have much time for each other in the initial couple of decades of their independence. There was little contact till consular relations were established in 1962.

Korea was prominent in the post-independence activities of both the Indian Ministry of External Affairs and the Ministry of Defence. The Indian delegation to the United Nations (UN) and Indian diplomats like K.P.S. Menon played a prominent role in the deliberations over the 'Korean

Question.' India was Chairman of the UN Temporary Commission on Korea (UNTCOK) as well as the Neutral Nations' Repatriation Commission established after the tragic Korean War (1950-1953) for the repatriation of the prisoners of war of the two sides. The exceptionally efficient services rendered by the 60th Indian Field Ambulance in the Korean War to both combatants and civilians are remembered with affection and gratitude by the Koreans to this day. India was honoured with a plaque by the President of Korea in 2010 on the day of remembrance of the 60th Anniversary of the Korean War.

However, political relations remained frosty in the context of the Cold War and superpower rivalries. Although both the Indian Prime Minister Jawaharlal Nehru and the Korean President Syngman Rhee were nationalistic and had strong personalities, their world views were different.. Nehru saw Rhee as a rabid anti-communist dictator and Rhee assessed Nehru as a crypto-communist. Also, India nursed the hope of early re-unification of the two Korean entities until the 1960s.

As a manifestation of India's evolving non-aligned policy, India treated both the ROK and the Democratic People's Republic of Korea (DPRK) in an even-handed and equitable manner till DPRK chose to endorse the Chinese line in the unfortunate India-China border conflict of 1962. With the fading away of President Syngman Rhee, the new leadership of ROK under President Park Chung-hee had a fresh look at India as a force ranged against the Peoples' Republic of China. Both ROK and DPRK had opened their Consulates General in New Delhi in 1962 and some tentative steps were taken to encourage bilateral cultural activity. However, because of a tight budgetary situation, India opened its Consulates in Seoul and Pyongyang only in 1968.

The beginning of 1970s ushered historic changes on both the Indian and Korean Peninsulas. In 1971, Indian military intervention led to the emergence of Bangladesh. Rapprochement between US and China led to some nervousness in both Koreas and the opening of direct dialogue between the DPRK and ROK in 1972. ROK finally gave up its unrealistic 'Hallstein Doctrine' in 1972, which required that other countries recognise it as the sole representative of the undivided nation of Korea.

ROK's efforts to upgrade relations with India to ambassador level received a positive response from India. Kyu-hap Choi visited India in August 1973 as the special envoy of President Park Chung-hee. India also sent a mission to Seoul to study the desirability of raising the level of bilateral relationship. Eventually, India announced on December 10, 1973, its decision to establish full Ambassador level diplomatic relations with both ROK and DPRK.

The relations started on a hopeful note. The Korean Ambassador to India during 1976-1980, Lee Bun-suk, later rose to become the Foreign Minister and subsequently the Prime Minister. The first Indian Foreign Minister to visit Seoul was Sardar Swaran Singh in August 1974. However, the 1970s may be termed as the 'Lost Decade' for the growth of bilateral relations between ROK and India. India, at that time, faced serious internal disturbances, a period of emergency (1975-1977), the chaotic interlude of the Janata Regime (1977-1979) and the return of Indira Gandhi as the Prime Minster in 1980. ROK witnessed enviable economic growth led by exports but on the back of suppression of labour and human rights.

The relations were nurtured by the two foreign offices in a formal manner without any long-term vision or expectations of a future close relationship. ROK Foreign Minister Dong-jo Kim came to India on a goodwill visit in April 1975, which was reciprocated by External Affairs Minister Atal Behari Vajpayee in August 1978.

There is some indication that the Park Administration looked at India as a source of nuclear technology. The Chairman of ROK Atomic Research Institute came to India in October 1973, but India decided to cooperate with ROK only through the International Atomic Energy Agency (IAEA). The decade ended with the assassination of President Park in October 1979.

In the 1980s, ROK caught the attention of the world as an emerging economic powerhouse, a source of heavy machinery and ships, and an exporter of engineering and manufactured goods. Indian planners looked at the 10 per cent annual growth rate of ROK with envy and had a fresh look at the overall relationship. In the 7th Non-aligned Summit at New Delhi in 1983, India played a moderating role on the discussion over the Korean Peninsula and it was well appreciated in Seoul. Although authoritarian, General Chun Doo-hwan's regime also started to marginally re-orient ROK's US-centric foreign policy to enhance engagement with the developing world. And, India was one of the new focus areas of ROK's diplomatic initiatives.

Korean Foreign Minister Bum-suk Lee's January 1983 visit to India and External Affairs Minister P.V. Narasimha Rao's return visit in May 1983 took the dialogue further. The deliberations led to a significant decision—a proposal for the first ever Presidential visit from ROK to India. Both sides moved quickly and India was one of the destinations for President Chun's five-country trip in October 1983.

At that time, India had some reservations about a close political relationship with the ROK leadership and focused more on strengthening economic contacts. A Trade Promotion and Economic and Technical Cooperation Agreement had been signed in 1974 and another agreement for cooperation in the field of science and technology in 1976. Two-way trade had risen to US$ 500 million in 1982, augmented by the acquisition of a floating oil drilling platform by Oil and Natural Gas Corporation (ONGC) for the Bombay High Offshore fields and import of around 30 Korean small and medium ships by Indian shipping lines. India's major export was naphtha and other chemicals, iron ore, etc. India's Minerals and Metal Trading Corporation (MMTC) had a long-term contract with Pohang Iron and Steel Works (POSCO) to supply 2-3 million tonnes of iron ore annually.

The primary objective of President Chun's visit to India was to give a new direction to the India-ROK economic engagement and raise it from a mere trading relationship to a higher level. ROK was keen to offer technology to develop India's coal mines. India was keen to invite Korean companies to invest in newly established free-trade zones for manufacture in 100 per cent export-oriented units.

Nevertheless, in those days of early contacts, India chose to keep some distance from the unpopular Chun regime. India did not respond favourably to the ROK proposal to create a ministerial level bilateral joint commission. The Korean Sherpas for the visit were understandably unhappy when India declined to have a joint communiqué after the visit, which is a normal practice. Perhaps the formulation on the situation on the Korean Peninsula would have posed a formidable drafting challenge to the two sides. As it so happened, the tour was called off in Burma in the aftermath of a terrorist attack on the ROK delegation in Yangon.

The growing bilateral relationship had a slight hiccup when India refused to lay all the blame on the Soviet Union for the shooting down of a Korean Airlines flight by the Soviet Air Force on September 1, 1983, when it had strayed over Soviet airspace. The reason why the Korean plane drifted so far from its flight path was never credibly explained. I was an Under Secretary in the UN Division at that time and had handled the incident. The view of Indian Air Force was that in a similar situation, if a foreign civilian plane was to fly over sensitive Indian airspace without flight clearance and would not respond to the ATC, they would have also taken offensive action against the unauthorised flight.

In the mid-1980s, the world, including India, took increasing notice of the miracle on the Han. ROK's international prestige grew when it won the bid to host the 10th Asian Games in 1986 and the Summer Olympic Games in 1988. The boost in bilateral relations came from ROK Prime Minister Cho Shin-yong's visit to India in March 1986 and his very fruitful meeting with Prime Minister Rajiv Gandhi. ROK agreed to participate in the development of Paradeep Port, particularly for enhanced export of iron ore. But the proposal fell victim to procedural delays and policy ambivalence on the Indian side and could not be implemented despite Korean willingness. This was a missed opportunity for opening a new door for bilateral collaboration leveraging Korean skills in the construction of ports and shipyards.

By the end of 1980s, the practice of regular dialogue between the two foreign ministers had been established. In May 1987, External Affairs Minister N.D. Tiwari made a very successful visit to Korea. In September 1987, Prime Minister Rajiv Gandhi dispatched Planning Commission member Y.K. Alagh to Korea to study the policy framework for the country's impressive economic growth.

The momentum for growing India-ROK ties was lost when both countries went through a phase of political changes from 1988 to 1990. The world itself changed dramatically with the dismantling of the Berlin Wall, the collapse of the Soviet Union and the end of the Cold War.

Prime Minister P.V. Narasimha Rao came to the helm of affairs in India in 1991 and had the wisdom and foresight to have a fresh look at India's dogmatic and static policies in the framework of a dynamic international order. The Rao Government introduced major policy reforms to liberalise and open up the Indian economy. Prime Minister Rao also formulated India's 'Look East Policy' to deepen India's engagement with East Asia. With its growing economy and shift towards democracy, ROK was an attractive partner as India set its eyes towards the East to seek new friends and partners.

Prime Minister Rao's visit to Seoul in September 1993 and his future-oriented discussions with President Kim Yong-sam led to a qualitative leap in bilateral relations. Both the leaders had a high regard for each other's civilisation and political heritage. Prime Minister Rao invited Korean *chaebols* to invest in India and had detailed discussions with the Chairman of Samsung Electronics Company, Lucky Goldstar Group and the Hyundai business group. The Hyundai group had ambitious plans for India, which included the establishment of an automobile plant, bidding for offshore oil fields, setting up a container factory, etc. The Lucky Goldstar group had its eyes on the manufacture of air conditioners and chemicals. The Samsung group focused on electronics, and engineering and construction.

Korean corporate leaders' assessment of India's huge consumer market and policy reforms to ease entry of foreign companies to manufacture in India was positive. These companies took a policy decision to enter the Indian market and over time, have won the trust of Indian consumers.

Since then, many of these proposals have come to fruition and have positioned Korean companies high on the Indian industrial scene as manufacturers of quality products. President Kim Young-sam and his successor Presidents have also encouraged the participation of Korean companies in the development of India's infrastructure.

Another important decision by India was to appoint an honorary Consul General in Busan. Recognising the Buddhist connection between the two countries, a proposal to establish a Korean temple at Bodhgaya was also mooted.

The state visit of President Kim Young-sam in February 1996 further cemented the foundation on which a strong bilateral economic superstructure was later built. Accompanying the President were 38 top Korean industrialists. On its part, in a major policy reform, India announced the approval of proposals by Samsung Electronics and Hyundai Motors to establish manufacturing units in India with 100 per cent foreign direct investment (FDI). This move convinced the Korean *chaebols* of India's sincerity in welcoming Korean investment. A much required Bilateral Investment Promotion Agreement was signed during the visit. Another important decision was to set up a Joint Commission at the level of foreign ministers. Its implementation, however, had to wait till 2002.

UN Secretary-General Ban Ki-Moon offers an interesting example in India-ROK relations. His first posting abroad was at the ROK embassy in New Delhi in the early 1970s. He was a member of President Kim Young-sam delegation in 1996 as Deputy Minister of Foreign Affairs. He later visited India as Foreign Minister in 2005. His Chef de Cabinet in his first term as the UN Secretary General was a senior Indian diplomat Vijai Nambiar. To cap it all, his son-in-law is of Indian origin.

Another missed opportunity for a potentially major collaboration between the two countries has been in the field of aircraft manufacture. In the 1990s, Hindustan Aeronautics Limited (HAL) had supplied some spare parts for Korean naval helicopters. At that time, India had also offered to maintain and service the Russian equipment which the Koreans had acquired as repayment of Russian debt. In 1994, the Samsung group mooted the possibility of a partnership with HAL to co-produce a 100-seat civilian aircraft. However, the Indian side did not have the foresight to jump start its aircraft manufacturing capacity and offered only a sub-contracting role for HAL. Samsung then turned towards China with a similar proposal.

The practice of regular foreign office consultations was started in the 1990s at the level of Director General/Head of Division. Korea appointed an Honorary Consul in Calcutta in November 1998 and another Honorary Consul in Chennai in 2002. Korea upgraded its office in Mumbai, opened in 1996, to a Consulate General in 2005. In 1999, ROK was deeply appreciative when Indian Customs arrested a DPRK ship carrying components for missiles to Pakistan. The ROK diplomats were allowed to inspect the ship along with diplomats of a few other countries.

ROK Minister of Foreign Affairs and Trade Lee Joung-binn visited India in July 2000 when he and Foreign Minister Jaswant Singh decided to initiate the Joint Commission process. The new Korean President Kim Dae-jung was a known admirer of Mahatma Gandhi, a founder member of the India-Korea Association and a descendent of the Princess of Ayodhya belonging to Gimhae Kim Clan. Unfortunately, his scheduled visit to India in October 2001 had to be called off in the aftermath of the September 11 terrorist attacks on the US and the resulting tense international situation.

The first meeting of the Joint Commission took place in April 2002 in Seoul. The two sides decided to deepen economic collaboration and strengthen defence cooperation. Since then, the Joint Commission has become an important forum to review the entire gamut of bilateral relations and chart a road map for the future growth of relations. However, the Joint Commission meetings have been rather irregular and the sixth meeting of the Joint Commission took place in Seoul in 2010.

India's nuclear tests of May 1998, which were a manifestation of India's search for security and recognition as a major power, introduced some dissonance in bilateral relations. Initially, ROK chose to endorse the adverse Western reaction to the nuclear tests. ROK was also apprehensive of the conclusions DPRK might draw from the international reaction to these tests. However, ROK gradually toned down its strong reaction. The major convergence between the two countries was the shared deep concern regarding the nexus between DPRK and Pakistan for the illegal and clandestine exchange of missile and uranium enrichment technologies. It is expected that the intelligence agencies of the two countries shared information on this noxious conspiracy between these two difficult states, which threatens regional security and stability.

Bilateral relations were on a sound footing when the 30th anniversary of establishing of diplomatic relations came in 2003. Warm greetings were exchanged between the top leaders of the two countries, special commemorative stamps were issued, and a number of cultural and economic events were held in both the countries. At the 2nd Joint Commission meeting in 2003, a proposal was mooted to move towards a long-term cooperative partnership.

By this time, democratic practices had taken deep roots in South Korea and the two Asian countries shared a largely similar world view. The over-arching policy of both the countries was centred on promoting a conducive international environment for domestic economic growth.

The two countries established a 'Long-Term Co-operative Partnership for Peace and Prosperity' during President Roh Moo-hyun's visit in October 2004. The legal framework for bilateral cooperation was strengthened by signing of an extradition treaty and a mutual legal assistance treaty. Looking ahead, a group of officials and economists was charged with the responsibility to devise a mechanism for a long-term economic partnership. The Memorandum of Understanding (MoU) between POSCO and Odisha state government for a 12 million tonnes steel plant in Odisha was signed in June 2005.

It is regrettable that the project has got embroiled in India's procedural delays and social contradictions. The project has now been scaled down to 8 million tonnes for which the state government may be able to hand over the required approx 3000 ha of land. It is, however, still a mega project and POSCO is unlikely to walk away from the project, despite the frustrating delays. Nevertheless, the project is very important for the credibility of India as a reliable economic partner. The establishment of the POSCO steel plant would also encourage Korean ship builders to set up ship-building capacity in India as custom-cut high quality steel is a prime requirement for efficient ship-building.

President A.P.J. Abdul Kalam's February 2006 visit to Seoul further cemented the bilateral relationship. In a decision of far reaching significance, a Joint Task Force was established to draft a Comprehensive Economic Partnership Agreement. In 2005-2007, ROK and India were competitors in the bid to host the 2014 Asian Games as well as for the post of UN Secretary General. It is to the credit of both the countries that canvassing was done without any rancour or negative propaganda.

The India-ROK relations matured under President Lee Myung-bak, who had come to India on a familiarisation visit as a Presidential candidate in April 2007. He and President A.P.J. Abdul Kalam shared the vision of promoting a 'world knowledge platform.' India announced to the world the strength of bilateral relationship by inviting President Lee as the Chief

Guest at the 61st Republic Day parade in January 2010. ROK reciprocated warmly and the bilateral relationship was raised to the level of a 'strategic partnership.' An MoU between the Indian Space Research Organisation and the Korean Aero Space Research Institute was also signed. The level of the foreign policy and security dialogue was raised to secretary/vice minister level. To have a well-directed collaboration in science and technology, a US$ 10 million fund was created for joint R&D.

The Indian President Pratibha Patil undertook a state visit to ROK in July 2011. The highlight of the visit was the signing of the India-ROK civil nuclear cooperation agreement. In appreciation of his wisdom and knowledge, President Lee invited former President A.P.J. Abdul Kalam to be a part of the 'Eminent Persons' Group' for the 2nd Nuclear Security Summit to be held in Seoul in March 2012. In 2012, Prime Minister Manmohan Singh and President Lee issued a joint statement on 'Deepening the Strategic Partnership.' The two leaders endorsed the initiation of a trilateral dialogue among designated think tanks of India, ROK and Japan, and the first dialogue was held in New Delhi in June 2012.

Cooperation

The delegation for President Chun Doo-hwan's abortive visit in October 1982 had included the Chairman, Joint Chief of Staff of Korea and ROK had evinced an interest in posting a Military Attaché in their embassy in New Delhi. However, India was wary of this proposal as it was envisaged that North Korea would request the same if the South Korean request was accepted. After much deliberation, a South Korean Military Attaché was finally posted to New Delhi in 1990.

On the other hand, groups from the respective national defence colleges have been visiting each other since 1984. The two navies and coast guards have interacted regularly and the two countries' naval ships have often undertaken goodwill visits.

The interaction between the two Ministries of Defence was placed on a formal framework with the signing of the MoU on Defence Industry and Logistics Cooperation in 2005. This has been supplemented with a broader agreement on defence cooperation and another agreement on R&D signed between Defence Acquisition Program Administration of ROK and Defence Research and Development Organisation of India.

ROK has been keen to sell its defence equipment to India. In 2012, Kangnam Corporation won a contract worth approx US$ 1 billion to supply eight advanced mine sweepers to the Indian Navy. Recognising the future potential of defence collaboration, India posted a Defence Attaché in its embassy in Seoul in 2012.

Trade and Investment

Trade between India and ROK has grown rapidly over the decades. In the 1970s and early 1980s, the trade balance was in India's favour. But as Korean export of manufactured goods increased, the balance shifted in ROK's favour and reflected the strength of Korea's industrialisation.

Bilateral trade was US$ 1.95 billion in 1995 and the 1996 Rao-Kim Summit set a target of raising it to US$ 5 billion by the year 2000. From the then figure of US$ 250 million, an ambitious target of US$ 3 billion Korean investment in India was also set. Korea was the partner country in the India Engineering Trade Fair in February 1999. Prime Minister Kim Jong-pil visited India on that occasion and visitors to the Korean pavilion were impressed by their manufacturing prowess.

During the visit of President Roh Moo-hyun in 2004, a target of US$ 10 billion bilateral trade by 2008 was set. The target was achieved before that date. Recognising this surge in bilateral trade, a target of US$ 30 billion by the year 2014 was set in January 2010, which was further hiked to a target of US$ 40 billion by 2015 in March 2012 during the two summit meetings between Prime Minister Manmohan Singh and President Lee Myung-bak. Bilateral trade was around US$ 20 billion in 2013 and, given the global economic slowdown, it may be difficult to achieve these ambitious targets. However, there is no doubt that India-Korea trade is on an upward trajectory and the future is bright.

The major chambers of commerce and industry in both countries have been instrumental in boosting bilateral trade and investment. The Confederation of Indian Industry (CII) and Federation of Indian Chambers of Commerce and Industry (FICCI) on the Indian side and Korean Chambers of Commerce and Industry (KCCI) and Federation of Korean Industries (FKI) on the Korean side have had regular interaction since the 1980s. Korea's trade and investment promotion agency Korea Trade-

Investment Promotion Agency (KOTRA) has done admirable work, acting as a bridge between Korean and Indian corporates and entrepreneurs.

The operationalisation of the Comprehensive Economic Partnership Agreement (CEPA) in 2010 has been a major accomplishment of the respective ministries of commerce and foreign trade. The CEPA has led to an across-the-board reduction in tariffs and smoothened the way for 163 categories of Indian professionals to work in ROK.

From India's point of view, the widening gap between its exports to and imports from Korea is a matter of some concern. In 2012, the Korean exports amounted to US$ 12 billion while India's exports were only US$ 7 billion. Korea needs to take proactive steps to facilitate imports of Indian pharmaceuticals, agricultural products and IT-enabled services to stem this rising imbalance.

The Korean investments in India are of the order of US$ 4 billion with companies reinvesting their profits in India. Indian companies like Tata Motors, Mahindra Group and Aditya Birla Group have also invested more than US$ 1 billion in Korea. In a major difference in strategy, while Korean investment has been mainly in green field projects, Indian companies have invested largely through the mergers and acquisitions (M&A) route.

Civil Nuclear Cooperation

Exchange of atomic energy scientists and experts between India and ROK through the International Atomic Energy Agency (IAEA) has occurred since the 1970s, but bilateral cooperation is more recent. While India was ahead of ROK in nuclear technology in the 1970s, ROK forged ahead in the 1990s with an extensive nuclear power programme. In 1996, India supplied heavy water to Korea's research nuclear reactors. Subsequently, direct relations were established between the atomic energy agencies of the two countries.

In recent years, ROK has been keen on entering the Indian nuclear power market and in 2008, as a member of the Nuclear Suppliers Group (NSG), supported the exemption of India from the sanctions imposed after the May 1998 nuclear tests. India responded positively and the India-ROK Civil Nuclear Cooperation Agreement was signed during President Pratibha Patil's state visit to ROK in July 2011.

ROK has developed its own nuclear power technology and has a proven track record of safety and efficiency. However, ROK does not have control over the full nuclear fuel cycle, as it is prohibited from enriching uranium under an ROK-US bilateral agreement. As India desires guaranteed supply of nuclear fuel for the entire life of a nuclear reactor from a foreign supplier, this constraint on ROK's capacity stands in the way of future award of a complete nuclear plant to ROK. However, the door is now open for procurement and exchange of civil nuclear equipment, technology and expertise between the two countries.

People-to-People Contacts

In the last 40 years of diplomatic relations between India and Korea, contacts between think tanks of the two countries have grown steadily. The annual dialogue between the Indian Council for Research in International Economic Relations (ICRIER) and the Seoul Forum for International Affairs (SFIA) is now well established and the 12th dialogue in 2013 at New Delhi focused on intensifying and deepening the partnership between the two countries. There are also regular interactions between the Indian Council of World Affairs and the Korean Institute of Foreign Affairs and National Security. In 2012, an MoU was signed between the Korea National Diplomatic Academy and India's Foreign Service Institute.

There are active India-ROK friendship societies in both the countries. Yet, the growth in people-to-people contacts and cultural exchanges has been less than their potential. Only about 80,000 Koreans visit India and about 60,000 Indians visit Korea for business or tourism.

It is an encouraging sign that the popularity of Bollywood films in Korea and K-Pop in India is growing. In a smart move, the two countries have opened their cultural centres in the respective capitals. Hindi is taught in Hankuk University of Foreign Studies and Busan University of Foreign Studies. Korean studies are popular in Delhi University and Jawaharlal Nehru University and have also been introduced in several colleges across the country. The role that a sizeable body of students and scholars well informed about each other's language, society, economy and polity can play in enhancing mutual understanding and goodwill is immense.

Future Perspectives

The last 40 years have created a strong foundation for deep engagement between the polity, economy and civil society of the two countries. There is a large reservoir of goodwill for each other among leaders, policy makers and the peoples of the two countries. A strong framework has been created for close future relations with the forging of the 'strategic partnership,' the Comprehensive Economic Partnership Agreement, and the growing relationship in the field of defence and security.

Today, India and Korea share a similar world view and aim to ensure peace and tranquillity in Asia, safety of maritime transport, strong action against terrorism, and to promote economic growth with open trade and investment. It would be in the long-term interests of both democracies to work towards a multi-polar Asia.

On the bilateral front, more content needs to be added to the strategic aspect of the relationship. The two countries should intensify collaboration in anti-piracy measures, cyber security and safety of satellites in space. The two navies need to formulate a long-term vision for collaboration. It would also be useful for both sides to identify a few platforms or weapons systems for joint R&D on the lines of India's development of the 'BRAHMOS' missile with Russia. The visit of India's National Security Advisor Shiv Shankar Menon to Seoul in July 2013 augurs well for deepening the future security relationship between the two countries.

India and ROK should make efforts to harmonise their positions on controversial issues in the East Asia Summit process, the Asean Regional Forum, the United Nations and other regional and global multilateral agencies. It is important that ROK finds a way to recognise and support India's aspirations for permanent membership of the UN Security Council. India and Korea can play an important collaborative role in reconstruction projects in Afghanistan, Iraq, Myanmar, etc., where Indian manpower and Korean technology could bring significant synergy for the execution of major projects.

On the economic front, India would continue to look at ROK for investments and technology. There is immense potential in India's infrastructure sector; however, unless the Korean *chaebols* offer soft credit to the Indian infrastructure and power sectors, they are likely to lose market share to their competitors. For Korea, India offers a huge market, skilled low-cost manpower for manufacturing and a base for exports to South Asia and the Middle East. Korean companies would do well to leverage their strong acceptance by the Indian consumer and establish more manufacturing bases in India. Bilateral trade would get a much needed push if the Korean side were to address the issues impeding Indian exports of generic drugs, agricultural products and IT-enabled services (ITESs) from India. It is also important that the ROK government devises ways for the future launch of Korean satellites on Indian launch vehicles.

The awareness of each other's culture, society and history is likely to gradually increase with the growing popularity of each other's cuisine, films and soap-operas and through increased tourism. But concerned agencies on both sides need to take concerted steps for speedy growth in soft diplomacy to fully mobilise the positive sentiments among the people to cement the overall bilateral relationship.

Regular high-level contacts between the leaders of the two countries are likely to continue as President Park Geun-hye is very upbeat about India. President Park believes that it is very hard to find countries that have as much potential as India. The Indian leadership has a similar assessment of ROK. The growth in overall India-ROK relations in coming decades would be incremental, stable and permanent. In the words of ROK Ambassador Joon Gyu Lee, while other countries may be more important for them, India and ROK are poised to be the closest friends with mutual goodwill, no conflict of interest and a stake in each other's prosperity and progress. Similarly, India's Ambassador to ROK Vishnu Prakash has observed: "Our issue-free bilateral relations have literally been transformed in recent years, given growing convergences." These forward looking and optimistic sentiments underscore the future steady growth of bilateral relations.

References

Ahn, Chong Yong and Pravakar Sahoo (eds.) (2012). *India-Korea Dialogue for a 21st Century Partnership*. New Delhi: Academic Foundation.

Raghavan, Vyjyanti (ed.) (2009). *India and Korea through the Ages: Historical, Religious and Cultural Perspectives*. New Delhi: Manck Publications.

Tayal, Skand R. and Sandip Kumar Mishra (2012). "India and Republic of Korea: A Growing Strategic Partnership", *Indian Foreign Affairs Journal* 7(3) : 321-30.

3 Analysis of Korea-India Security Relations and its Future Direction

Changhee Park

Introduction

The geopolitical landscape in Asia has been changing radically. China is at the centre of power dynamics in the region. With its economic development, Beijing thinks that it is very important to secure an unimpeded, stable supply of energy and resources. Without securing the sea lanes of communications (SLOC) from its ports in East China Sea through Indian Ocean to the Middle East and Africa, China cannot expect ongoing economic growth, public support for the political leadership, and thus, social stability (Song, 2013). For that reason, China has sought to develop safer, shorter and more cost-effective maritime trade routes following the coast line of Myanmar, Bangladesh, Sri Lanka and Pakistan, shaping the so-called "String of Pearls" (Pehrson, 2006: 3-4). The rise of China as a strong power is definitely related to securing and expanding its maritime interests.

The US is rebalancing its military and diplomatic resources toward this region to prepare for the possibility that China could undermine global commons such as the freedom of navigation and commerce with its anti-access and area denial (A2/AD) strategy. Washington has been enhancing regional defence alliances with South Korea, Japan, Australia, the Philippines and Thailand, and partnerships with India, Singapore, Vietnam, Myanmar and others. In particular, the Philippines agreed last year on the limited redeployment of US troops to a naval base in Subic Bay and Clark Air Force Base; Vietnam allowed the US to use its naval bases as calling ports amid its own territorial dispute with China over the Spratly Islands; Australia showed its strong alliance with the US by permitting the rotational deployment of up to 25,000 US marines in the northern city of

Darwin (Song, 2013). The aim of the US rebalancing seems to be to check expanding Chinese maritime influence through redeploying its naval assets.

In this environment, Korea-India security relations have developed rapidly in recent years. The 21st century security environment, contrary to the Cold War era when the two superpowers dominated the rest of the countries, involves a critical role for middle powers and even weaker states. As the US and China call their allies and friends to line with them, the role of middle powers, including Korea and India, in dealing with regional and global issues becomes larger than ever before. In this respect, enhancing security relations would have a serious impact on the regional balance of power. Realising this strategic implication, the two countries signed a 'Strategic Partnership' agreement and have consulted on regional security issues through the mechanisms of the Joint Commission, the Foreign Policy and Security Dialogue, and nuclear energy cooperation. Besides, defence cooperation, such as R&D, transfer of technology and exchange between defence institutes, has been promoted.

What is the current status of the Korea-India strategic partnership in the dynamic security environment in Asia? What are the limits and possibilities in the development of their relations? How can they promote their security ties in the future?

This paper analyses Korea-India security relations and its future direction. I will argue that security relations between Korea and India should develop further into a strategic partnership. Of course, there exist clear limits in enhancing their strategic linkage due to the differences in strategic objectives, security issues, and perceptions on China and Japan. Nevertheless, there is considerable room for Korea and India to strengthen their strategic ties, and enough reason why they should do so. More importantly, changing global power dynamics, shaped by the rise of China and an exhausted America, provide an opportunity for middle powers like Korea and India to assume a more active role in regional peace and stability. And enhancing Korea-India strategic cooperation will not only contribute to shape a 'healthy balance of power' in Asia, but also enable them to enjoy mutual benefits in other areas.

I will evaluate in the next section the development of Korea-India security relations since the outbreak of the Korean War. The third section will deal with the limits on and the possibilities of their security relations, and the fourth section outlines the future direction of their relations. The last section suggests some of the implications of security ties between Seoul and Delhi for the Korean Peninsula.

Evaluation of Current Korea-India Security Relations

Constrained Relations during the Cold War Era

In March 1947, Jawaharlal Nehru mentioned at the Asian Relations Conference in New Delhi that "we are of Asia and the people of Asia are nearer and closer to us than others" (Nehru, 1949 and 1953; Strachan *et al.*, 2009: 5). Even though it clearly underlined the rationale and significance of Asia's resurgence in India's world view, India's foreign policy during the Cold War era had seldom met what he proposed earlier. Being addicted to emotional decolonisation and ideology in its foreign relations, India failed to achieve anything very tangible in terms of commercial and economic development. Disappointingly enough, the Bandung Conference could not produce any Asian relations organisation as envisioned in the Asian Relations Conference.

Republic of Korea (ROK)-India security relations go back to the Korean War. In 1951, India dispatched the 60th Parachute Field Military Ambulance Platoon, a mobile army surgical hospital that treated wounded soldiers during the UN operations. In 1953, India was involved in the Korean Armistice negotiation and played a constructive role between China and the West. After the war, Korea and India established consular relations in 1962, and began diplomatic relations by upgrading their relations to ambassador level in December 1973. There were two agreements in economic and cultural fields in August 1974. One of them was the Agreement for Trade Promotion, Economic and Technical Cooperation to facilitate imports to develop and to diversify trade between the two countries (Indian Ministry of External Affairs, 1974a). The other was the Cultural Agreement to establish and develop closer cultural relations, which could contribute to a better understanding of each other's culture, art and education (Indian Ministry of External Affairs, 1974b).

However, during the Cold War era, Korea-India relations remained in a state of "strategic disconnect" (Panda, 2012: 64). India pursued a 'non-alignment policy' and maintained close relations with the Soviet Union. Korea, a strong ally of the US, saw India with ideological suspicion, and had little interest in improving state relations. Besides, due to its autarkic economic policy, India was insulated from the outer world and did not offer a favourable environment for economic trade with Korea, or with neighbouring South-east Asian countries.

India's 'Look East' and ROK's 'Northern Diplomacy' in the 1990s

The 1991 economic and financial crisis in India, which coincided with the collapse of the Soviet Union, compelled India to take a fresh look at its foreign policy. To overcome its severe balance of payments (BoP) crisis, Prime Minister P.V. Narasimha Rao proposed a new strategic vision of 'Looking East' in 1993 for the first time, changing the economic and strategic paradigms of international relations (Strachan *et al.*, 2009: 3). The Association of Southeast Asian Nations (ASEAN), with Japan, Korea and China put together, constituted economically the most dynamic region not only in Asia but in the whole world, and got a priority in India's search for Asian partnerships (Ibid.: 10).

Korea's 'Northern Diplomacy' since the end of the 1980s, pursued by Korean President Roh Tae-woo, extended its diplomatic relations with countries of the Communist world including Poland, Hungary, Czechoslovakia, Bulgaria, Romania and Mongolia. Moreover, Seoul normalised its relations with the Soviet Union in 1991 and China in 1992, bringing a truly global aspect to its new diplomacy. In the process, Seoul got a chance to explore ways to improve relations with Delhi.

So, it was a kind of 'policy rendezvous' between Seoul and Delhi to activate economic and commercial cooperation in the early 1990s. India's reform toward a market economy in 1991 and the Look East policy (LEP) under Prime Minister Narasimha Rao spurred economic and political relations with Korea. Being open-minded with the former anti-US bloc, Korea responded positively to India's cautious approach. As a result, in 1996, the two countries established the Korea-India Joint Commission for bilateral cooperation, which was chaired by Korean Minister of Foreign Affairs and Trade and the Indian External Affairs Minister.

However, Korea-India security cooperation during this period had clear restraints. India focused its LEP more on Southeast Asian countries than the far eastern region. Korea also concentrated its diplomatic efforts to improve relations with her northern neighbours rather than with western countries. As a result, their contacts were intermittent and remained confined to trade.

Establishment of 'Cooperative Partnership'

At the turn of the century, India's LEP was transformed not just 'beyond ASEAN' but also 'beyond economic cooperation.' The LEP in the 21st century, after a decade since its official declaration in 1993, has been expanded to non-ASEAN members like Australia, Japan and Korea. India's Foreign Minister Yashwant Sinha described the second phase of the LEP in 2003 as follows:

> The first phase of India's Look East policy was ASEAN-centred and focused primarily on trade and investment linkages. The new phase of this policy is characterised by an expanded definition of 'East', extending from Australia to East Asia, with ASEAN at its core. The new phase also marks a shift from trade to wider economic and security issues including joint efforts to protect sea lanes and co-ordinate counter-terrorism activities.[1]

India's strategic vision for the East extends to the whole Asia-Pacific region as India manifested both its willingness and capability to play a critical role in the emerging strategic dynamics and architecture for this region (Muni, 2011: 2). India has developed close strategic understanding and cooperation with Japan, Australia, Korea and even China, and established various forms of partnerships with these countries.

In October 2004, Korean President Roh Moo-hyun visited India at the invitation of President A.P.J. Abdul Kalam. The two leaders agreed to take ROK-India relations to a higher level of "Long Term Cooperative Partnership for Peace and Prosperity" to fully utilise the substantial potential and opportunities for deepening mutually beneficial cooperation, taking advantage of their economic complementarities and political convergence, and furthermore, pursuing peace and prosperity in the region and the world. They evaluated the importance of the ROK-India Joint Commission, co-chaired by the foreign ministers of the two countries, and

1. Yashwant Sinha's speech at Harvard University (Cambridge, September 29, 2003). The full text of the speech is available at *www.meaindia.nic.in/*

established the ROK-India Foreign Policy and Security Dialogue (FPSD), to be held alternately in Korea and India from the year 2005. They also noted the useful exchanges and interaction in the defence field and agreed to further promote such exchanges and interaction (Ministry of External Affairs, 2004).

Next year, Korea and India signed a Memorandum of Understanding (MoU) on cooperation in defence and logistics. This facilitated cooperation in the defence industry and the joint development of self-propelled artillery and mine-countermeasure vessels. This was followed by another MoU in March 2006 on cooperation between the coast guards of the two countries, leading to a joint exercise in July 2006 (Panda, 2012: 68).

Toward 'Strategic Partnership'

In 2010, Korean President Lee Myung-bak paid a historic visit to Delhi to celebrate India's Republic Day, and elevated their bilateral relations to a 'strategic partnership.' There were four main items for security cooperation: the two leaders agreed to maintain regular contacts; they acknowledged the necessity of holding the ROK-India Joint Commission meeting on an annual basis; they agreed that the FPSD will be raised to the level of vice minister; the two leaders agreed to strengthen dialogue and exchanges in the area of defence through regular high-level military exchanges. They also agreed on the need for greater cooperation between the navies and coast guards in areas pertaining to the safety and security of international maritime traffic.[2]

Since the signing of the 'strategic partnership', security ties between Seoul and Delhi have been strengthened. India's Defence Minister Mr A.K. Anthony visited Korea in September 2010, and signed MoUs on defence cooperation between the Defence Research and Development Organisation of India and the Defense Acquisition Program Administration of Korea. In July 2011, Indian President Pratibha Patil also visited Seoul, and agreed to develop their nuclear partnership with the conclusion of the Agreement for Cooperation in the Peaceful Uses of Nuclear Energy. In addition, South Korean Minister of Foreign Affairs and Trade, Kim Sung-Hwan, met with

2. ROK Ministry of Foreign Affairs: "Text of "Republic of Korea-India Joint Statement: Toward a Strategic Partnership," *http://www.mofa.go.kr/webmodule/htsboard/template/*

Secretary of Department of Atomic Energy, Srikumar Banerjee, during the signing of the nuclear cooperation deal.

In March 2012, India Prime Minister Manmohan Singh visited Seoul to attend the second Nuclear Security Summit in Seoul. He had a summit meeting with ROK President Lee Myung-bak for the second time, which ended with the issue of a joint statement that showed deepening state relations (Panda, 2012: 65). It is worth mentioning several points regarding security cooperation between the two countries. The two leaders appreciated the positive role of the ROK-India Joint Commission and reaffirmed that the commission would meet every year regularly. They also shared the view that the FPSD at the level of vice foreign ministers was a useful instrument to exchange views and harmonise positions on a vast variety of bilateral, regional and international issues. There was also a shared view on the need to actively pursue consultations and cooperation in the field of maritime security and in maintaining regional stability both bilaterally and in association with other countries of the region. The most notable agreement was on deepening defence cooperation, including joint ventures in research & development (R&D) and manufacture of military equipment, transfer of technology and co-production, and exchange between defence establishments of the two countries.[3]

The visits of high-level officials continue. In November 2012, Korean Defence Minister Kim Kwan-jin visited India, following that of his predecessor Kim Jang-soo in May 2008. In July 2013, Indian National Security Adviser Shiv Shankar Menon visited Seoul as a special envoy of Indian Prime Minister Manmohan Singh to mark the 40th anniversary of establishing diplomatic relations between the two countries. The envoy conveyed Dr Manmohan Singh's message that called for the development of strategic relations between Korea and India to promote regional stability and maritime security, where both have similar values and interests.[4]

As indicated in Table 3.1, ROK-India security relations have rapidly improved since 2010. President Lee's visit to Delhi and the conclusion

3. "Full Test of India-Korea Strategic Partnership Deal," *IBNLive.com*, March 25, 2012. *http://ibnlive.in.com/news/full-text-of-indiakorea-strategic-partnership-deal*

4. *UPKOREA.net*, July 3, 2013. *http://www.upkorea.net/news/*

of the strategic partnership was a watershed event that improved ties by institutionalising high-level exchanges on various security issues.

Table 3.1

High-level Visits Related to Security Area

Year	*From India to ROK*	*ROK to India*
2013	National Security Adviser Shiv Shankar Menon	
2012	Prime Minister Manmohan Singh	Defence Minister Kim Kwan-jin Vice Minister of Foreign Affairs Ahn Ho-young
2011	President Pratibha Patil External Affairs Minister E. Ahmed	Chairman of DAPA Noh Dae-lae
2010	Prime Minister Manmohan Singh Defence Minister A.K. Antony External Affairs Minister S.M. Krishna	President Lee Myung-bak
2009		Foreign Minister Yu Myung-hwan
2008		Defence Minister Kim Jang-soo
2007	External Affairs Minister Pranab Mukherjee	Foreign Minister Song Min-soon
2006	Defence Minister Pallam Raju	
2005		Foreign Minister Ban Ki-moon
2004	External Affairs Minister Natwar Singh	President Rho Moo-hyun
2003		Foreign Minister Yoon Young-kwan
2002	External Affairs Minister Yashwant Sinha External Affairs Minister Jaswant Singh	
2000		Foreign Minister Lee Jeong-bin
1999		Prime Minister Kim Jong-pil
		President Kim Young-sam
1993	Prime Minister Narasimha Rao	
1992	External Affairs Minister Madhavsinh Solanki	
1990		Foreign Minister Choi Ho-joong

Limits and Possibilities of Korea-India Security Relations

Limits of Bilateral Security Relations

Even though Korea-India security relations have surged recently, there exist apparent limits that restrain the development of their security ties. First, the strategic aims of Korea and India may be shared in broad terms, but differ in detail. For example, India's LEP in the second phase has reflected its strategic intention to contain the growing influence of China. Seoul shares the same concerns in that the People Liberation Army's navy modernisation programme would be a threat to Korea's maritime security. Besides, an empowered China could destabilise the regional balance of power and bully its neighbouring states. Both Korea and India consider China a cause for concern. Their strategic calculations, however, are different. While India wants to form an anti-Sino coalition consisting of several US allies and friends to contain the rise of China, Korea is reluctant to join such a coalition because Seoul thinks a stronger China should be a neighbour to engage or cooperate with, not to contain or challenge.

Second, strategic issues that both are most concerned about may not be shared. India has faced external and internal destabilising factors. Surrounded by vulnerable states such as Afghanistan, Pakistan, Myanmar, Bangladesh, Sri Lanka, Nepal and Bhutan, South Asia already seems to be the most dangerous place on earth with the threat of global terrorism. The border conflict with China does not appear to be amenable to a diplomatic resolution and recently, military incursions from the Chinese side have increased. The resurgence of radical political ideologies of mass mobilisation, including religious extremism, ethnic fundamentalism, and Maoism has intensified across wide regions (Sahni, 2012: 5-13). Korea has also encountered several security issues. Deterring North Korea's military provocation and maintaining peace on the Korean Peninsula have been the urgent and most important tasks for Seoul recently. Preventing Pyongyang's nuclear development and improving relations with North Korea are priorities since this would help pave the way to turn the current armistice to peace on the peninsula. In addition, Korea has been challenged by Japan's territorial claim of Tokdo on the East Sea.

Unfortunately, Korea and India have not been able to pay attention to each other's more delicate security issues due to geographical distance and the geopolitical environment. Koreans are unaware of Sino-Indo territorial disputes and the threat of terrorism in India. Similarly, Indians do not have much knowledge of North Korea's military provocation of South Korea. In this regard, it would be hard to expect that the two countries will go beyond verbal support for regional peace and stability, and form a common stance on major security issues and provide diplomatic and political support to the other. As an arms supplier to North Korea in the 1990s, India may not be able to take bold measures against North Korea in conformity with the United Nations Security Council (UNSC) resolutions.[5] Korea also cannot side with Delhi on the Indo-China border conflict ignoring Beijing's position.

Third, the strategic approach that the two governments prefer may differ. While New Delhi hopes to form a coalition with Korea, Japan and the US, Seoul wants to improve bilateral relations first. Delhi thinks that India, Korea and Japan should develop and build trilateral cooperation in security matters because of their shared concerns. According to the Indian perspective, they shared common values of democracy and market economy, and shared cordial relations with the US, all of which could propel the three countries to promote such an initiative to formalise trilateral cooperation (Panda, 2012: 73). India's view, however, underestimates the seriousness of historical issues in Korea-Japan relations. It overlooks why, even though they are allies of the US and have actively engaged in economic cooperation, the two countries have failed to sign any public agreement on security relations. Sixty-eight years after the end of Japanese rule, the Koreans are still anti-Japanese, mainly because of insensitive remarks by Japanese politicians on the history of Imperial Japan.

Fourth, there seems to be a big perception gap on the role of Japan in regional security between the two countries. Since the announcement of the strategic partnership with Japan in 2005, India supported Prime Minister Abe Shinzo's proposal for a new grouping of Asian democracies in 2006, held massive multilateral naval exercises in the Bay of Bengal in 2007, and unveiled a declaration on military security cooperation in 2008 (Raja, 2012: 31-2). The first 'Two Plus Two Dialogue' at the senior defence and foreign affairs official level was held between the two countries on July 6, 2010, and the second one in October 2012. Bilateral defence and military ties were enhanced by the first-ever exercise between the Indian Navy and the Japanese Maritime Self-Defence Force in June 2012 off the coast of Japan (Limaye, 2013). In addition, they have the same goal for reforms in the UN and their seats in the Security Council as permanent members. Being

5. Until 1990s, India was supplying weaponry made in the USSR and using its expertise in Soviet weapons to assist North Korea in upgrading MiG-21 planes and extending life of other Soviet supplied equipment.

positioned at the opposite ends of a rising China, their strategic ties were by no means spectacular.

Korea has been wary of Japan's policy to expand its military capability and role in the region. Currently, the Abe Shinzo cabinet is trying to reform the Japanese Constitution and legalise the right of collective defence, transform its Self-Defence Force into a 'National Defence Force,' and has the capability to attack, all of which are in violation of current Constitution. Even though these moves can be understood as a response to the increasing threats from North Korea's nuclear development and Chinese assertiveness in the territorial dispute over the Senkaku Islands recently, Korea has watched Tokyo's radical policy change toward re-militarisation with great concern. Without Japan sincerely regretting its past history, Seoul is unlikely to either consider Japan a 'normal state' or tolerate its becoming a permanent member of the UNSC.

Possibilities of Bilateral Security Relations

Despite the limits mentioned above, Korea and India can improve their security relations. First, they have just begun to recognise the imperatives of cooperation for a future balance of power. India has made no secret of its desire and capabilities to play a crucial role in ensuring Asian regional security. On November 28, 2005, Foreign Secretary Shyam Saran, speaking at the Economic Forum in New Delhi, said:

> India and the United States can contribute to a much better balance in the region... We believe in terms of managing the emerging security scenario in Asia, we need to bring more and more countries within the discipline of a mutually agreed security paradigm for the region (Muni, 2011: 21).

In June 2006, Defence Minister Pranab Mukherjee, speaking at the Fifth Shangri-La Dialogue in Singapore said that "India is one of the important legs of the Asian Juggernaut along with China, Japan and Indonesia... India's role is crucial for ensuring and maintaining long-term peace, stable balance of power, economic growth and security in Asia."[6]

Korea also understands the importance of regional balancing as China's military gains more power in Asia. With the financial difficulty of sustaining a huge military presence in Asia due to the 2008 economic

---

6. Text of the speech, June 3, 2006, *www.iiss.org/conference/the-shangri-la-dialogue/shangri-la-dialogue-archive/shangri-la-dialogue-2006/*

crisis, the US wants regional allies, especially Japan, to take on more responsibility to maintain strategic stability. US silence on Japan's rightist moves can be understood in this respect. As long as Korea views Japan's expanding its role in checking and balancing Chinese military activism unfavourably, India could be an alternative. That is, aligning with India could restrain Japan's increasing its balancing role against China in the future.

Second, they could provide mutual support on some critical issues, if not all, such as the nuclear issue, India's border conflict, and transnational threats like piracy and terrorism. Korean Foreign Minister Lee Jeong-bin during his visit to India in August 2000 said:

> India and South Korea are now fully conscious of the new security linkages between the subcontinent and the Korean peninsula. There have been disturbing reports, over recent years, of nuclear and missile cooperation between Pakistan and North Korea. Both India and the ROK are already moving to strengthen cooperation for mutual reinforcement of peace and stability between our respective regions (Panda, 2011).

This shows that the two countries share some concerns on strategic issues and can benefit from mutual support despite their geographical distance. Additionally, when Korea President Roh visited Delhi in 2004, he and the Indian Prime Minister criticised international terrorism and agreed to continue their consultations for cooperation in fighting against it. Moreover, they expressed their support for efforts at denuclearising the Korean Peninsula.[7]

Third, they could reach a deal on different approaches to their security cooperation. Korea will not admit the expansion of Japan military operations beyond its islands in this region. However, this does not mean that Seoul will rule out any security and military cooperation with Tokyo. When it comes to transnational threats or nuclear proliferation, bilateral or multilateral security cooperation would be possible. Of course, this presumes that Japan would adopt an appropriate attitude on past history and giving up revising the current Constitution and re-militarisation, which seems unlikely under the leadership of Abe Shinzo. Anyway, Korea

7. *http://www.mea.gov.in/bilateral-documents.htm?dtl/7467/Joint+Statement+State+Visit+to+ India+of+HE+Mr+Roh+MooHyun+President+of+the+Republic+of+Korea+ROK+46+October+2004*

and India can develop bilateral security cooperation first, which might be transformed into a multilateral mechanism later.

Future Directions of Korea-India Security Relations

Keeping the limits and possibilities in mind, it is necessary to work out some principles for Korea-India security relations. First of all, their security relations should not be directed against a third country. 'Partnership' is different from 'alliance' in that the former does not assume that another party is an enemy, while the latter does. That is the reason why partnerships can be universalised. Likewise, it would not be desirable for Korea-India security ties to pursue containing China. Second, the two countries should concentrate their efforts on shaping a 'healthy balance of power' in Asia. Their ties could supplement US military power in part to restrain the growth in the PLA's military capabilities without directly confronting China. Third, their security ties should be based on international norms and universal values. If the Korea-India partnership is to be recognised as a credible one by regional states and develop into more strategic relations, then their ties should respect and comply with global standards. These include promoting democracy, protecting human rights, securing global commons, preventing proliferation and so on. Based on these principles, Korea and India should spur their efforts to develop security relations as follows.

First, Korea-India cooperation should focus on maritime security from the Indian Ocean through South-east Asia to East Asia. Freedom of navigation in the Indo-Pacific Ocean is directly related to the strategic interests of both countries as well as others. If there is disruption in the global commons in this area by a trouble maker, it would cause political tension and military conflict, thus bringing about a negative impact on global economic activity. That is the reason why the US considers the freedom of navigation the first priority of its strategy toward the Asia-Pacific region. At a time when the US monopoly role in providing public goods is being challenged and questioned, Korea and India can play a positive role and help the 'weary giant' in managing the global commons.

If agreed, it will be a good starting point for building Korea-India security relations later. They could protect sea lanes of communication, cooperate on counter-piracy operations and support international efforts for freedom of navigation, thus contributing to regional peace and stability. This will lay the foundation for deepening their relations further in strategic terms. Such bilateral cooperation, if successfully managed, could provide an opportunity to further develop into a more expanded, multilateral maritime security mechanism that the US, China, Australia and Japan might join.

Second, both countries need to be more sensitive to each other's concerns. It is true that Korea cannot support or take a role in solving the Sino-Indian border conflict or issues relating to India's oil exploration in the South China Sea. Similarly, India has limitations in participating in resolving issues on the Korean Peninsula, such as North Korea's military provocations. Nevertheless, they should be sensitive to the other's issues and try to link these with their own security interests. Not all issues can necessarily be linked. But, they should take a more transparent stance on some critical issues based on global standards. For example, India could support the Korean government on North Korea's nuclear tests by criticising and participating in international sanctions outlined in the UNSC resolutions. As the North has cooperated with Pakistan in providing missile technology in exchange for its uranium enrichment programme, it is apparent that this issue is linked with India's national security. On the other hand, Korea could also provide diplomatic support to the Indian government on issues of terrorism initiated by Islamabad and Pakistan's nuclear deal with North Korea. Terrorism and nuclear proliferation is not only strictly prohibited by international norms and rules, but could also directly threaten Korean security. As long as such issue linkage is clear and recognised, it should be possible for the two countries to extend mutual support.

Third, they should promote military cooperation further, which is considered a criterion to estimate the level of strategic relations. Korea and India have earnestly upgraded their relations with frequent visits of high-level officials and holding strategic dialogues on a regular basis. Now is the time to expedite more tangible and concrete measures to achieve strategic outcomes. Their military cooperation might include participation in the other's military exercises as an observer, having combined naval exercises, combined counter-piracy operations, exchange of military information, and so on. There have been several occasions for the two countries to promote military cooperation further every time high-ranking official visits, such as India's Defence Minister A.K. Antony's visit to Korea in September 2010 and Prime Minister Manmohan Singh's visit to Seoul in 2012, take place. Unfortunately, even though they agreed to increase defence cooperation, their main concerns were focused on joint ventures in R&D, military equipment, and transfer of technology. To upgrade their relations to a strategic partnership, Korea and India should strengthen military-to-military cooperation more vigorously.

Fourth, both countries should enhance defence cooperation, especially in the fields of arms imports and exports, technology transfer, joint development of military equipment, and space development. Their structures of weapon systems and technologies seem to be mutually complementary and reciprocal in nature. For example, India has the fifth largest fleet in the world. But the Indian Navy continues to have difficulty in procuring modern equipment. Both domestically produced weapon systems and foreign purchases have been delayed, raising questions regarding its role in the Indian Ocean. To overcome current hardships, the Indian government took a bold measure increasing its defence budget by 34 per cent in fiscal year 2009 to US$ 30 billion. Moscow remains the country's main source of defence equipment, but currently New Delhi has revived procurement from Europe and has begun to buy equipment from the US [International Institute of Strategic Studies (IISS), 2012: 243]. In this regard, there is scope for the ROK to sell some of its military products to India, because shipbuilding is one area where the ROK enjoys a competitive edge. For instance, Hyundai Heavy Industries has jointly developed the KDX-III Aegis destroyer with the US Lockheed Martin. As India hopes to introduce the high-tech Aegis ships designed to trace incoming missiles and shoot them down, it could be the first target customer for this joint venture (Panda, 2011: 31).

India may also have an interest in the world's first-ever supersonic T-50 trainer jets and unmanned aerial vehicles produced by Korea Aerospace Industries. Although the Indian market for arms is already crowded with European countries, there is room for the ROK to penetrate the market because its products are cost-effective and therefore, competitive. Defence R&D cooperation between Korea and India is another area yet to be exploited. The countries have already signed an MoU on sharing of military expertise and technology in 2010. They can initiate joint development of a jet fighter. Indian Defence Minister A.K. Antony mentioned after signing the MoU that the defence industry relationship should be more than a buyer-seller relationship and evolve into transfer of technology, joint production and joint R&D (*World DNA*, 2010)

Korea, instead of providing some defence equipment and technology to India, can benefit from India's advanced capability in space programmes. Space has become another area of military operation. Satellite systems can provide information, facilitate command and control, and share necessary data on weather and positioning. Without space dominance, it would be impossible to expect efficient military operation in the battlefield. Korea has tried to launch various kinds of satellite into orbit, but has experienced failure several times because it lacks launching technology. If India can assist the launch of Korean satellites and transfer related technology, this could be another case of security cooperation that not only has critical meaning for Korea's space exploration programme, but will also enhance Korea-India security ties.

Conclusion

India's role as a stabiliser becomes critical in the evolving balance of power. Currently, India is part of the South-east Asian balance of forces and a counterweight to China in the Indian Ocean. In future, it is also likely to emerge as a balancing force in the Indo-Pacific region. Up to now, regional states have been concerned about how to deal with China. From now on, we should be more focused on how to co-operate with India.

India's security strategy should be seen as part of a US-led multilateral coalition in which Japan and South Korea are key players. India is a too big a country to stay calm without having a separate bilateral coalition with other countries, even though it became a member of the US-led 'hub and spoke, system. With a rising India, the US's regional allies, including Japan, South Korea and Australia, have been put under pressure to review their relationships with Delhi.

In this regard, an enhanced Korea-India strategic partnership will bring about positive results in the Korean Peninsula as well as in Asian security. First, it will contribute to developing Korea's maritime strategy and national interests, thus enabling Korea to be a maritime power. Korea and India have the common feature that they are land and sea powers, and it would be necessary and desirable for them to pursue a land and maritime strategy at the same time. Korea can learn India's strategy, analyse her strength and weakness, and incorporate the findings of these analyses in developing its own maritime strategy.

Second, Korea can use India as a strategic foothold to expand its maritime power into the Middle East, Africa and Europe. India has a geostrategic value in that despite its distance from the Korean Peninsula, it is located in the middle of the southern coast line of the Eurasian Continent. A strategic alignment with India, therefore, will provide Seoul a huge advantage in terms of access to a critical region and in pursuing its ambitious national policy of a 'global Korea.'

Third, their strategic ties will be conducive to settle issues in the Korean Peninsula. Until now, issues of Pyongyang's denuclearisation, North Korea's military provocation and the establishment of a peace regime on the peninsula have been dealt by the four regional powers and two Koreas. But, such a framework did not work, as concerned parties pursued their own interests, ignoring international norms and global standards. If those issues are regionalised and other Asian states including India raise their voices, they could be considered on the basis of broader universal values and standards rather than narrow interests, thereby increasing the possibility of reaching a consensus.

Korea and India should go beyond trade and promote security cooperation. They need the big picture of basic principles, strategic aims and linkage of issues, and need to search for more practical ways of interaction.

References

IISS (2012). *The Military Balance 2012*. London: Routledge.

Limaye, Satu (2013). "India-US and East Asia Relations: A Year of Notable Visits and Anniversaries", *Comparative Connections*. January.

Ministry of External Affairs (1974a). "Agreement for Trade Promotion Economic and Technical Cooperation", August 12. *http://www.mea.gov.in/bilateral-documents.htm?dtl/6248/*

———. (1974b). "Cultural Agreement", August 12. *http://www.mea.gov.in/bilateral-documents.htm?dtl/6248/*

———. (2004). "India: Joint Statement, State Visit to India of H.E. Mr. Roh Moo-Hyun, President of the Republic of Korea (ROK), October 4-6, 2004", October 6. *http://www.mea.gov.in/bilateral-documents.htm?dtl/7467/*

Muni, S.D. (2011). "India's 'Look East' Policy: The Strategic Dimension", *ISAS Working Paper.* February 1.

Nehru, Jawaharlal (1949 and 1953). *Speeches*, Vol. 1 (1946-1949). Delhi: Government of India.

Panda, Rajaram (2011). "India-Republic of Korea Military Diplomacy: Past and Future Projections", *Journal of Defense Studies* 5(1): 23. January.

———. (2012). "India and South Korea Relations: Past and Future Trends", *Portuguese Journal of International Affairs*, 6 (Spring/Summer).

Pehrson, Christopher J. (2006). *String of Pearls: Meeting the Challenge of China's Rising Power Across the Asian Littoral*. Carlisle: SSI.

Raja, Mohan, C. (2012). "Managing Multipolarity: India's Security Strategy in a Changing World", *India's Security Challenges at Home and Abroad*. NBR Special Report #39. The National Bureau of Asia Research. May.

Sahni, Ajai (2002). "India's Internal Security Challenges", *India's Security Challenges at Home and Abroad.* NBR Special Report #39. The National Bureau of Asia Research. May.

Song Sang-ho (2013). "U.S. Steps Up Policy for Asia-Pacific Rebalancing", *The Korea Herald*, January 13.

Strachan, Anna Louise *et al.* (2009). "India's Look East Policy: A Critical Assessment", *IPCS Special Report*. October.

World DNA (2010). "India, South Korea Sign Five-year Defence Cooperation Agreement", September 3. *http://www.dnaindia.com/world/1433007/*

4 India and Korea in a Changing Asia

From Distant Neighbours to Strategic Partners

C. Raja Mohan

Introduction

Although the Indian subcontinent and the Korean Peninsula have had contacts dating back to centuries, it is only in the last two decades that India and South Korea have drawn close. Despite the belated mutual discovery of each other, Delhi and Seoul will have a lot to do with each other in the coming years and shape the geopolitical destiny of Asia. This essay begins by reviewing the evolution of India-Korea relations over the last century. In the second part, it examines the changing geopolitics of Asia and concludes with a discussion of the imperatives for enduring and, consequentially, strategic cooperation between India and South Korea.

Estrangement and Endearment

At the dawn of the 21th century, India and Korea were deeply moved by the new forces of anti-imperialism and nationalism that swept across Asia. The discovery of the rich and shared heritage among Asian nations saw the articulation of new ideas about Asian unity by leading Asian intellectuals, including Rabindranath Tagore. As he constructed a new sense of Asian universalism, Tagore also helped build one of the first bridges between the peoples of India and Korea. His poem "The Lamp of the East" offered a great evocation of Korea's potential role in transforming the East (See Yang-shik, 1988). Nehru and many other internationalist leaders in India as well as in Korea were deeply inspired by the ideal of Asian unity. Yet the liberation from colonialism was accompanied by tragedies in the subcontinent and the Korean Peninsula. The partition of the subcontinent and the Korean

War and the division of the Korean Peninsula left the political elites in Delhi and Seoul coping with extraordinary security challenges that would preoccupy them for decades.

One of the first casualties of the Cold War between the United States (US) and the Soviet Union was the idea of Asian unity. Even before India gained full independence, Nehru, as the Prime Minister of the interim government, convened a conference of Asian nations in Delhi in March 1947. The conference itself had roots in the popularity of the idea for an 'Asian Federation' in India and across the continent, including in Korea. Yet the Asian Relations Conference underlined all the potential problems that Asia would face in translating the aspirations for unity into practical collaboration. The conference was deeply divided on the choices to be made for economic development, the extent of cooperation with Western capital in the post-colonial era and by divisions among themselves to the spectre of communism that confronted Asia. If the divisions within the Asian nations prevented the emergence of a region-wide mechanism for cooperation, the American effort to construct an anti-Communist alliance in the region too was unsuccessful. The Southeast Asia Treaty Organization (SEATO) and Central Treaty Organization (CENTO) did not survive for long. The US ended with the construction of the hub and spokes system of security in Asia—the alliance with South Korea was central to this. Meanwhile, disappointed by the meagre results of the Bandung conference, India moved away from the Asianist agenda to a larger global agenda that focused on non-alignment (Abraham, 2008).

Nehru's post-War diplomatic activism in Asia was visionary but could not alter the dynamics of the region's geopolitics defined by the great powers. Nehru's deep involvement in the Korean crisis did not result in political warmth between Delhi and Seoul. On the economic front too, India and South Korea found themselves on different paths. India's focus on economic self-reliance saw the steady dissipation of India's historic economic and commercial links with East Asia. South Korea instead was embarked on a different path, of building a strong domestic production base through export-led growth in close collaboration with the US and soon emerged as a 'tiger economy.' If India proved the pessimism about Asia's future, Korea presaged the optimism about Asia, which has now become conventional wisdom. Put simply, when Delhi and Seoul established diplomatic relations in 1973, they were virtually on separate planets. Meanwhile, the idea of Asian regionalism was acquiring slow but certain traction. A modest approach of self-interested regional cooperation unveiled by the formation of the Association of Southeast Asian Nations (ASEAN) provided the basis for a comprehensive development of regional institutions in Asia. Asian regionalism, which seemed so elusive in the 1950s, became a reality by the first decade of the 21st century focused around the nomenclature of 'East Asia' (World Bank, 2003). The economic miracle in East Asia provided a whole new basis for imagining Asian regionalism and brought together all the major powers together to manage regional security. India was largely out of this story until it initiated its own economic reforms.

Only a fundamental change in its economic orientation brought India closer to the realisation of the Asian dream that its founding fathers had envisaged. And as the Indian economy looked outward, it was a matter of time that it would discover the virtues of cooperation with South Korea. While much of the world was sceptical about India's economic reforms at the turn of the 1990s, Seoul was more empathetic to India's prospects. As India looked outwards at the turn of the 1990s, South Korea, now an impressive industrial power, was looking beyond its traditional partners to new markets in Asia. South Korean conglomerates stepped into India when many others were afraid to tread what was seen as a forbidding market. The expanding economic engagement between the two was consummated in a Comprehensive Economic Partnership Agreement signed in 2009. With deepening economic ties came the inevitable strategic partnership between the two countries. The widening political consultations between the two countries were elevated into a strategic partnership when President Lee Myung-bak came to India in January 2010 as a special guest for India's annual Republic Day celebrations.[1] Since then, there has been rapid intensification of cooperation in high-technology areas, including the conclusion of an agreement on civil nuclear cooperation. The prospects for collaboration in the aerospace sector are widely recognised as immense.

1. See speech by Lee Joon-Gyu, Ambassador of South Korea to India, "India-South Korea Strategic Partnership" at the Institute of Peace and Conflict Studies, New Delhi, May 2013, available at <*http://www.ipcs.org/special-report/east-asia/india-south-korea-strategic-partnership-140.html*>

Delhi and Seoul have also stepped up defence consultations and drawn up plans for regular joint military exercises. Delhi is also considering the purchase of minesweeper ships from South Korea. As India looks to expand its defence industrial base, South Korea is likely to emerge as an important partner for collaboration in the arms industry. Within two decades, the bilateral relationship between Delhi and Seoul has altered beyond recognition. But India and South Korea may not have the luxury of resting on their oars for they confront a very dynamic security condition in Asia that demands even greater strategic imagination from the two nations.

Asia's New Geopolitics

Despite the impact of the Cold War and the emergence of two alternative paths to economic development, Asia was too large and diverse to fit into the rigid bipolar framework that defined the geopolitics of the era. While the Cold War provided the overarching framework for the political development in Asia, the region never lent itself to the regimen of a bipolar framework.

Unlike in Europe, where the Soviet Union was a dominant threat, Moscow's influence—military, economic and political—tended to be far more limited. The European colonial powers that initially resisted the decolonisation process and sought to regain their territorial possessions had to eventually retreat. Britain abandoned its security role East of Suez by 1971 and transferred most of its security burdens to the US. Japanese imperialism, which shook Asia to the core and accelerated the downfall of European colonialism, was defanged after the Second World War and consigned to a subordinate political position to the US.[2] While the US remained the dominant power in Asia, the inherent multipolar tendencies in the region were underlined by the strategies adopted by the two nations that had the potential to emerge as great powers—China and India.

Communist China demonstrated the capacity to align, de-align and realign rather than accept the constraining bipolar logic of the Cold War. After the initial deep alignment with the Soviet Union, Beijing broke away from Moscow by the early 1960s and drew closer to Washington

2. For a comprehensive recent review, see, Miller and Wich (2011); see also Yahuda (2011).

by the early 1970s. As concerns about unipolarity emerged in the 2000s, Beijing once again sought to establish a partnership with Moscow. India departed from its non-aligned ideology to seek US military support when it confronted China across its northern borders in 1962 and to build a *de facto* alliance with Moscow in the 1970s. If the logic of containing communism put countries like Japan and South Korea on the same side, the normalisation of US relations with Communist China in the 1970s added to the complexity of Asia's international relations. Much of Asia, which refused to recognise Communist China, restored political ties with Beijing from the 1970s. After Deng ended China's economic isolation at the end of the 1970s, the region began to deepen commercial ties with China. Strong economic partnerships with Beijing remain despite political suspicion in much of Asia about China's intentions.

The rise of China and India and the broader improvement in the economic fortunes of Asia along with the slowdown of the West amidst a financial crisis have begun to alter geopolitical conceptions of the world. This transformation is being framed in three different ways.

The first is focused on the changing balance between the East and the West.[3] The notion of Asia's uniqueness and the exceptionalism of its political values have gained some ground in recent years. This, in turn, is reinforced by a growing sense of threat, economic and political, from Asia to the West. If there was triumphalism in the East about the rise of Asia, there has been rising pessimism about the future of the West.[4]

A second frame looks at the implications of the changing distribution of power within Asia. Political scientists tend to argue that the changes in the distribution of power are among the principal threats to international peace. If that proposition points to conflict between rising Asian powers and those in the West, it must apply equally to Asia itself. For the rise of Asia involves a significant reordering of Asia itself. The central driver for this is China, which has overtaken Japan as the second largest economy in the world in 2011. China is on the way to rapidly closing the gap with the US on aggregate GDP. Estimates vary on when China is expected to

3. For a provocative framing of the issue, see Mahbubani, 2008, and Lundestad, 2012.

4. See Peerenboom (2007) and Jacques (2009). For a critique of the view on the irresistible rise of Asia, see Pei (2009). For a balance view of the power shift, see Zakaria (2008).

overtake the US. Some expect that it could take place by the end of this decade. Meanwhile, China is expanding the gap between itself and India. At the turn of the 1990s, China and India were broadly level in terms of aggregate GDP and per capita incomes. By 2010, these indicators were nearly four times larger for the Chinese.

As Chinese economic power translates into military power, amidst a purposeful modernisation of the Chinese armed forces, there is no doubt that China will emerge as the foremost military power in Asia. As Beijing towers over most of its Asian neighbours, some analysts believe that the region is simply returning to the historic Sino-centric regional order. Others, however, would insist that the rise of China will lead to regional instability. Just as Germany's rise drove Europe into two world wars, so too might China's rise. Much will depend on how the rest of the region will react to the rise of China. From current indicators, it is quite clear that not all in Asia will accept a Sino-centric regional security order. While some Asian nations might choose to 'bandwagon' with China, others are likely to 'balance' the rise of China by tighter alliances and security cooperation with the other powers, especially the US (Ross, 2006).

The third frame of reference examines the role of external powers, especially the US, in shaping the security environment in the region. For decades now, the US has been the principal security provider in Asia, and had few peer competitors in managing the security order in the region. How might the US role in the region evolve amidst the weakening of the US economy, the exhaustion of its military power in the Middle East during the 2000s and the rise of China?

While the US insists that it will remain a 'resident power,' there is a widespread perception of the US decline. To be sure, most Asian nations have welcomed the policy of 'return to Asia' under the Obama Administration. Amidst Chinese assertiveness in the region, the East Asian nations have invited the US to be part of the East Asia Summit and join the defence ministerial consultations of the ASEAN.

On its part, the US has signalled its commitment to strengthen its alliances and proclaimed an interest in the peaceful resolution of maritime territorial disputes between China and its Southeast Asian neighbours. Nevertheless, the US is deeply divided on how to deal with the rising

Chinese power. Some in Washington believe a conflict with China is inevitable and demand an aggressive containment of Beijing's power before it is too late. At the other extreme are those who say a confrontation with China would be disastrous and propose the development of a framework for 'co-evolution' with Beijing in managing the global order (Kissinger, 2011). Some have called for a more explicit 'Group of Two' to manage the international system (Brzezinski, 2009). While the Obama Administration itself has not used the term G-2, during the first year of its tenure, it sought to develop a framework of reassurance towards China that involved US respect to Chinese interests and Beijing's commitment to develop a rule-based international system. Beijing, however, was largely cold to the idea of a G-2 and made it clear that it is not amenable to construct a duopoly on American terms (European Council on Foreign Relations, 2009).

Amidst the difficulties of structuring an accommodation with China, President Obama announced new defence guidance in January 2012 that called for a rebalancing of US military forces to the Asia-Pacific theatre: "US economic and security interests are inextricably linked to developments in the arc extending from the Western Pacific and East Asia into the Indian Ocean region and South Asia, creating a mix of evolving challenges and opportunities. Accordingly, while the US military will continue to contribute to security globally, we will of necessity rebalance toward the Asia-Pacific region. Our relationships with Asian allies and key partners are critical to the future stability and growth of the region. We will emphasize our existing alliances, which provide a vital foundation for Asia-Pacific security. We will also expand our networks of cooperation with emerging partners throughout the Asia-Pacific to ensure collective capability and capacity for securing common interests" (U.S. Department of Defense, 2012).

Besides declaring the US political will to devote sufficient resources to the defence of its strategic objectives in Asia, Washington has outlined plans to deploy an increasingly larger portion of its military resources in the Pacific. Washington is also debating a new military strategy called the 'air-sea battle' that can cope with China's growing military capabilities and Beijing's new ability to constrain American military movements near China's coast line. China's political assertiveness in Asia and America's strategic response have begun to end a prolonged period of great power peace in Asia. If this peace provided the basis for the region's economic growth and prosperity, the unfolding rivalry between Beijing and Washington makes much of Asia a contested zone between the two in the coming decades.[5] This contestation, in turn, will pose significant challenges to Asian regionalism, which had made considerable progress in the last few decades and demands much greater security cooperation between India and South Korea.

India, Korea and Asian Security

At the end of the Cold War, the ASEAN took the initiative to set up a regional forum, the Asian Regional Forum (ARF), to create an institutional framework to discuss region-wide political and security challenges. It brought together all the members of the ASEAN and all the dialogue partners of the organisation into a single, security-oriented platform in the early 1990s. But the record of the ARF has been less than impressive. Many have dismissed it as a 'talk shop' of little consequence for regional security. Others point to its limited impact on the development of cooperative security norms in the region (Haacke and Morada, 2010). Recognising the limitations of the ARF, the ASEAN took the initiative to establish in 2005 the East Asia Summit (EAS), which has emerged as the new institutional framework to consider security problems of Asia at the highest political level. India and South Korea have both been founding members of the organisation.[6] Despite the emergence of new regional institutions, the prospects for regional conflict have not diminished. Asia is looking at three broad types of regional conflict in the early 21st century.

The first is the prospect of war between great powers. Until a rising China grabbed the attention of the region, there has been little fear of great power rivalry in the region. The facts that all major powers interested in Asia are armed with nuclear weapons and that there is growing economic interdependence among them have led many to argue that great power conflict is not likely to occur. Economic interdependence, as historians might say by citing the experience of the First World War, is not a guarantee

5. For a discussion of the strategic implications of the US rebalancing in Asia, see a series of essays in the section on "Asia Pivot", *Orbis* 56(3): 333-502, Summer 2012.

6. For a comprehensive review of the founding and early evolution of the EAS, see Emmers *et al.* (2010).

for peace in Asia. Europe saw great power conflict despite the growing interdependence in the first half of the 20st century. Nuclear weapons surely are a bigger dampener on great power wars. Yet we have seen military tensions build up between China and the US in the waters of the Western Pacific in recent years. The contradiction between China's efforts to enforce a Monroe Doctrine on its maritime periphery and the US commitment to maintain forward presence in the Western Pacific is real and can only deepen over time.[7]

We also know from the Cold War that while nuclear weapons prevent a conventional war between great powers, they do not prevent competition and conflict by proxy. Great power rivalry then could express itself in two other forms of conflict: inter-state wars and intra-state conflict. If the outcomes in these conflicts are seen as threatening to one or the other great powers, they are likely to influence the outcome. This can be done either through support for one of the parties in inter-state conflicts or through civil wars. Often the stakes could be very high, when a great power decides to directly inject itself into conflicts. In the coming years, it is possible to visualise conflicts along all these axes in Asia. Although the last few decades have seen relative tranquillity in Asia, the same cannot be said for the future.

As Asia looks ahead, it is quite clear that regional powers will and must undertake a large part of the burden securing the region. Unlike in the past, when Asia was a mere theatre of confrontation for Western powers, today the regional actors have considerable capacity to shape the strategic outcomes. That is true especially of India and the Republic of Korea (ROK). The military capacities of both countries have grown significantly in the last two decades and are being called to contribute to the security of the region as a whole. While both countries have huge problems on their own borders, Delhi and Seoul have no option but to devote considerable resources in shaping the Asian security order, which could evolve in many different ways.[8] Two broad pathways stand out: one is the construction of a collective security mechanism and the other is the emergence of a balance of power system.

---

7. For a review, see Yoshihara and Holmes (2010).

8. For a discussion of the possible security orders in Asia, see Cook *et al.* (2009).

Although collective security systems are the best in a normative sense, achieving them in the real world has always been difficult. A more achievable goal is 'cooperative security' that seeks to develop mechanisms to reduce mutual suspicion, build confidence, promote transparency and mitigate, if not resolve, sources of conflict. The ARF and EAS are largely conceived within this framework, but the former has disappointed while the latter is yet to demonstrate its full potential. They are being severely tested by the growing intensity of China's territorial disputes with its maritime neighbours in the East and South China Seas. The Obama Administration's decision to interpose itself into these disputes and the deepening naval tensions between China and the US are adding additional layers of complexity to the regional dynamic.

ASEAN has found itself largely paralysed in dealing with the gathering territorial conflict in the South China Sea between China on the one hand and its two important members, Vietnam and the Philippines, on the other. Maintaining ASEAN unity in the face of these conflicts, let alone rallying behind its member states against China, has become very difficult for the organisation. The annual meetings of the ASEAN foreign ministers in Phnom Penh, Cambodia, in July 2012, ended in political disarray over the question of territorial disputes in the South China Sea. For the first time in the history of the organisation, the ministers failed to issue an agreed joint statement, and many analysts have attributed this outcome to Beijing's new ability to influence the internal dynamic in the ASEAN.

Beijing, on the other hand, has accused the US of trying to provoke the ASEAN members against it (Storey, 2012; see also Xinhua, 2012). The ASEAN has also found it increasingly difficult to cope with the new contours of Sino-American contestation in Asia. While many would like to see a strong US presence in Asia to provide an effective balance in the region, few of them would want to be caught in the crossfire between Washington and Beijing (Thayer, 2011).

A second approach emphasises the importance of power, especially military power to deter one's adversaries and the building of countervailing coalitions against a threatening state. A balance of power system, as many critics of the idea point out, promotes arms races, is inherently unstable and breaks down frequently, leading to systemic wars. There is growing concern in Asia that amidst the rise of Chinese military power and the sense of American decline, many large and small states are stepping up expenditures on acquiring advanced weapons systems. Some analysts think an expansive arms race is already a structural condition of the new Asia (see Calder, 1997; Bracken, 2000; Tan, 2012). Contrary to the arguments that America is in terminal decline, few doubt that America will remain a decisive power in Asia. It is beginning to strengthen its traditional alliances in the region and deepening special relationships with new partners like India, Indonesia and Vietnam. China, meanwhile, is trying to loosen American alliances in the region, alter the local military balance of power with the US and end nearly a century of American primacy in the Western Pacific.

As the emerging tensions now play out in Asia, the many large nations of the region face a complex set of challenges. All countries in Asia, including India and Korea, see China as an economic opportunity and are seeking deeper interdependence with it. At the same time, many of them are concerned about the prospect that China's rise may not necessarily be peaceful. Many of them want the US to stay in Asia and balance the Chinese power but do not want to be caught in the cross-fire between Washington and Beijing. Some of them are equally worried about a potential Sino-US condominium in Asia limiting their freedom of action.

Delhi and Seoul, then, must adopt a number of approaches even as they hold on to the traditional anchors of their foreign policy—India's non-alignment and Korea's alliance with the US. The first is to actively contribute to the success of regional security institutions in Asia. As members of the ARF, EAS and ADMM plus, they have much work to do to strengthen these institutions and prevent them from becoming vulnerable to great power politics. As major trading nations, India and Korea have a great stake in securing the sea lines of communication in Asia's waters, promoting respect for maritime laws and helping defend good order at sea.

Second, while emphasising cooperative security, prudence demands that India and Korea insure against the breakdown of security regionalism in Asia. Korea will be right to strengthen its military partnership with the US and India will continue to build stronger security partnerships with the US, Japan, Australia, Vietnam and Indonesia within the broad framework of strategic autonomy.

Third, given the complexity of current Asian geopolitics, it makes sense for Delhi and Seoul to develop trilateral and quadrilateral engagements with other critical regional powers. India and Korea have done well to launch a triangular track 1.5 consultation with Japan. Delhi and Seoul could consider extending that framework to involve other countries like Indonesia and Vietnam. Greater security cooperation among the middle powers of Asia, without prejudicing their pre-existing special relationships, will contribute to regional stability and reduce the vulnerabilities arising from twists and turns in great power politics.

Finally, Delhi and Seoul ought to recognise that bilateral security cooperation between them must form the bedrock of expanding their own comprehensive national power and improving their overall impact on regional affairs. The changed nature of their domestic capabilities, the absence of any clash of national interests, the growing comfort among the political elites of the two countries, and the larger circumstances in Asia make it possible and very necessary for a stronger strategic partnership between India and Korea.

References

Abraham, Itty (2008). "From Bandung to NAM: Nonalignment and Indian Foreign Policy, 1947-65", *Commonwealth and Comparative Politics* 46(2): 195-219.

Bracken, Paul (2000). *Fire in the East: The Rise of Asian Military Power and the Second Nuclear Age*. New York: Harper Collins.

Brzezinski, Zbigniew (2009). "The Group of Two that Could Change the World", *Financial Times*. January 13.

Calder, Kent (1997). *Asia's Deadly Triangle: How Arms, Energy and Growth Threaten to Destabilize Asia*. New York: Nicholas Brearly.

Cook, Malcolm, Raoul Heinrichs, Rory Medcalf and Andrew Shearer (2009). *Power and Choice: Asian Security Futures*. Sydney: Lowy Institute.

Emmers, Ralf, Joseph Chinyong Liow and See Seng Tan (2010). "The East Asia Summit and the Regional Security Architecture", *Maryland Series in Contemporary Asian Studies* 3.

European Council on Foreign Relations (2009). 'No Rush into Marriage: China's Response to the G2", *Asia Analysis* 22, June 2009. Available at *<http://ecfr.eu/page/-/documents/china_analysis_22.pdf>*. Accessed on September 12, 2011

Haacke, Jurgen and Noel M. Morada (eds.) (2010). Cooperative *Security in the Asia Pacific: The ASEAN Regional Forum*. Oxford: Routledge

Jacques, Martin (2009). *When China Rules the World: The Rise of the Middle Kingdom and the End of the Western World*. London: Allen Lane.

Kissinger, Henry (2011). *On China*. New York: Penguin.

Lundestad, Geir (2012). *The Rise & Decline of the American 'Empire': Power and Its Limits in Comparative Perspective*. New York: Oxford University Press.

Mahbubani, Kishore (2008). *The New Asian Hemisphere: The Irresistible Shift of Global Power to the East*. New York: Public Affairs.

Miller, Alice Lyman and Richard Wich (2011), *Becoming Asia: Change and Continuity in Asian International Relations since World War II*. Stanford: Stanford University Press.

Peerenboom, Randall (2007). *China Modernizes: Threat to the West or Model for the Rest*? New York: Oxford University Press.

Pei, Minxin (2009). "Think Again: Asia's Rise", *Foreign Policy*. July-August.

Ross, Robert (2006). "Balance of Power Politics and the Rise of China: Accommodation and Balancing in East Asia", *Security Studies* 15(3): 355-95, July-September.

Storey, Ian (2012). "China Pushes on the South China Sea, ASEAN Unity Collapses", *China Brief* 12(15), August 3.

Tan, A.T.H (2012). *The Arms Race in Asia: Trends, Concepts, Implications*. New York: Routledge.

Thayer, Carlyle A. (2011). "The United States, China and Southeast Asia", in Daljit Singh (ed.), *Southeast Asian Affairs 2011*. Singapore: Institute of Southeast Asian Studies. pp.16-25.

U.S. Department of Defense (2012). *Priorities for 21st Century Defense*. Washington, DC. January. p.2.

World Bank (2003). *The East Asian Miracle: Economic Growth and Public Policy*. Washington, DC.

Yahuda, Michael (2011). *The International Politics of the Asia Pacific*, Third Edition. New York: Routledge.

Yang-shik, Kim (1988). "Rabindranath Tagore and Korea", *Korea Journal* 28(12): 23-7, December.

Yoshihara, Toshi and James Holmes (2010). *Red Star Over the Pacific: China's Rise and the Challenge to U.S. Maritime Strategy*. Annapolis: Naval Institute Press.

Xinhua (2012). "US Needs to Behave Itself in South China Sea", *Global Times*, August 4, available at <*http://www.globaltimes.cn/content/725124.shtml*>

Zakaria, Fareed (2008). *The Post-American World*. New York: W.W. Norton,

5 South Korea's Economic Development from a Historical Perspective and Implications for Korea-India Economic Cooperation

Choong Yong Ahn

Introduction

In the past half century or so, South Korea (hereafter Korea) emerged from being one of the poorest agrarian societies in the world to being a near-developed country by joining the Organisation for Economic Cooperation and Development (OECD) in 1996. Korea dramatically shortened the usual phase of industrial transformation, which most of today's developed nations experienced over a span of at least a century and a half. The World Bank (1993) recognised Korea as the representative economy of the East Asian miracles. Korea achieved such remarkable industrial expansion despite considerable odds. To begin with, the country had no significant mineral resource deposits. Furthermore, the partition of Korea after liberation (1945) from Japanese colonial rule and then the devastating Korean War (1950-1953) caused political chaos, leading to a vicious circle of poverty, hyperinflation and chronic unemployment in the post-war period.

Korea's income per capita in 1962 was a meagre US$ 87 but increased to US$ 10,000 in 1995, about US$ 14,000 in 2004 and finally to US$ 23,000 in 2012. In 1960, the share of industry, including utilities and construction, in gross domestic product (GDP) was only 20.1 per cent but swelled to 45.0 per cent in 1991 and tapered off substantially to 36.2 per cent in 2004 as the services sector rose dramatically, a phenomenon seen in advanced matured economies. During this industrial transformation period,

Korea's total trade volume increased to US$ 1.07 trillion in 2011 from US$ 0.48 billion in 1962.[1] By any international standard, Korea demonstrated unprecedented trade-oriented industrialisation in a little over four decades.

From 1962 to the late 1990s, Korea's gross national product (GNP) grew at an average rate of 8 per cent per year in real terms, making it one of the highest performing economies in the world. In its quest for long-term high growth, Korea was seriously hit by the Asian financial crisis in 1998, which slowed economic growth to 5.1 per cent annually between 1995 and 2004. Again in 2008, Korea was engulfed in the serious economic downturn arising from the global financial crisis like most developed economies. Since then, Korea, like many other advanced economies, has had a structured, slow, jobless growth with a persistently declining potential growth rate, a kind of a maturing economy syndrome.

It is widely agreed that Korea's modern industrial development after the adoption of the first Five Year Economic Development Plan in 1962 was made under the unique paradigm of an export-based industrialisation strategy, with varying degrees of government involvement. In the 1960s, various incentives and disincentives were put in place to ensure the export of labour-intensive products. In the 1970s, the government's credit allocation policy toward target industries promoted the development of heavy and chemical industries. However, the 1980s witnessed the initial phase of domestic market opening for consumer goods.

On the political side, Korea's rapid industrial growth was accompanied by rapid political democratisation, which was characterised by a continued demand for new labour-management relations. With the advent of the World Trade Organization (WTO) in 1995, liberalisation and deregulation have been pursued both to promote a more open trade regime and to produce more technology-intensive products for export.

In retrospect, however, Korea's hitherto remarkable growth masked some structural weaknesses that left the economy vulnerable to external shocks and adverse shifts in investor confidence. When the Asian financial crisis broke out in 1997, Korea had faced unprecedented challenges. With the rapid depletion of foreign exchange reserves and the refusal of

1. Korea's trade volume surpassed for the first time the US$ 1 trillion benchmark in 2011, becoming the 8th nation to join the US$ 1 trillion trade club in world trade history.

foreign creditors to reschedule debt, Korea, in December 1997, agreed to receive then the largest the International Monetary Fund (IMF) emergency financial assistance on the condition that Korea would undertake far-reaching structural reforms to remove serious caveats contained in its high-growth economic model over four decades, namely a comprehensive restructuring of the financial, corporate, labour and public sectors. As Korea enters the 21st century, it has been in search of a new engine of growth in an increasingly globalising world economy.

The main purpose of this paper is to give an overview of the evolution of Korea's unique economic development in terms of industrial and trade policies over time, which have adjusted to changing market environments at home and abroad, and then briefly explain some practical lessons and policy implications for India-Korea economic cooperation. Overall, the main message of this paper is that Korea's policy instruments designed for trade expansion and industrial development toward a matured advanced economy have been automatic, transparent and moving toward an open trade regime step by step. The second section describes the initiation of export-led industrialisation and the major policy instruments mobilised to do so; the third section discusses industrial policies for the development of heavy and chemical industries; the fourth section describes Korea's industrial rationalisation and shift to an open trade regime; the fifth section assesses the effectiveness of outward-looking industrialisation; the sixth section presents Korea's shift to new trade and economic policies geared toward realising Korea's long-term economic vision and rapid integration in the globalising world economy; the seventh section draws a broad set of lessons from Korea's economic development. The paper concludes with some suggestions to strengthen ongoing India-Korea economic cooperation.

The Initiation of Export-led Industrialisation[2]

In the midst of economic chaos after the Korean War (1950-1953), the Syngman Rhee administration carried out two institutional reforms: land reforms based on the cultivator-owner principle and the enforcement of a compulsory primary education system. These two reforms helped increase greatly the necessary human capital for future rapid industrialisation. On

2. This section heavily draws from Ahn (1999).

the economic policy side, in the 1950s, the Rhee government adopted an import-substitution policy for non-durable consumer goods to ensure post-war economic stability above all.

With the installation of a military government headed by General Park Chung Hee in 1961, economic policy shifted to an export-led industrialisation strategy. The Park administration recognised that an increase in foreign exchange earnings was necessary to meet the rapidly rising import bill for energy and food. The Park administration also recognised that Korea's domestic market was insufficient for sustainable growth and totally lacked capital to build productive facilities to utilise a massive and unemployed but educated labour force. These changes in the economic development strategy were formally presented in the first Five-Year Economic Development Plan (1962-1966). Drafting and finalising the series of five-year plans allowed economic agents to share basic policy objectives and established a consensus-building process to identify national priorities and policy measures. The series of Korea's five-year plans contained the following special features.

Reliance on Foreign Capital Rather than Foreign Direct Investment

The goal of the outward-looking development strategy by the Park administration was to make maximum use of Korea's comparative advantage in labour-intensive manufactured food items for export (Ahn, 1986). The financing of ever-increasing investments to build up export capabilities and industrial development was made by borrowing foreign capital rather than by inducing foreign direct investment (FDI) (Ahn, 2001b). By doing so, Korea was able to cultivate the indigenous capabilities of exporting firms for industrial development through learning-by-doing and the reverse engineering processes of advanced overseas economies. To facilitate this, the government provided the business sector with official payment guarantees for foreign loans. The proportion of foreign capital to total capital formation was approximately 40 per cent during the latter half of the 1960s. It declined gradually, but was still 30.4 per cent in 1981. The share of FDI in Korea's gross domestic investment for the periods of 1984-1989 and 1990-1994 was only 1.4 and 0.7 per cent respectively. In comparison, the share of FDI in Malaysia's GDP was 8.8 and 22.4 per cent respectively for the same two periods.

Exchange Rate and Interest Rate Reforms

One of the important policy actions taken by the Park administration to promote export-led growth was to devalue the local currency (KRW) by almost 100 per cent. In 1964, the exchange rate went from 130 KRW/US$ to 255 KRW/US$. The government also switched to a unitary floating exchange rate system from the multiple exchange rate system so that a single rate would be applied to import and export transactions.

Korea consistently attempted to provide realistic exchange rates for exporters through a mixture of major devaluations and flexible adjustments with occasional time lags. The Korean government also attempted to compensate for periodic domestic currency overvaluation by means of financial and tax incentives for exporters. Rhee (1985) observed that Korea's managed foreign exchange system had a number of benefits. It prevented capital flight and selectively allowed capital inflows.

Following the exchange rate reforms in September 1965, the government raised the interest rate from 15 per cent to 30 per cent for a year's fixed deposits and loans. The goal was to increase voluntary private savings and discourage unproductive use of bank credit. To encourage further the flow of private savings to financial intermediaries, financial transactions under false names were allowed until 1993 to provide savers with a tax shelter. These efforts to mobilise both domestic and foreign savings made possible a significantly high ratio of investment to national income.

Incentive Schemes for Export Promotion

Korea's basic incentive system for export promotion was designed to eliminate discrimination against export activities. Unlike most developing countries, access to basic incentives in Korea in the 1960s was automatic for all production and commercial transactions related to exports. There were two key systems for administering the incentives for export promotion in Korea. One was related to unrestricted and tariff-free access to imported intermediate inputs and raw material needed in export production. The exporters could buy those inputs at world prices and suffered no disadvantage in the prices they paid for their raw material (Rhee *et al.*, 1984).

The other system granted automatic access to bank loans for working capital needed for all export activity, often with preferential interest rates. One of the key requirements of exporting is readily available credit for pre-shipment activity. One important reason to provide automatic access to bank loans was that it helped export activity without discriminating between large conglomerates and small firms. The system was able to minimise the case-by-case whims of bank managers and tax officials. Because of its underdeveloped money and financial markets and the predominance of credit rationing, Korea's export financing system made a significant contribution to ensure that its manufactured exports were not adversely affected by the weaknesses of its financial system.

Both direct and indirect exporters were required to present documentation of completed exports and input-coefficient certificates to prevent abuse of export incentives. To ensure tariff-free import of intermediate goods for export production, exporters were required to pay tariffs on intermediate goods and later received an immediate automatic rebate when proof of export based on the input-output coefficient requirement formulated by the Office of Industry Promotion was provided. In 1965, the Korean government also invented the local letter-of-credit system to extend the same benefits to all firms that generate export value added by providing necessary inputs but do not export directly.

Throughout the 1960s, a variety of additional incentives were provided to reduce the bias against exporting. They include corporate income tax reductions for export firms; the rationing of medium- and long-term loans for investment in heavy and chemical industry, which have a long gestation period; wastage allowance to give producers duty-free imports that could be used for production for the domestic market; import-export links, which permitted the import of restricted luxury goods in exchange for exporting specified goods having low profit margins; reduced rates for electricity and rail transport to reduce operating costs for the export firms; tariff exemptions on the imports of capital goods for long-term export production; post-shipment export loans by the Korea Export-Import Bank; and a system of export credit insurance and guarantees to diversify exports in emerging markets.

Administrative Supportive System

To complement the incentive system for export promotion, the Park administration also established a key administrative support system. Monthly export promotion meetings were held and export targeting was done to enhance the effectiveness of various export incentives. The monthly export meetings basically reviewed the progress made and initiated necessary measures to reach export targets. Chaired by the president and attended by economic ministers and leaders from the business community, political parties, and representatives from academia, the monthly meeting regularly brought the country's political leadership face to face with the major economic agents in the county, providing appropriate guidelines for action from both the government and exporting firms.

The export targets were set by each firm, based on projected sales abroad. The government used the aggregate as an important macroeconomic policy variable. For the exporting firms, the export targets were used as an informal basis to obtain long-term investment loans. As a result, the rules and regulations became transparent to every major economic agent. In order to implement the government's export-led industrial policy, the government instituted the economic planning board as a 'super ministry' with elite bureaucrats playing a pivotal role in development planning, budgeting and policy co-ordination. A reward and punishment system based on performance criteria was employed.

Public recognition was bestowed on successful exporters by awarding them with achievement medals. This was recognition of a good performance record, which enhanced a firm's credit worthiness. More importantly, government decorations provided entrepreneurs with enormous social prestige.

Industrial Policy for Heavy and Chemicals Industries[3]

In the early 1970s, Korea shifted the economic policy focus from light labour-intensive manufacturing exports to the "Heavy and Chemical Industry (HCI) Development Plan." The sudden shift to industrial deepening was motivated by the need to upgrade the industrial structure

3. For details, see Ahn and Kim (1997).

ahead of emerging labour-abundant competitors and to improve national defence capabilities after a one-third reduction of US troops stationed in Korea. Korea's HCI drive was very unique in the following aspects.

Direct Government Intervention

The HCI Development Plan identified shipbuilding, automobiles, steel products, machinery, non-ferrous metals, textiles, electronics and petrochemicals as future strategic industries. Government involvement became industry specific and sometimes firm specific. In this regard, the earlier industry-neutral incentives of the 1960s provided for exports as a whole were replaced by target industries or target firms for the promotion of these industries (Sakong, 1993). The government provided those 'strategic HCIs' with central bank credit at preferential interest rates, foreign loans, tax incentives including investment tax credit, accelerated depreciation allowances and tax holidays. They also constructed industrial parks such as the Changwon Machinery Complex and the Yeochon Petrochemical Complex.

The HCI promotion policy fostered the creation of Korean conglomerates known as *chaebols* in order to reap both economies of scale and scope. The government's industrial policy permitted the *chaebols* to grow very rapidly through diversification, cross-shareholdings among their subsidiaries and mutual repayment guarantees among subsidiary firms. Consequently, most large firms continue to register much higher debt-to-equity ratios than those in other competing economies. The expansion and increase in the number of *chaebols* created a monopolistic and oligopolistic market structure in Korea. The government's strategic allocation of financial resources resulted in shallow financial development.

Although some military and political objectives were envisioned by President Park, the sudden HCI expansion resulted in a crisis of major proportions in the late 1970s. The targeted HCIs were highly energy-intensive and seriously harmed by the first oil shock in 1973. The government's support of HCI business with virtually 'unlimited' financial support and preferential credit resulted in accelerated inflation, a growing deficit in the balance of payments (BoP), and a high degree of idle capacity. However, it should be pointed out that although the HCI drive contained import substitution elements, export was continuously emphasised. Thus, export promotion and import substitution were pursued simultaneously in a mutually reinforcing manner.

Financial and Other Incentive Schemes for HCIs

In order to finance the massive investment requirements of the HCIs, the government established the National Investment Fund, which provided long-term subsidised loans to strategically selected heavy and chemical industries to develop their capital formation in an effective and orderly manner. The fund was created through the compulsory mobilisation of private deposits from commercial banking institutions. In addition, most of Korea's concessionary loans were given by specialised banks and non-bank financial institutions, many of which were under the direct control of the Ministry of Finance. In addition, government intervention was visible in other ways, such as putting in place high tariff barriers to protect targeted HCI projects. Entry barriers were also erected for certain industries to limit competition from home and abroad.

In order to support the ever-increasing capital requirements of the HCI drive, the government issued an unusual presidential emergency decree in 1972 stating that all borrowings by business corporations from the unofficial financial markets would be subject to a repayment moratorium. The purpose of the presidential decree was to reduce the debt burden of the business corporations in order to boost their production and investment activities. Investment and finance companies were also established to undertake short-term dealings in commercial paper issued by business firms. Financial support mechanisms on the part of the government to ration long-term domestic and foreign loans were one of the most important instruments of government control over *chaebols* until the early 1980s. The government also controlled domestic banks by appointing their managers as the major shareholder.

Economic Consequences of HCI Promotion

The HCI promotion in the 1970s substantially decreased the effectiveness of Korea's export-led development machinery. Due to the HCI's long gestation period, huge idle capacities, a lack of appropriate technologies and uncertain rates of return, distortions caused by the government policy became increasingly visible. In order to induce private investment in these industries, the government had to provide ever-more distorted incentives in the form of preferential loans. To facilitate such an allocation, government authorities had to keep nominal bank lending rates below market levels, resulting in negative real interest rates and rapid expansion of the kerb market, i.e., over-the-counter (OTC) market. Economic policy became increasingly rigid and resulted in a syndrome usually associated with import substitution regimes.

In order to develop HCIs, the government took on the major burdens of investment risk. With the risk of investment reduced, and the prospects of return buoyed by the government drive, major corporations, primarily *chaebols*, made excessive investments in certain sectors such as machinery. Premature and excessive investments in HCIs caused severe distortions in resource allocation at the expense of upgrading labour-intensive industries. Furthermore, the oil shocks had resulted in a long global recession and had a severely unfavourable impact on Korea's HCI projects.

Despite some negative economic consequences of the HCI projects, the share of HCI in total manufacturing output rose from 33 per cent in 1970 to 50 per cent in 1980. By the late 1970s, some HCI products such as electronics, machinery, ships, and iron and steel products began to appear in the export commodity list. The sense of contained managerial crisis on the part of *chaebol* owners forced them to focus on high value-added technological development as the only way of overcoming the crisis instead of the traditional approach of using the comparative advantage due to low wages (Kim, 1995). Ironically, an inevitable switch to technological deepening by the HCI-based *chaebols* enabled them later to produce global brand names in electronics, automobiles, and shipbuilding through learning-by-doing and fierce competition in the international market.

Industrial Rationalisation and the Shift to an Open Trade Regime (1980s and 1990s)

While the HCI industries suffered major setbacks because of the two oil shocks in the early and late 1970s, some HCI projects in industries such as power generation, automobiles and machinery became excessive and redundant. As a result, some HCI companies experienced severe financial losses due to idle capacities and inadequate technology, requiring major rationalisation efforts.

Industrial Rationalisation and Reform of the Industrial Support System[4]

The Park administration implemented the first phase of the investment coordination plan in May 1979 to reduce excess capacity caused by the HCI projects. Then, the Chun Doo Hwan administration (1980-1988) put a higher priority on rationalising the economy. This comprehensive stabilisation programme included technological and human resource development, selective support for HCI subsectors with a focus on international competitiveness, and reduction or cancellation of scheduled projects. Power generation facilities, automobiles, diesel engines, heavy electric equipment and copper refinery smelting industries underwent substantial downsizing.

In line with an industrial rationalisation plan, Korean policy makers also recognised that import liberalisation was an effective way to bring in the competitive element to the protected but stagnant HCI and light manufacturing sectors in the economy. While pursuing an export-oriented development strategy, the import of consumer goods and other expenditures that would result in the outflow of foreign currency were very tightly controlled. Obviously, these selective import restrictions helped protect domestic industries from foreign competition in the early stage of development.

Korea's import liberalisation efforts date back to 1967, when the import regulation system was changed from a positive list system to a negative list system. In order to maximise the benefits of market opening in a still-protectionist environment, the government announced in the early 1980s a five-year import liberalisation schedule, which would gradually reduce tariff rates and eliminate non-tariff barriers. As a result, the import liberalisation ratio of manufactured foods, measured by the ratio of automatic approval items to total tradable items, rose from 37 per cent in 1965 to 95.4 per cent by 1988.

While carrying out the industrial rationalisation programmes, industrial policy in the 1980s relied more heavily on market functions by taking several measures to reduce government intervention and encourage

---

4. For details, see Ahn and Kim (1995).

private sector initiatives. First, the industry-specific support system was replaced by functional support systems dealing with technological and human resource development and energy conservation. Second, a fair and competitive market environment was encouraged by removing import restrictions and entry barriers. Third, the government provided temporary support to only those industries that were essential to the national economy but did not have adequate supportive infrastructure at the time for sustained growth.

Trade Liberalisation under the World Trade Organization

As the US and other western economies suffered stagnation and chronic trade deficits throughout the 1970s, the US demanded a reciprocal opening of the market of all trading partners. Korea has traditionally shipped the largest share of its exports to the US. It registered a trade surplus of US$ 1.9 billion for the first time in 1985, and reached a peak surplus of US$ 9.5 billion in 1987. The consequence was that new protectionist measures were applied against US trading partners, including rapidly growing economies. Korea faced voluntary export restraints, quantity restrictions and anti-dumping measures, especially by the US.

Since the mid-1980s, efforts have been made to resolve bilateral trade frictions by opening Korea's market to selected agricultural products to accede to the terms of Article XI of General Agreement on Tariffs and Trade (GATT) in 1989; it accelerated the pace of liberalisation, raising the liberalisation ratio to 99 per cent in 1994. The motivation behind import liberalisation in Korea was the international competitiveness of domestic industries rather than consumer welfare. Domestic firms exposed to international competition had to do more than simply raise market prices and assemble imported parts to earn profits. Since 1984, comprehensive import liberalisation reform measures have had positive effects on expanding the import substitution of fabricated metals and mechanical equipment industries by substantially raising their import dependency ratio.

While initiating export-led growth, Korea joined the GATT as a full member in 1967. When the WTO was formally launched in 1995, open and fair competition became a new directional guideline in formulating Korea's industrial policy. This new policy accelerated the industrial restructuring process. An important government policy was geared to induce FDI, especially in the high-tech areas, by simplifying government permission procedures and other regulations.

The shift to a new development paradigm was inevitable for various internal reasons. The government's fair competition law started to get strictly enforced. Under this environment, government direct intervention was neither effective nor feasible anymore. As a result, the government-business interface became more transparent and more market based. The industrial policy shifted to infrastructure and necessary social overhead capital (SOC) building to promote technological innovation by private initiatives. The 'globalisation' slogan of the Kim Young Sam administration (1993-1997) was also a manifestation of this trend.

Assessment of the Outward-oriented Industrialisation Strategy in the High Growth Era

Since the adoption of an outward-looking development strategy, the annual growth rate of both GNP and export rose very sharply, as shown in Table 5.1. The annual real growth rate of commodity exports was 36.8 per cent under the export expansion regime between 1962 and 1976, whereas the growth rate under the import substitution regime was only 7.6 per cent over the same period.

Table 5.1

Annual Real Growth Rates of GNP by Industrial Origin and Exports, 1953-1976

(Unit: %)

Period	*Primary*	*Secondary*	*(Manufacture)*	*Tertiary*	*GNP*	*Commodity Exports*
1953-1961	2.5	10.8	(11.1)	4.3	4.1	7.6
1962-1976	4.5	17.9	(18.5)	9.4	9.6	36.8

Source: Bank of Korea, Economic Statistics, various years.

The role of export-led growth is further evident when comparing the contribution of import substitution to manufacturing growth, as shown in Table 5.2. The direct contribution of exports to the growth of manufacturing increased from 5 per cent in 1960 to 36 per cent in 1973 and averaged 26.8 per cent for the entire period. However, import substitution contributed little and was even negative in the final period of 1970-1973.

Table 5.2

Direct Contribution to Growth in Manufacturing, 1960-1973

Source of Growth	1960-1963	1963-1966	1966-1968	1968-1970	1970-1973
Export expansion	4.8	14.2	12.4	15.1	35.9
Import substitution	-2.8	0.2	11.4	7.2	-4.0

Source: Westphal and Kim, 1977.

Effectiveness of the Neutral Exchange Rate Policy

A crucial variable in explaining the main features of the trade regime in an outward-oriented economy is the exchange rate policy. Since the exchange rate reforms of 1964-65, the export-incentive system in Korea has been formulated to reduce consistently trade-distorting effects on the export side. This is clearly reflected in the time series of nominal and purchasing power parity (PPP)-adjusted effective exchange rates for exports and imports, as shown in Table 5.3.

Table 5.3

Nominal and PPP-adjusted Effective Exchange Rates

Year	Nominal Exchange Rate (Won/US$)			PPP-adjusted Exchange Rate (Won/US$)			
		Effective			Effective		Anti-export Bias
	Official	Exports (1)	Imports (2)	Official (3)	Exports (4)	Imports (5)	(4)/(5)
1965	265.4	275.3	293.1	265.4	275.3	293.1	0.94
1970	310.7	331.5	336.4	240.2	256.2	260.0	0.99
1973	398.3	407.0	417.7	320.6	327.6	336.2	0.97
1975	484.4	496.9	508.9	274.4	281.7	288.5	0.98
1978	484.0	495.0	526.9	272.0	278.2	296.1	0.94
1980	607.4	628.0	641.8	250.1	260.0	265.7	0.98
1983	775.8	775.8	831.7	264.5	264.5	283.6	0.93
1985	870.0	870.0	920.3	290.6	290.6	307.4	0.95
1988	730.6	730.6	780.3	319.3	319.3	341.0	0.94
1990	708.6	708.6	748.0	289.1	289.1	305.2	0.95

Note: (1) Official exchange rate plus net export subsidies per US dollar of exports.

(2) Official exchange rate plus actual tariffs and tariff equivalents per US dollar of import.

(3) Multiplying nominal official exchange rate by the PPP index divided by 100. The PPP index is the average weighted by their respective average shares in Korea's total trade volume.

Source: Kim, 1991.

The net export subsidies per US dollar of exports have been gradually reduced over time so that the effective exchange rate for export is identical to the official exchange rate in Korea. Despite substantial price inflation, particularly before 1982, the anti-export bias index has remained consistently near one, indicating that the nominal exchange rate had been flexibly adjusted to prevent any significant overvaluation of the won. It should be noted that the relative stability in the PPP-adjusted exchange rate since 1965 and the removal of the anti-export bias significantly contributed to the rapid expansion of Korea's exports (Kim, 1995).

Effectiveness of Protection for Domestic Industries

While removing the anti-export bias, the Korean government also selectively adopted protective measures for strategic industries in the domestic market to ensure self-sustaining growth. Korea also pursued an import substitution policy for machinery and transport equipment and consumer durables until they gained international competitiveness while actively promoting the export of finished goods of these manufacturing sub-sectors during the sample period. The upshot of Korea's industrial policy was to ensure that both import substitution and export promotion complemented each other.

Contribution of Exports to Industrial Growth and Structural Transformation

During the export promotion period, both domestic demand and exports contributed most to Korea's industrial growth. Table 5.4 shows that Korea's production and exports had similar compositions. Manufactured goods increased from about 61 per cent to about 94 per cent of total exports by 1990. Furthermore, within the category of manufactured export, machinery and transport equipment increased from 3.1 per cent to nearly 40 per cent of the total between 1965 and 1990.

Two points are clear regarding the role of exports in Korea's industrialisation process. First, the structural change in manufacturing exports generally led to the pattern of change observed in manufacturing production. Considering the dominance of HCIs within manufacturing in the 1980s, the industrial deepening from the HCI drive and the upgrading of export commodities were mutually reinforcing. Second, export expansion was more critical to Korea's rapid industrialisation than import substitution, suggesting that the policy shift to export-led growth was quite effective in altering the pattern of industrialisation.

Table 5.4

Production and Export Structure of Manufacturing

(Unit: %)

	Food Processing	*Textiles*	*Finished Consumer Goods*	*Inter-mediate Goods*	*Machinery & Transport Equipment*	*Manufacturing Total*
1. Production structure						
1963	27.8	15.4	18.0	30.0	8.8	100.0
1975	15.7	14.9	18.3	32.2	18.9	100.0
1985	10.5	12.1	16.8	40.8	13.6	100.0
2. Exports structure						
1963	20.7	20.8	13.9	38.6	6.0	100.0
1975	4.2	15.5	33.6	18.3	28.4	100.0
1985	1.5	9.5	20.7	27.9	40.3	100.0

Source: Kim and Hong (1990).

Contribution of Technology to Economic Growth

Korea's consistent efforts to improve allocative efficiency within a market framework are reflected in the important contribution of technological progress to economic growth. According to estimates derived by Hong (1994) and Park (1994), technology factors contributed significantly to economic growth in the past three decades, beginning in the early 1970s, as shown in Table 5.5.

Table 5.5

Contribution of Technology Factor to Economic Growth in Korea

(Unit: %)

	1963-1972	*1972-1982*	*1982-1992*	*1963-1992*
Growth Rate of GNP	8.22	7.09	9.49	8.26
Labour	2.74	2.95	2.18	2.61
Capital	1.14	2.02	1.93	1.71
Scale Merits	1.52	1.51	1.81	1.65
Technology	1.89	0.64	0.95	1.14
Others*	0.94	0.97	1.24	1.07

Note: * Includes effect of improved resource allocation, grading level of education, and deregulation of trade barriers.

Source: Hong, 1994.

The Shift to New Trade and Economic Policies in the 21st Century

Korea's rapid growth since the early 1960s until the mid-1990s was indeed a wonder but contained a serious caveat due to long-term, highly leveraged business expansion. Surprisingly, the Korean economy was seriously hit by the Asian financial crisis, which erupted in Thailand and rapidly spread to other Asian countries in July 1997. It seems that some inherent structural weaknesses in Korea's economy had not been seriously raised prior to the outbreak of the Asian financial crisis, except in Krugman's assertion (1994) that the East Asian economic miracle was nothing but an input-driven model.

A vicious chain of inefficiency that existed across the financial sector and the corporate sector in Korea had been growing since the second stage of the heavy chemical industrial drive in the early 1980s. *Chaebols* were promoted by means of government-administered credit allocation to take advantage of economies of scale, which resulted in excessive lending without prudential rules. Yet, the *chaebols'* focus on increasing market share and pursuing diversification through debt financing with little attention to profitability caused an inefficiency syndrome in Korea's economy. Consequently, the demise of both the corporate and financial sectors was intertwined. As corporate bankruptcies rose, financial institutions became burdened with bad debts and were no longer able to roll over their domestic or foreign liabilities.

As a result, Korea had no choice but to draw a financial bailout package on the condition that Korea would carry out the International Monetary Fund's mandates to undertake comprehensive reforms in four sectors: banks, corporations, labour and public enterprises. Both the Asian financial crisis and the launch of the WTO system demanded that Korea modify its conventional high growth-oriented model and adjust to new trade and industrial policies to match the increasingly globalised world economy and increasingly integrated capital markets. The key to overcoming Korea's economic crisis and promote sustainable growth involves the development of effective financial intermediaries with international best practices, an advanced governance system, and frontier technologies. Korea's conventional industrial policy *via* subsidised credit allocation to target industries is no longer allowed under the WTO's policy of a level playing field.

With the advent of the 21st century with rapid globalisation and given the stalled Doha round, Korea adopted a multi-track free trade agreement (FTA) policy to maintain its outward-looking development orientation. As shown in Table 5.6, Korea became the first significant economy to have an effective FTA with the US and the EU. Korea now aims to serve as an FTA hub nation in East Asia.

Table 5.6

FTA Trends in Korea

Classification	*Remarks*
In Effect (9)	Chile (April 2004), Singapore (March 2006), EFTA (September 2006), ASEAN (September 2009), India (January 2010), EU (July 2011), Peru (August 2011), USA (March 2012), Turkey (May 2013)
Concluded (1)	Colombia (June 2012)
Under Negotiation (5)	Indonesia, Vietnam, China, China-Japan, RCEP
Under Consideration (10)	Canada, Japan, Mexico, GCC, Australia, New Zealand, MERCOSUR, Israel, Central America, Malaysia

Note: EFTA (4): Switzerland, Norway, Ireland, Liechtenstein.

ASEAN (10): Indonesia, Malaysia, Singapore, Thailand, Vietnam, Cambodia, Brunei, Myanmar, the Philippines, Laos.

EU (27): Austria, Belgium, England, Czech, Cyprus, Denmark, Estonia, Finland, France, Germany, Greece, Hungary, Ireland, Italy, Latvia, Lithuania, Luxemburg, Malta, Netherland, Poland, Portugal, Slovakia, Slovenia, Spain, Sweden, Bulgaria, Rumania.

MERCOSUR (4): Argentina, Brazil, Paraguay, Uruguay.

Central America (5): Costa Rica, El Salvador, Guatemala, Honduras, Panama.

Source: Ministry of Trade, Industry and Energy, Korea.

In trade as well as in industrial development, Korea now needs to develop world-class products to ensure a sustainable and trade-oriented economy. In a borderless economy, it is increasingly difficult to distinguish between the objectives of trade policy and industrial policy. In order to meet the single converging objective of trade and industrial policies, Korea has to develop frontier-technology products in an open, fair and competitive manner in the global market. The essence of new industrial policies is (a) to promote a virtuous circle of manufacturing and manufacturing-related service industries to utilise the fusion effects of information and communication technologies, (b) to focus on a market-based innovation system and (c) to cultivate frontier-technology products or a functional support system.

In a nutshell, Korea now has to establish a knowledge-based economy to nurture a competitive industrial structure based on market-driven innovation rather than a visible government hand. During the post-crisis period, indeed, most of the needed 'hardware' improvements to the regulatory and institutional framework were largely completed, but important steps remain in developing the necessary 'software' in order to change the financial practices and ways of doing business that prevailed in the high growth era. The Korean government needs to continue to play a critical role in monitoring and enforcing its regulations to ensure fair trade practices and the removal of moral hazards on the part of businesses and financial institutions.

Thanks to the heavy and chemical industry drive in the early stages of industrialisation and private and public R&D efforts, Korea succeeded in catching up with global leaders in selected industries. For example, in the semiconductor, shipbuilding and digital electronics industries, Korea has been firmly secured as a global leader. Automobile and petrochemical industries are on the verge of entering the world's top four in terms of production and exports. Steel and some machinery parts and materials have also become highly competitive in the global market. Korea also recognises e-business, distribution and logistics as leading sub-sectors of service industries.

The Korean government is planning to establish a world-class industrial foundation and develop advanced strategic technologies such as information technology (IT), bio technology (BT), and nano technology (NT) that will be critical for a knowledge-based economy. According to the Ministry of Commerce, Industry and Energy, Korea's vision for industrial development can be seen in Table 5.7.

Table 5.7

Korea's Industrial Vision by Group

Basic Industries Towards World-class Competitiveness	*Future Strategic Industries*	*Service Industries*
Shipbuilding, Semiconductors, Automobiles, Textiles, Steel, Petrochemicals	Digital electronic industry, Electronic medical equipment, Bio industry	Business service, E-business

Source: Ministry of Commerce, Industry and Energy homepage (*http://www.most.go.kr/*).

Lessons from Korea's Economic Development

Since the early 1960s, the guidelines directing trade and industrial policies have shifted from the calculus of intervention to a focus on market function and liberalisation. As a result, it is very hard to generalise about Korea's trade and industrial policies over time. At each stage of industrial development, a different element has been more dominant than others, even under the outward-oriented development regime. Several lessons drawn from Korean experiences can be shared with other emerging and developing economies.

Consistently Outward-looking Development Policies

The export-driven industrialisation strategy operated with clear objective performance criteria to reward or punish subsidised industries because exporters had to compete in the world market. An export promotion-type industrial policy had a much better chance of succeeding and was consistent with market-guided resource allocation. Kruger (1997) points out that there is no doubt that Korea's economic performance with respect to exports and industrial growth has been truly remarkable. Korea's unique industrialisation model is something more than a neo-classical growth model. Since switching to an outward-oriented development strategy in the early 1960s, Korea has developed a general consensus to push 'the export-first doctrine' through cooperation among government, entrepreneurs and workers.

In sum, Korea's development policies for export-led industrialisation were basically formulated to ensure that potential exporters would be on equal footing with international competitors. Rules have been largely nondiscretionary and transparent for every agent in the market. Korea used export as the criterion with which success was judged. However, whenever market functions were beneficially available, the policy was to let the market determine production.

There are conflicting views about the nature of the Korean industrialisation model. *The 1987 World Development Report* characterised the South Korean growth model as an outward-oriented growth model based on a free market and free trade system. Other schools, like Alam (1989) and Kirkpatrik (1987), view Korean industrialisation as completely interventionist, with a 'strict state' that differs little from an import substitution growth strategy. There are several studies between the two extremes—for example, the *1991 World Development Report* or the "East Asian Miracle Study of Fundamentals and Interventions" (*The East Asian Miracles*, 1993: 22). Professor Amsden describes Korea's industrial development model as "the market augmenting paradigm of late industrialisation" (Amsden, 1989: 150). Overall, the Korean government-led HCI promotion policies maintained performance-based 'stick and carrot' policies to ensure the survival-of-the-fittest principle.

Korea's industrial development has mostly been associated with effective but carefully designed government activism that left exports largely free to market principles. The underlying spirit of this approach could be described as a 'market friendly strategy,' in which market solutions were sought whenever market functions were sound. However, the government intervened aggressively whenever market development was still in a rudimentary stage.

The Role of Entrepreneurs and *Chaebols*

In a market economy, any industrial policy implementation is finally achieved through private entrepreneurial responses. Jones and Sakong (1980) suggested that there was a substantial stock of entrepreneurial talent even in the 1950s. However, it was only in the 1960s that these entrepreneurial energies were channelled into socially productive activities such as exports, mostly through the policy efforts of the government. Most importantly, Korean entrepreneurs always emphasised indigenous efforts in mastering advanced technology and business practices in the world market. The export orientation of national economic policy provided them with ready access to world-class products. Korean entrepreneurs relied on indigenous efforts to gain industrial competence through various forms of learning-by-doing (Ahn, 2001a). Korea's entrepreneurial talents responded positively to various government incentives to build up Korea's indigenous technological capability. In this regard, both Chairman Lee Byung Chul of the Samsung Group and Chairman Chung Ju Yong of the Hyundai Group were ahead of their time in pioneering new industries such as electronics, shipbuilding, automobiles and semiconductors.

Despite the positive role played by Korean entrepreneurs and *chaebols*, Korea's big businesses created a concentrated economic power in comparison with small- and medium-sized companies. In addition to the monopolistic or oligopolistic nature of major industries where *chaebols* are most visible, their sheer size and diversification also distorted competition in a relatively closed trading regime.

Despite Korea's high economic performance, Korea's rapid industrialisation and high growth created some weaknesses in terms of sustainable growth. The rapid economic expansion of the *chaebols vis-à-vis* small- and medium-sized companies created a dualistic structure in the business sector. Korea's sandwich position in the international technology competition is still apparent. The financial sector had been depressed during the HCI promotion period.

Korea's industrial development pattern largely followed the flying geese model. Declining industries from advanced countries were introduced and turned into mature industries in Korea. In recent years, many Korean firms have been expanding their business operations overseas to exploit cheaper wages, natural resource deposits and local market access. Especially, as domestic wages increased, they were moved to other developing countries. Many countries focus on offering functional support to enhance science and technology (S&T) to nurture world-class high-tech MNCs. It should be noted that Korea's top *chaebols* began to operate their businesses on a global scale and were able to attract the best and brightest personnel. The consistent global orientation of Korea's top *chaebols* allowed them to gather international market information and create innovative practices.

Although Korea introduced the proactive inducement of FDI after the Asian financial crisis, Korea's outbound FDI in the past six years was three times the inbound FDI. As cross-border supply chains are becoming the new business life, Korea needs to create a more robust, friendly business environment for inbound FDI. In the domestic as well as overseas markets, Korea must now compete head-to-head with advanced countries in high-tech industries, such as the semiconductor, automobile, machinery and information industries. It is clear that *chaebols* should develop close partnerships with small- and medium-sized firms because assembly-type industries such as electronics, automobiles and machinery are becoming increasingly important in Korea.

Korea now faces the problem of competing in a fair and competitive, globalised world economy. In this regard, Korea needs to dismantle existing rigidities and regulations on entry and exit with more vigour. How to foster competition and cooperation between local and multinational firms and the extent to which Korea should maximise the existing R&D capabilities of *chaebols* and mould them into institutions that operate on a fair and anti-monopolistic basis in a market friendly environment are important issues. In the WTO era, Korea's financial sector must be developed side-by-side with the rest of the economy. Financial liberalisation and deregulation should be pursued to bring in more efficiency as well as transparency in the economy.

By and large, the administrations of Park, Chun, Roh and both Kims consistently sought the industrial policy of 'getting the basics right' within a market-conforming framework with varying degrees of success. However, both incentives and disincentives were designed to promote efficiency in the allocation of limited resources with the help of market forces as much as possible. During the rapid growth phase, policy mistakes were made. As Kruger (1997) points out, a hallmark of Korea's economic policy seems to have been a rapid feedback mechanism, which enabled relatively rapid correction of policy mistakes.

Other developing countries at various stages of industrial development can draw general lessons from Korea's experiences. First, government incentive systems in the initial stages of industrialisation need to be outward looking and should be closely linked to quantifiable, transparent and performance-based criteria. Winning export orders from the competitive international market means that firms have passed an international efficiency test. Even during the HCI drive, the government penalised badly performing chaebols and rewarded good performers with new licences in more lucrative sectors. As a result, incentives reinforced allocative efficiency.

Second, financial sector development should not be neglected in favour of more tangible real-sector activities. In recent years, this has become a top priority issue. Progress to date has included interest rate liberalisation and capital market opening. Henceforth, the evaluation of a firm's creditworthiness and monitoring firms' risks should be transferred from the state to financial institutions.

Third, entrepreneurship is essential in implementing government policies at all stages of industrialisation. Therefore, it is critical to foster a cadre of entrepreneurs who display business leadership.

Fourth, a disciplined workforce as well as capable bureaucrats is fundamental in moving the export-led development machinery forward. Fifth, it is crucial that competition is fostered within regulatory and legal boundaries to ensure fair play; equally, the leadership should be able to build a national consensus to achieve development goals.

Korea faces daunting challenges in preparing for ongoing globalisation and the WTO era. Korea should continue to adhere fully to the international rules of fair competition as an OECD member. Upgrading Korea's business environment and taking advantage of its geo-economic location in rapidly growing northeast Asia, especially due to China's economic rise, could result in Korea becoming a regional business and financial hub in northeast Asia. If successful in restructuring its industries and service sectors toward a knowledge-based economy by the early 21st century, Korea could be one of the few countries to become an advanced industrial economy with a political democracy within a little over a half century after the initiation of export-based industrialisation in the early 1960s.

Implications for Korea-India Economic Cooperation[5]

Korea adopted outward-oriented economic policies with the inception of its first five-year economic development plan in 1962, which resulted in high growth and the integration of the Korean economy with the rest of the world. India, on the other hand, adopted an import-substitution policy from its independence until the early 1990s. Since 1991, India has introduced wide-ranging economic policy reforms to enhance the efficiency of both the manufacturing and fragmented service sectors toward an outward-looking and market-driven economy. This has resulted in consistent high economic growth over the past decade and a half, making India the 10th largest economy in the world.

At present, India and South Korea are the third- and fourth-largest economies in Asia. They have shared a close relationship since the establishment of formal diplomatic ties in 1973. The past four decades have seen tremendous economic transformation in both countries. Given the great difference in factor endowment and once markedly different development paradigms, the two countries can benefit a lot by looking at each other's policy instruments. As the Indian economy has launched its economic reform programme with a focus on liberalisation and globalisation, India might take a look at Korea's quest for international competition through export promotion policies with a clear and transparent incentive and disincentive system.

The greater openness of the Indian economy has not only enhanced market access for Korean goods but has also provided investment opportunities for internationally competitive Korean companies. However, the current size of trade and investment is very low compared to the size and structural complementarities of the two economies. There is immense potential to enhance economic cooperation between the two sides. As a part of its 'Look East Policy' (LEP), India has been making efforts to intensify its economic relations with East Asian economies. On the other hand, Korea is looking beyond its traditional trading partners, like the US and China, to sustain its trade and economic progress.

---

5. For comprehensive coverage of India-Korea economic cooperation, see Ahn and Sahoo (2012).

Both India and Korea have been getting integrated in the world economy, enhancing their role in the international economic order. The increasing scale of globalisation not only holds potential for greater cooperation at various multilateral forums like the WTO and the IMF, but also offers immense scope at the regional level to strengthen bilateral ties, given the deadlock and slow growth of negotiations in the Doha Round in the WTO. Realising the need for greater economic cooperation, both countries agreed in 2005 to establish a Joint Study Group (JSG) to comprehensively evaluate their economic relations and the feasibility of an India-Korea Comprehensive Economic Partnership Agreement (CEPA). After several rounds of negotiations, the CEPA was finally signed on August 7, 2009. This is also India's first FTA with an OECD country.

Given the outward-looking and liberalising economic orientation, economic diversity and factor endowments in India and Korea, the two countries are likely to benefit from each other by maximising the potential benefit of the CEPA. It is fortunate and timely that the ICRIER and Seoul Forum for International Affairs (SFIA) have conducted annual dialogues over a decade to deepen mutual cooperation and understanding between the two countries. As global economic gravity shifts to Asia, the mutual cooperation between two like-minded countries, India and Korea, can serve as an important step toward the early completion of the Regional Comprehensive Economic Partnership (RCEP)[6] and eventually the Asia-Pacific economic community.

References

Ahn, Choong Yong (1986), "Economic Development of South Korea, 1945-1985: Strategies and Performance", *Korea and World Affairs* 10(1), Spring.

———. (1999), "Newly Industrializing Economies: The Case of the Republic of Korea", Francisco Sercovich with others (ed.), *Competition and the World Economy*. Edward Elgar and the UNIDO.

———. (2001a), "A Search for Robust East Asian Development Model after the Financial Crisis: Mutual Learning from East Asian Experiences", *Journal of Asian Economics* 12(3).

———. (2001b), "Financial and Corporate Sector Restructuring in South Korea: Accomplishments and Unfinished Agenda", *Japanese Economic Review* 52(4).

6. The participating countries in the RCEP negotiations include ASEAN 10 economies, China, Japan, Korea, Australia, India and New Zealand. They intend to complete a free trade and investment agreement by the end of 2015.

———. (2003), "A Vision for Korea as a Business Hub", *Joint U.S.-Korea Academic Studies* 13.

Ahn, Choong Yong and Baekin Cha (2004), Financial Sector Restructuring in South Korea: Accomplishments and Unfinished Agenda", *Asian Economic Papers* 3(1): 1-21.

Ahn, Choong Yong and Joo-Hoon Kim (1995). "The Outward-looking Trade Policy and the Industrial Development", in Dong-Se Cha and Kwang Suk Kim (eds.), *The Korean Economy 1945-1995: Performance and Vision for the 21st Century* (in Korean). Korea Development Institute. pp.312-69.

———. (1997). "Outward Looking Trade Policies and Industrial Development", in Cha Dong Se, Kim Kwang Suk and Dwight Prekins (eds.), *The Korean Economy 1945-1995: Performance and Vision for the 21st Century.* Korea Development Institute Press.

Ahn, Choong Yong and Pravakar Sahoo (2012), "Introduction", in Choong Yong Ahn and Pravakar Sahoo (eds.), *India Korea: Dialogue for a 21st Century Partnership*. New Delhi: Academic Foundation.

Alam, M. Shahid (1989). *Government and Market in Economic Development Strategies: Lessons from Korea, Taiwan, and Japan*. New York: Praeger.

Amsden, Alice H. (1989). *Asia's Next Giant: South Korea and Late Industrialization.* New York: Oxford University Press.

Balassa, Bela (1976), "Reforming the System of Incentives in Developing Countries", *World Development* 3(6).

Chopra, Ajai, Kenneth Kang, Meral Karasulu, Hong Liang, Henry Ma and Anthony Richards (2002). "From Crisis to Recovery in Korea: Strategy, Achievements, and Lessons", in *Korean Crisis and Recovery*. International Monetary Fund and Korea Institute for International Economic Policy.

Frankel, Jeffery (1997). *Regional Trading Blocs in the World Economic System*. Washington, D.C.: Institute for International Economics.

Hong, Sung Duk (1994), "Analysis of Factor Contribution to Korea's Economic Growth" (in Korean), *Korea Development Review* 16(3), Korea Development Institute.

Jones, Leroy P. and Sakong Il (1980). *Government, Business, and Entrepreneurship in Economic Development: The Korean Case*. Harvard University Press.

Kim, K.S, (1991). "Korea", in D. Papageorgiou, M. Michaely and A.M. Choksi (eds.), *Liberalizing Foreign Trade: Korea, the Philippines and Singapore*, Vol. 2. Cambridge: Basil Blackwell, pp.1-131.

Kim, Kwang-Suk (1994). "Trade and Industrialization Policies in Korea: An Overview", Garry K. Helleiner (ed.), *Trade Policy and Industrialization in Turbulent Times*. London: Routledge.

Kim, Kwang-Suk and Sung Duk Hong (1990). *Analysis of the Long-term Industrial Growth and Their Contribution to the Structural Changes in Korea: 1955-85*, (in Korean). Korea Development Institute

Kim, Linsu (1993). "National System of Industrial Innovation: Dynamics of Capacity Building in Korea," John Nelson (ed.), *National Innovation Systems: A Comparative Analysis.* New York: Oxford University Press

Kirkpatrik, Colin (1987). "Trade Policy and Industrialization in LDCs", in Norman Gemmel (ed.), *Surveys in Development Economics.* Basil Blackwell, pp.56-89.

Kruger, Anne O. (1997). "Korean Industry and Trade over Fifty Years", in *The Korean Economy 1945-1995: Performance and Vision for the 21st Century*, Korea Development Institute.

Krugman, Paul (1994). "The Myth of Asia's Miracle", *Foreign Affairs* 73(6). November/ December.

Lieberman, Ira W. and William Mako (1998). "Korea's Corporate Crisis: Its Origins and Strategy for Financial Restructuring", in *Korean Economic Restructuring: Evaluation and Prospects*. Korea Institute for International Economic Policy.

Park, Yung Chul (1994). "Development and Structural Change of the Financial System", in Hugh T. Patrick and Yung Chul Park (eds.), *The Financial Development of Japan, Korea, and Taiwan*. Oxford University Press.

Rhee, Yung Whee, Bruce Ross-Larson and Garry Purshell (1984). *Korea's Competitive Edge: Managing the Entry into World Markets*. Johns Hopkins University Press.

Rhee, Yung Whee (1985). "Instruments for Export Policy and Administration: Lessons from the East Asian Experience", *World Bank Staff Working Papers* No. 725.

Sakong Il (1993). *Korea in the World Economy*. Washington, DC: Institute for International Economics.

Westphal, Larry E. and Kwang Suk Kim (1977). "Industrial Policy and Development in Korea", *The World Bank Staff Working Paper*, No. 263, World Bank.

World Bank (1993). *The East Asian Miracle: Economic Growth and Public Policy*. New York: Oxford University Press.

6 Korea's Institutional Resolve

Lessons for India

Rajat Kathuria

Introduction

Despite many apparent and obvious differences in their growth paths, India and Korea have both emerged as strong Asian economies demonstrating increasing resilience to deal with crises. Both states emerged from decades of colonial rule after World War II, suffering fractious and violent divisions that fashioned their initial approach to economic growth. Starting from a war-destroyed, impoverished economy in the mid-1950s, South Korea industrialised rapidly and, in 1996, joined the 'rich man's club,' the Organization for Economic Co-operation and Development (OECD). India, on the other hand, did not begin market friendly reforms until 1991 when a beleaguered government cut tariffs, eased foreign entry restrictions and significantly dismantled industrial licensing. The pre-reform era had skewed India's development in ways that locked India into a suboptimal growth trajectory. It was the deep macroeconomic crisis of 1991 that forced dismantling of the dirigiste controls.

Around the middle of the last century, both India and South Korea were poor developing economies. At the end of Korean War in 1953, South Korea's GDP per capita was roughly US$ 800, while India's was only slightly lower than that. Sixty years on, South Korea's GDP per capita has soared to US$ 31,950, whereas India's has witnessed a moderate increase to US$ 3,843 in international dollars.[1] The period immediately prior to liberalisation in both countries reflected the dominant thinking amongst

1. International Monetary Fund (2013). *World Economic Outlook Database*. An international dollar buys in the cited country a comparable amount of goods and services a US dollar would buy in the US. This is often referred to as purchasing power parity (PPP) exchange rate.

development economists of that time.[2] As labour abundant economies, South Korea and India adopted an inward-looking growth agenda that manifested itself in import substitution industrialisation (ISI) that was prompted largely by the scepticism of the benefits of free trade and competition.

Displeased with its own performance, South Korea pressed the reform button much earlier than India and reaped the corresponding rewards. By the early 1960s, South Korea embarked upon an outward-looking development model and experienced rapid growth over the next two decades (see Box 6.1). On the other hand, the public sector took on a more prominent role in India. Government intervention was seen as the best way to achieve multiple national economic objectives, including growth and equity.[3] The origins of government ownership and the consequent controls were, in the words of Jagdish Bhagwati, "the result of two major factors: first, the inability to trust the market and its outcomes and secondly, the failure to understand that markets [would] generally work better than central planning as a resource-allocation device" (Bhagwati, 1993). Centralised planning thus dominated decentralised markets and decision making until the dismantling of the draconian Licence Permit Raj in 1991.

There is ample evidence from across the world suggesting that protected state-owned monopolies have failed to respond to demands for expanded service or improved quality (Brown *et al.*, 2006). Public funding dulls the incentive to respond to customers, while government mandates to provide services may be simply infeasible if they are not accompanied by sufficient financial, technology and human resources to deliver these outcomes. Inclusive, efficient production cannot simply be decreed without an institutional framework that guides investment and management toward public goals. Students of economic history repeatedly emphasise the significance of institutions and the role of the state. According to Lloyd Reynolds (1985), government matters. W. Arthur Lewis (2013)

---

2. The seminal papers are Prebisch (1950) and Singer (1950). For a more recent survey of the issues, see Bruton (1998). There are also recent studies of the empirical observation of declining relative primary commodity prices, as in Harvey *et al.* (2010).

3. In the 19th century, however, a good portion of infrastructure investments, particularly investments required to open up access to natural resources or new areas for development, were provided by the private sector. See Rakesh Mohan's *India Infrastructure Report* (2003).

noted that growth theory is incomplete without a role for government, where government is as much the problem as the solution. More recently, a number of scholars have gone further, suggesting that an activist state has been a key ingredient of rapid development, especially in parts of East Asia, and that, conversely, malfunctioning states have contributed heavily to developmental failures, say, in sub-Saharan Africa (Kohli, 2004). The *prima facie* case for a broad focus on state and development is thus strong. Acemoglu *et al.* (2012) develop the empirical and theoretical case that differences in [economic] institutions are the fundamental cause of differences in economic development, citing evidence from the division of Korea into two parts with very different institutions, among others, to back the claim. And therefore, even though a broad consensus has emerged on the increasing role of the market in almost all countries including in South Korea and India, state intervention through its institutions remains critical to achieving several development objectives.

The reason is straightforward. At the microeconomic level, there are fundamental problems with competitive capitalism and yet, if it is not clear where the market has failed, government through its several instruments will be able to improve the outcomes (Nolan, 2004). The experience of a wide range of successfully industrialising countries, from France, Germany and Japan in the 19th century through to Singapore, Taiwan and South Korea since the 1950s, demonstrates that a key element in rapid growth is devising appropriate ways in which the state can offset market failure (Ibid.). But it is also possible that state intervention could produce worse results for growth than those obtaining with market failure and an absence of state intervention. According to Lin (2010), states that possess a well-informed, effective bureaucracy embedded in the realities and needs of local industry are more likely to succeed.[4] The historical record indicates that in all successful economies, the state has always played an important role in facilitating structural change (Lin and Monga, 2010). There is, however, considerable variation in state capacities to implement economic transformation. While the South Korean case points to the capacity of the state to effectively implement its own policies, the results from India are mixed. According to Kohli (2004), the creation of effective states within

4. Peter Evans calls this 'embedded autonomy.'

the developing world has generally preceded industrialisation. This is because state intervention in support of investor profits has proved to be a precondition for industry to emerge and flourish among late-late-developers. Of late, even the World Bank, after decades of consensus that industrial policy does not work for developing nations, is now recommending its use (Ibid.).

State intervention, however, is not always successful. Defined as an attempt by the government to promote economy-wide growth or even support-specific industries, there have been successes and, as expected, failures. There are many variables that are likely to determine success, such as the choice of sectors, the prevailing global economic conditions, the status of international agreements and, above all, the capacity of the state to implement its own policies. Even if the costs and benefits of the policies are measured properly, it is possible that costs could far exceed the benefits. For example, a study by the McKinsey Global Institute argues that although America, South Korea and Taiwan established enduringly successful semiconductor industries, other countries have so far wasted billions (see Table 6.1). The IT sector is usually preferred for government support due to the significant spillover benefits it can produce for the domestic economy in term of reduction in transactions costs, efficiency enhancements and job creation.

Table 6.1

Attempts to Establish Semiconductor Industries

Country	*Date*	*Estimated Subsidies ($ bn)*	*Sustainable Competitive Edge?*
United States	1976-1980	12-36	√
Japan	1980-1982	19-54	×
Taiwan	1990	15-43	√
South Korea	1990	9-26	√
Singapore	1995	5-16	×
Germany	1996	2-7	×
China	1999	6-17	×
Malaysia	2001	1-3	×

Source: McKinsey Global Institute.

The state and market debate in today's deeply competitive landscape is, therefore, best seen as one in which state intervention is perceived as an instrument that can help produce a range of economic outcomes. In rapid industrialising countries such as Korea, it has been characterised by market-reinforcing behaviour, supporting profitability for private investors. This is contrary to the claim that state intervention generates distortions that hurt economic growth. Admittedly, it has to be nuanced and carefully calibrated. While state intervention in Korea has been largely deemed to be successful, in India it has suffered on several counts. During the colonial period, economic development was severely handicapped by the absence of any consistent state support to a process of industrialisation (Mazumdar, 2010). After independence and more recently, state intervention has been mired in charges of corruption, reflecting the state's weakness in implementing its own policies. Judicial intervention became necessary in the light of serious institutional failures. While pronouncing judgement, the Supreme Court was conscious of its intrusion into the policy domain, and recognised that such judicial interventions should be made only in exceptional circumstances. The court maintained that the policy of allocating airwave spectrum, a renewable natural resource, on a first-come, first-serve basis—as opposed to an auction—was deliberately devised to confer largesse on a chosen few, and, therefore, violated public interest. It was also contrary to principles enshrined in the Indian Constitution, and in these exceptional circumstances, an exercise of judicial authority in the larger public interest was justified.

Institutional failures in India have stretched well beyond the telecom sector. While 'crony capitalism' in India has declined since economic liberalisation in 1991, it would be premature to suggest that the practice has been eradicated. The allocation of land to real estate developers and mining rights to private interests are but two examples in a long list of public resources that have been stealthily distributed for private benefit. In fact, economist Raghuram Rajan recently stated that many of India's billionaires have made money through their proximity to government.

If anything, in India, the government's evolving role in creating enabling conditions could be the difference between good and 'not so good' outcomes. Effective governance—including creating robust institutions—is the most critical enabling condition for further reform. The new agenda, therefore, calls for the introduction of a strong framework for regulation, including for public-private partnerships so that much needed investments can fructify. A vast amount of empirical evidence gathered over the years suggests that the quality of regulation matters for performance. Among the most critical tasks for policy makers, therefore, is the designing and implementation of stable and effective regulation for crucial sectors,

Box 6.1

South Korea's Growth Story

From having a GDP per capita that was $100 lower than the Philippines in the 1950s to advancing to the ranks of OECD countries, South Korea's growth story has been remarkable and has been facilitated by policy measures that promoted export-oriented industrialisation and large investments in human capital. South Korea's policies took into account the country's unique socio-political context as evidenced by General Park Chung Hee's statement that 'Western democratic institutions do not harmonise with the underdeveloped conditions of Korea.' Emerging from the destruction of the Korean War in 1953, South Korea's economy was weak and the subsequent period of development was characterised by heavy government intervention, import liberalisation and the active control of exchange rates to bolster export competitiveness. In the early 1970s, when current account deficit grew, Korean authorities decided to devalue the Won such that exports rose and, as a precautionary measure, the government bailed out firms holding large external debt. Towards the end of the 1970s, the Government of Korea began the 'Big Push'; the government invested directly in heavy chemical industries and manufacturing. A testament to South Korea's success was the 90 per cent increase in Korea's exports and a record breaking increase in output by 16 per cent in 1973. From 1961 to 1979, the South Korean economy experienced an average annual growth rate of 9 per cent. Several social policies also accompanied General Hee's economic measures including land reforms, which wiped out the traditional landed aristocracy and set the stage for greater income equality and heavy investment in human capital through educational reform. South Korea's growth path, like that of other nations, was not free from debt crises and large current account deficits but thanks to its export-oriented exchange rate policy and large investments in human capital and manufacturing, the nation grew to become a global leader and has successfully transitioned from being a centrally-planned economy to a market-driven one. South Korea's growth trajectory demonstrates that government intervention in the short-term coupled with an outward-oriented focus can deliver success. In contrast, countries in Latin America and Asia that were inward-focused and engaged in heavy import substitution have not experienced the same success although they were wealthier than South Korea in the 1950s.

Source: Collins and Park (1989) and Cho (2011).

thereby reducing a lot of existing and unwarranted governmental intrusion. Second, certain types of states and thus certain types of state interventions have proved to be more successful than others at promoting growth—the Korean example readily comes to mind. While it may not be possible or indeed desirable to replicate successful models fully, India can learn from successful stories (see Box 6.1). This learning can especially be useful to stress the link between institutional capability and growth and the embedded need to create a positive working relationship between the state and business. On the other hand, a strong state can slip into using 'absolute power' and has often been criticised for being totalitarian. A difficult balance, therefore, needs to emerge where the state's role is decisive and yet inclusive so that the benefits of pro-market growth can be democratised. This is needed in India much more at the current juncture than at any other time in its history. The rest of the paper is organised as follows. The next section briefly compares India's and Korea's growth trajectories. The third section points to the robust nature of Korea's institutions in striking contrast to India's, including Korea's response to the two recent crises in their history and highlights the decisive nature of those interventions. The fourth section concludes.

Comparison of Growth Trajectories in India and Korea

Growth theorists recognise the importance of organised markets, factor accumulation, R&D and innovation, and institutions, among other variables, as being crucial to the growth process. Economic reform and the introduction of market-based transactions boosted growth in both India and Korea, but the impact has been significantly larger and more long-lived in Korea. While Korea's GDP per capita increased to the current US$ 22,590 in 2012[5] following the reforms of the 1950s and 1960s, India's is a study in contrast. Even after reform, India remains a low- to middle-income country with an estimated 680 million people living in deprivation or below the 'empowerment line' (McKinsey Global Institute, 2014).

---

5. *http://data.worldbank.org/indicator/NY.GDP.PCAP.CD*

Figure 6.1

Comparison of GDP Growth Rates of India and Korea

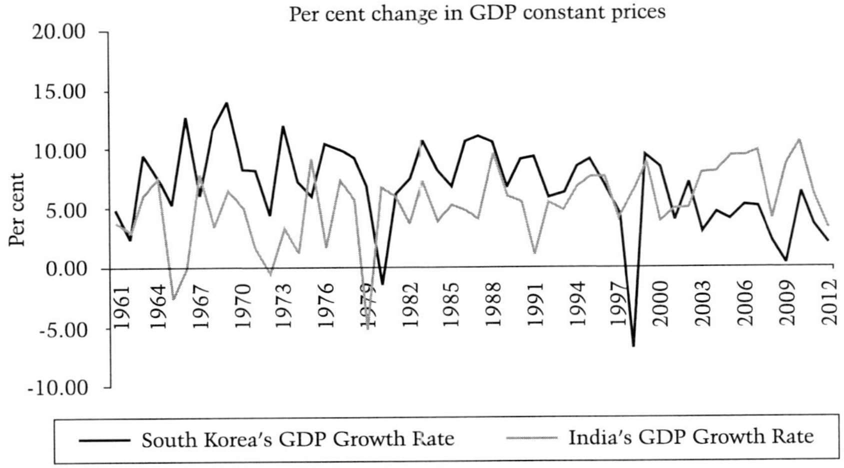

Source: IMF, 2013.

It is instructive to investigate the factors that shaped the divergent pathways of economic growth in the two countries. South Korea's economic success is often attributed to pragmatic market reforms. Rodrik (1996) argues in favour of market-oriented policies combined with reduced, yet effective, government intervention. He also places considerable importance to the better-educated labour force that led to the creation of a competent bureaucracy that enhanced the productivity of interventions and facilitated private investment. In a growing economy, the crucial role of appropriate human capital to absorb new investments cannot be overemphasised. Harvie and Pahlavani (2006) specify the impressive investment in human capital that boosted South Korea's economic growth far beyond the level of other South and East Asian economies. By contrast, India's record on investment in human capital and educational attainment has been modest.[6]

It is, of course, true that South Korea embarked upon economic reform much ahead of India in the early 1960s and experienced rapid growth over the next 20 years (see Figure 6.1). Accordingly, structural change associated with economic growth occurred much sooner; besides, it had a much more

6. Annual Status of Educational Report (ASER) 2013.

profound and transformative impact on the Korean economy. During its rapid industrialisation, Korea was able to achieve astonishing growth with sudden reductions in poverty and inequality. Between 1960 and 2002, i.e., for more than four decades, the compound annual growth rate (CAGR) of real GDP was 7.5 per cent. Manufacturing value added increased sharply to 30 per cent and that of agriculture fell to 4 per cent during this period (World Bank, 2006). Only 9 per cent of employment was attributed to agriculture, while the share of employment in services has increased continuously during the last decade, reaching 64 per cent in 2003. With rapid economic growth, absolute poverty decreased sharply in Korea. In the late 1960s, poverty was widespread, but by the mid to late 1990s, the share of population living on less than US$ 1 a day (PPP) was only 2 per cent (World Bank, 2004).

Export-oriented industrialisation, which generated rapid economic growth, played a vital role in Korea's development. It helped create demand for labour and led to a rapid expansion of employment, increased incomes and reduced poverty. The initial focus on export of labour-intensive manufactures subsequently gave way to manufacture of high-value, sophisticated products that were made possible by the existence of a highly educated and skilled work force. This had a positive impact on productivity and increased the ability to absorb technology developed elsewhere, all of which contributed to sustained high growth. Compared to many other developing countries, investment in human resources was extensive and decisive in Korea.[7]

The South Korean example that has now come to be known as the 'Korean model' drew inspiration from the 'Japanese model,' wherein the focus was on extensive government intervention and cooperative R&D projects (Sakakibara and Cho, 2002). This is in stark contrast to India. For example, the huge gulf in R&D investments in India and Korea in the last decade revealed in Table 6.2 is indicative of the difference in emphasis and the prevailing state of development. According to Kohli (2004), South Korea's rapid industrialisation and growth is best understood by recognising

7. In addition to growth based on industrialisation, land reform in the late 1940s also contributed to the reduction of poverty, especially in rural areas, Henderson *et al.*, 2002.

the roles played by a growth-oriented, cohesive, capitalist state and by neighbouring Japan.

Table 6.2

Research and Development Expenditure

(% of GDP)

Years	*India*	*South Korea*
2008	0.89	3.36
2009	0.87	3.56
2010	0.87	3.74

Source: South Korea: World Bank data on Research and Development Expenditure (% of GDP), *http://data.worldbank.org/indicator/GB.XPD.RSDV.GD.ZS*.

India: Selected Statistical Indicators for India, Department of Science and Technology, *http://www.nstmis-dst.org/PDF/TableNo45.pdf*.

While India's post-independence economic policy was also characterised by a [heavily] statist approach, it owed its inspiration to the Soviet planning system (Mohan, 2004b). The overarching objective of India's economic policy after Independence was to achieve self-sufficiency, with a focus on public provision of what were then characterised as the commanding heights of the economy (Yergin and Stanislaw, 1998). Industrialisation driven by the state was seen as a necessary condition to achieve economic development and protect national sovereignty (Jadhav, 2005). India's planned economy model used industrial policy as an instrument to promote manufacturing to achieve higher economic growth, an equitable distribution of income and greater employment opportunities and ensure spillover effects on other sectors of the economy (Panagariya, 2008). Transplanting the Soviet style planning system meant that India ended up with a command economy and an economic administration more suited to regulation and control than to development (Ibid.). It is now well documented that this strategy was singularly ineffective, created perverse incentives resulting in bureaucratic overreach and rampant rent-seeking behaviour (Bhagwati, 1993).

Policy reforms were started in the 1980s, and some provisional attempts to encourage capital-goods imports, rationalise the tax system and relax industrial regulations were made but these became pervasive only in 1991 following a disruptive macroeconomic crisis. With the 1991 reforms, resource allocation shifted in favour of the market, although labour legislation and the agricultural sector were left out of the purview of reform. In general, India's approach to liberalisation has been gradual and calibrated, in which sudden privatisation and capital account liberalisation have been avoided until now. While this signalled a systemic shift to a more open economy with greater reliance upon market forces, a larger role for the private sector including foreign investment, and a restructuring of the role of government, the failure to implement these reforms effectively has often led to a criticism of the gradualist model itself (Ahluwalia, 2002). We discuss this further in the next section.

Structural transformation, i.e., the reallocation of economic activity across the broad sectors, namely agriculture, manufacturing and services, is a feature of modern economic growth (Kuznets, 1971). In Korea, the role of structural transformation was profound, leading to the accumulation of new complex capabilities, including high value production, especially for export. During the past four decades and more, the Indian economy has witnessed structural change as well, although there has been remarkable stagnation in the share of manufacturing (15% in 2013 *versus* 14% in 1965). The share of agricultural value added in GDP has fallen from 45 per cent in 1965 to approximately 3 per cent in 2012.[8] Despite structural changes, agriculture still accounts for a very high share of employment. At the same time, the expansion of services has been sizable, with its share in GDP increasing from 35 per cent in 1965 to almost 60 per cent in 2013. A services 'revolution' gripped India, beginning in the 1990s. Empirical literature cites high income elasticity of demand, splintering of industrial activity, rising demand for services exports and the distinctive role of economic reforms in prompting services-led growth in India (Gordon and Gupta, 2004). Figure 6.2 exhibits the sharp contrast in the growth rates of the agricultural, manufacturing and services sectors in the last four decades. According to India's recent National Manufacturing Policy (NMP 2011), the contribution of manufacturing to India's GDP is "much below potential." The target is to boost the share to 25 per cent, comparable to other Asian economies where it has consistently been 25 per cent or

8. *http://data.worldbank.org/indicator/NV.AGR.TOTL.ZS*

higher.[9] The below potential performance of manufacturing in India has also raised fears of 'de-industrialisation.'[10]

India's growth stands in sharp contrast to the traditional pattern witnessed by developed economies in the West and in East Asia, including Korea. Growth driven by manufacturing has the ability to generate spillovers, technical progress, economies of scale and induce overall productivity improvements in the economy (Felipe *et al.*, 2010). The imminent additions to the labour force due to demographic changes in India underscore the need to revive manufacturing. It is estimated that there will be a net addition of 110 million to the workforce over the coming decade.[11]

Figure 6.2

Value Added as a Per cent of GDP for India

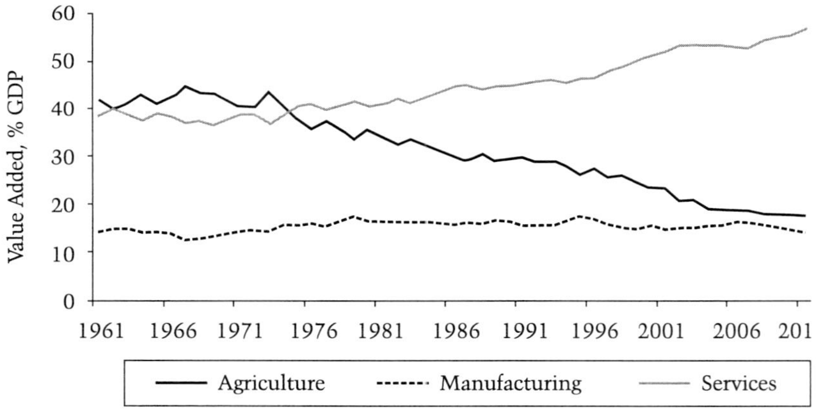

Source: World Bank, 2013.

Between 2003-04 and 2007-08 in the last decade, India experienced unprecedented growth at an average rate of 9 per cent per annum. It has

9. National Manufacturing Policy, 2011: The share of manufacturing in GDP for both China and Korea was 30 per cent in 2010.

10. Felipe and Estrada (2008), using a logistic regression and controlling for income per capita, population and the share of trade in GDP, estimate that India's manufacturing is about five percentage points smaller than it should be.

11. "India will Add 110 mn People to Global Workforce by 2020: Study", *The Economic Times*, July 28, 2010, *http://articles.economictimes.indiatimes.com/2010-07-28/news/27623896_1_labour-laws-gdp-growth-ilo*

been rightly referred to as the golden period of India's growth. The high growth rates of the golden period have been attributed to high investment, open trade policies and calibrated financial sector reforms. At the heart of the reform measures were the successful completion of several privatisation initiatives (as distinct from disinvestment of minority stakes) and the further relaxation of the FDI regime (Acharya, 2001). The *Economic Survey* (2012-13) underscores the strong correlation of growth with investment rate. In the period after 2003-04 and until 2011-12, the investment rate has averaged 34.5 per cent.[12] What is remarkable for India now is that the share of private sector in total investment is the major source of investment, the golden period of India's growth having largely been driven by the boom in private corporate investment. But today, the Indian economy faces significant challenges. Growth has slowed to 4.9 per cent in fiscal 2014, the lowest level in a decade and it is expected to rebound to only 5.5 per cent in 2015.[13] India's federal structure, however, makes policy formulation and implementation complex; moreover, it is often politicised, either because of centre-state conflicts or because the state is too weak to implement its own policies. In striking contrast, Korea was exceptionally successful in implementing industrial policy. According to Bardhan (2006), the lack of a coherent industrial policy played a key role in the fate of manufacturing in India. Industrial policy in South Korea (and other East Asian economies) suggests that well-designed state interventions were responsible for promoting cost and quality-efficient production that facilitated exports (Timothy, 1999). The quality of state intervention is likely to determine whether India can replicate Korea's success—private investors will need organised help to overcome obstacles to manufacturing such as capital scarcity, infrastructure constraints, regulatory inconsistencies and rigidities in labour markets that have become the bane of Indian business.[14] According to *The Economist*, India needs private sector engagement with infrastructure and with urbanisation. For this to succeed, the relationship between companies and the state needs to be repaired. Corruption has not

12. *Economic Survey of India 2013.*

13. IMF forecast chapter IV consultation.

14. *http://www.doingbusiness.org/data/exploreeconomies/india*

only produced bad decisions, it has also produced indecision. The damage is visible in stalled road, power and mining projects.[15]

In the recently released World Bank Report, "Connecting to Compete 2014: Trade Logistics in the Global Economy," India ranks 54th among 160 countries across the world on the basis of the logistics performance index (LPI). LPI is an indicator of on-the ground efficiency of trade supply chains, or logistics performance. According to the report, Korea ranks 35 places above India; Germany is reported as the best performing country with an LPI score of 4.12. We highlight India's LPI because it is established that the biggest gains to low-income countries typically come from improvements in infrastructure and basic border management. This means reforming customs procedures, improving efficiency in other agencies responsible for trade facilitation, including those responsible for sanitary and phyto-sanitary controls.

Table 6.3

Trade Logistics Performance Comparison with Select Countries

Countries	*Particulars*	*Customs*	*Infrastructure*	*International Shipments*	*Logistics, Quality & Competence*	*Tracking & Tracing*	*Timeliness*
India	Rank	65	58	44	52	57	51
	Score	2.72	2.88	3.2	3.03	3.11	3.51
China	Rank	38	23	22	35	29	36
	Score	3.21	3.67	3.5	3.46	3.5	3.87
Korea	Rank	24	18	21	21	28	56
	Score	3.47	3.79	3.44	3.66	3.69	4

Note: The LPI index is a multidimensional assessment of logistics performance, rated on a scale from 1 (worst) to 5 (best). The six core components captured by the LPI survey are rated by respondents on a scale of 1-5, where 1 is very low or very difficult and 5 is very high or very easy. Ranks are given out of 160 countries.

Source: Compiled from World Bank.

Korea's Institutional Push Compared to India's Weak Resolve

The neoclassical explanation of the Korean growth story, while plausible, is incomplete. The state in Korea not only contributed to economic growth by designing the right policies and carrying out

15. "A Bad Boom", *The Economist*, March 15, 2014.

investments in infrastructure, but also intervened in an extraordinarily active way in the technological development of the country. Rodrik (1995) has persuasively argued that initial conditions of Koreas' social infrastructure—a relatively high literacy rate and a high educational level—allowed the government to adopt aggressive investment policies without having to address issues of justice. The role of concentrated political power helped Korea to set the economic agenda. On the other hand, and as explained above, a weakening alliance between the state and capital is becoming increasingly difficult to hold together in India, necessitating deep institutional overhaul. Robust institutions reduce risk by imposing constraints on activities that impede development.

The role of institutions is central to understanding South Korean economic development. Rodrik (2000) argues that there are five types of institutions for growth: property rights, regulatory institutions, institutions for macroeconomic stabilisation, institutions of social insurance and institutions of conflict management. Korea has enjoyed good property rights and conflict management institutions, as well as good institutions for macroeconomic stabilisation. Using regression analysis, Garcia-Blanch (2001) empirically establish a positive relationship between Korean growth and institutional capacity, including protection of property rights and contract enforcement. Political stability and the uniform composition of race and language also favoured Korea as compared to India.

Acemoglu *et al.* (2005) also show the causal influence of institutions on Korea's prosperity through the 'natural experiment' of the division of the two Koreas into North and South. Since separation, the two Koreas have experienced dramatically diverging paths of economic development, their very different institutions accounting for a significant part of the explanation. Besides a strong interventionist state, simultaneous existence of helpful conditions such as the availability of high-quality, low-cost labour and growing world trade created a powerful blend for Korea's economic take-off. While replicating the Korean success is not possible due to several differences in space and timing, the lessons for India are worth keeping in mind. A strong state can be an effective safeguard against the risk of policy uncertainty and the rent-seeking and monopoly power of a narrow elite.

Institutional responses to periodic crises also serve to capture the relatively advanced nature of the Korean approach. Both India and South Korea have been subject to various economic crises. Beginning in the 1950s, India ran trade deficits that increased in magnitude in the 1960s. In 1966, foreign aid slowed, and the response was devaluation accompanied by partial liberalisation. By 1985, balance of payments (BoP) problems reappeared and by 1990, turned into a serious macroeconomic crisis. The government was perilously close to default since foreign exchange reserves could barely finance three weeks' worth of imports. India was forced to airlift gold reserves as a pledge for an IMF loan and began a series of reform and liberalisation measures that, in the two decades since they were introduced in 1991, have run their course. Without additional and second generation reforms, including reform of its institutions of governance, India runs the risk of foregoing the massive advantages of a young population.

Comparable to the 1991 crisis in India was the 1997 crisis in Korea that was triggered by the inordinate rise in short-term foreign debt, especially the high leverage of the *chaebols*.[16] Korea's government began its policy reaction to the crisis quickly and much ahead of the other affected economies such as Thailand and the Philippines. Several initiatives were undertaken to address problems associated with the *chaebol* system and the financial system even as the government began talks with the IMF in November 1997 for a bailout package (see Box 6.2).[17] The policy response was quick and decisive as illustrated by the fact that while GDP growth rate fell from 7.1 per cent in 1996 to -6.8 per cent in 1998, it rebounded just as rapidly to 10.7 per cent in 1999.

The Korean economy was better equipped to deal with the economic crisis in 2008 compared to 1997. First, sufficient foreign reserves had been built up in the interim that helped diminish the impact of a sudden reversal in capital flows. Although the large accumulated short-term foreign debt made the Korean economy vulnerable to a foreign liquidity shock, the amount of foreign reserves was still sizeable to cover all short-term foreign debt. The restructuring of *chaebols* in 1997 meant that the debt-

---

16. The term *chaebol* is used to describe a large family-owned business conglomerate usually with close ties with the government and banks.

17. *http://news.bbc.co.uk/2/hi/world/analysis/47496.stm*

to-equity ratio of the corporate sector had plunged to around 100 per cent in 2008 from over 400 per cent in 1997. This improvement in financial buffers greatly helped Korean firms withstand the credit constraints and demand contraction posed by the global crisis that was triggered by the now well-known Lehman Brothers collapse in 2008. In addition, banks were better placed to absorb shocks in 2008 than in 1997, based on improved prudential regulations. Increase in manufacturing exports to China, on which the Korean economy was heavily dependent, served to cushion the dramatic collapse in global trade. China's import recovered faster than that in other regions, which in turn was the result of the global rebalancing (International Monetary Fund, 2012). In retrospect, it is clear that sound pre-crisis fundamentals coupled with post-crisis macro-policy choices were crucial to Korea's performance. Thus, a large amount of foreign reserves, improved financial structures of firms and banks, a prudent government balance sheet and timely and focused interventions meant that Korea successfully recovered from the crisis. The value of pre-crisis fundamentals achieved by the restructuring processes since the 1997 crisis cannot be overemphasised.

Box 6.2

The Reverse Gold Rush

On a chilly January morning of 1998, South Korea sent the first shipment of 300 kilograms of gold collected in a public campaign to help the country out of its economic crisis. A nationwide campaign, "Collect Gold for the Love of Korea", was started by large business groups including Daewoo, Samsung and Hyundai and involved ordinary Koreans donating personal gold treasures, which were melted down into ingots ready for sale on the international markets. The BBC noted, "housewives gave up their wedding rings; athletes donated medals and trophies; many gave away gold 'luck' keys, a traditional present on the opening of a new business or a 60th birthday". According to some sources, within the first two days of the programme, over 100,000 South Koreans donated more than 20 tons of gold worth over $100 million. At the end, approximately $150 to $200 million in gold was collected through the campaign, which might seem an inconsequential amount, given the country received a bailout in excess of $50 billion. But the symbolic aspect of the Korean people's willingness to make personal sacrifices to save their national economy resonated. The managing director of IMF, who had just completed a visit to Seoul at that time, was moved by the campaign and called it "admirable".

Source: *http://news.bbc.co.uk/2/hi/world/analysis/47496.stm*

On the other hand, although India's response to the two crises in 1991 and 2008 was also measured and swift, the pre-crises fundamentals were much weaker when compared to Korea. In the run up to the 1991 BoP crisis, it was clear that the long-standing import substitution policy had failed. Several government reports documented the inefficiencies engendered by the high tariff regime and by the system of licensing that went with it (Agarwal and Whalley, 2013). The 1991 crisis provided the opportunity to bring about a fundamental change in development strategy, an abandonment of the import substitution model and a sharp reduction in the role of the public sector by de-licensing many sectors. While growth did revive, it did not pick up to the heady levels of 9 per cent until 2003-04. It was subsequently interrupted by the 2008 global crisis. According to Srinivasan and Tendulkar (2002), the relatively modest of success of Indian reforms cannot be attributed to their rapidity. At the same time, reform did not help increase the share of manufacturing in GDP—fast growing sectors remained either capital intensive or skilled-labour intensive (Panagariya, 2008). Transformation would, therefore, need a structural shift to labour-intensive manufacturing to absorb the huge surplus labour from the farm economy. This requires reform of labour laws and building of infrastructure, especially power (Ibid.).

The financial crisis of 2008 thus occurred when much reform was pending, although the political will to implement it naturally weakened after the onset of the crisis. While the crisis lowered the growth rate from 9.7 per cent in 2007-08 to 6.5 per cent in 2008-09, the economy recovered quickly to grow at 7.9 per cent in 2009-10 and 8.3 per cent in 2010-11 on the back of tax cuts and a fiscal stimulus (De, 2012). But the high rate of growth has not been sustained and declined to 5 per cent in 2012-13. It has also become more variable. India's self-confidence has also been shaken (Subramanian, 2013). While other economic indicators—rupee (1 Indian rupee = 0.016 US$), inflation [provisional annual inflation rate based on all-India general consumer price index (CPI) (combined) for February 2014 on point-to-point basis (8.10 per cent in February 2014),[18] current account deficit (CAD) (US$ 4.2 billion in February 2014)[19] and fiscal deficit

18. Ministry of Statistics and Programme Implementation, CSO, Government of India, Press Release (March 12, 2014).

19. Reserve Bank of India.

(₹ 5424.99 billion in 2013-14)][20]—have all taken a beating along with slowing growth, India's travails have a conspicuous domestic context.

Structural problems, infrastructure deficits and inflexible labour laws, among others, have resulted in a stagnating manufacturing sector that could absorb abundant and cheap unskilled labour. Manufacturing requires transparent rules and reliable infrastructure and India lacks both. Mounting corruption in the allocation of land, spectrum and mines led the Supreme Court to pronounce that all natural resources must be assigned by auction. The verdict must be seen in the context of a deep sense of resentment at the collective failure of India's institutions. But exclusively picking a market mechanism over an administrative allocation mechanism is an extreme reaction to institutional failure. The high-powered Committee on Allocation of Natural Resources opposes such a 'one-size-fits-all' straitjacket while recognising that there can be no substitute for strengthening institutions.[21]

The two crises of 1991 and 2008 both brought to the fore structural problems and institutional weaknesses in India that otherwise tend to get hidden in times of good economic performance. While reform has been gradual, it has also suffered from poor implementation. Going forward, it is equally, if not more, important to address institutional and implementation bottlenecks as it is to design better policy for improved economic outcomes. To reiterate, the Korean experience is instructive in this respect.

Conclusion

In striking contrast to Korea, the lack of a coherent industrial policy has played a key role in the fate of manufacturing in India. Industrial policy in South Korea suggests that well-designed state interventions were responsible for promoting cost and quality-efficient production that facilitated technology and high-value exports. The subsequent growth of the industrial sector is one of the principal factors behind South Korea's economic development. South Korea successfully transformed from a domestic economy based on agriculture to that of a leading world

20. Ibid.

21. See Kathuria (2012). Also see the Ashok Chawla Committee Report on Allocation of Natural Resources, May 31, 2011.

industrial power, with a constant increase in income per capita and a high growth pattern. The ingredients of success included strong and effective institutions, targeted creation of domestic industrial capacities, the development of education and skills, infrastructure building, and actively managed capital markets. Political stability and the uniform composition of race and language also favoured Korea. On the other hand, India's diversity and federal structure make policy formulation and implementation complex and, politicised at times, either because of centre-state conflicts or because implementation capacity is weak. Thus, part of the reason that economic reforms were much more efficient in South Korea is due to weak institutional capacity and implementation in India.

While India can certainly learn from the experience of Korea (and other countries), it must devise policy solutions that are appropriate to its unique context. This does not mean foregoing reform or maintaining the *status quo* to generate political consensus. It means creating appropriate institutions that are accountable and transparent; it means devising policy initiatives that clearly spell out long-term goals and above all, it means focused implementation. Only then will India be able to replicate the success of countries such as Korea that showed that transitioning from a low to high-income country is possible in a single generation.

References

Acemoglu, D., S. Johnson and J.A. Robinson (2005). "Institutions as a Fundamental Cause of Long-run Growth", in Philippe Aghion and Stephen Durlauf (eds.), *Handbook of Economic Growth*. Amsterdam: North Holland. pp.385-472.

Acemoglu, D., J.A. Robinson and D. Woren (2012). *Why Nations Fail: The Origins of Power, Prosperity, and Poverty* (Vol. 4). New York: Crown Business.

Acharya, S. (2001). "India's Macroeconomic Management in the Nineties", *ICRIER Occasional Paper*.

Agarwal, M. and J. Whalley (2013). "The 1991 Reforms, Indian Economic Growth, and Social Progress", *NBER Working Paper* No. 19024.

Ahluwalia, I.J. (2002). "Economic Reforms in India since 1991: Has Gradualism Worked?" *Journal of Economic Perspectives* 16(3): 67-88.

Bardhan, P. (2006). "Awakening Giants, Feet of Clay: A Brief Assessment of the Rise of China and India", *Journal of South Asian Development* 1: 1-17.

Bhagwati, J. (1993). *India in Transition: Freeing the Economy*. Oxford University Press.

Brown, A., J. Stern, B. Tenenbaum and D. Gencer (2006). *Handbook for Evaluating Infrastructure Regulatory Systems*. Washington: World Bank.

Bruton, H.J. (1998). "A Reconsideration of Import Substitution", *Journal of Economic Literature* 36(2): 903-36.

Cho, D. (2010). "Responses of the Korean Economy to the Global Crisis: Another Currency Crisis?" Paper presented at *EWC/KDI Conference on Global Economic Crisis: Impact, Transmission, and Recovery*. Honolulu, Hawaii

Cho, Hyunsu (2011). *Economic Development of South Korea under Park Chung Hee (1961-79)*. March 21. *http://www.slideshare.net/noblepylon/economic-development-of-south-korea-under-park-chung-hee-196179-7328748.*

Collins, Susan M. and Won-Am Park (1989). "External Debt and Macroeconomic Performance in South Korea", in *Developing Country Debt and the World Economy*. University of Chicago Press.

Crook, C. (1992). "Third World Economic Development", *The Concise Encyclopaedia of Economics, Library of Economics and Liberty, <http://www.econlib.org/library/Enc1/ThirdWorldEconomicDevelopment.html>.*

De, S. (2012). "Fiscal Policy in India: Trends and Trajectory", *Working Paper*. Ministry of Finance, Government of India (forthcoming).

Dong, Sohn Won and Kenney Martin (2006). *Universities, Clusters and Innovation System: The Case of Seoul*. Korea: Elsevier.

Felipe, J. and G. Estrada (2008). "Benchmarking Developing Asia's Manufacturing Sector", *International Journal of Development Issues* 7(2): 97-119.

Felipe, J., Utsav Kumar and Arnelyn Abdon (2010). "Exports, Capabilities and Industrial Policy in India", *Working Paper* No. 638. Annandale-on-Hudson, NY: Levy Economics Institute of Bard College.

Gordon, J. and P. Gupta (2004). "Understanding India's Services Revolution", *IMF Working Paper* WP/04/171, September.

Harvie, C. and M. Pahlavani (2006). "Sources of Economic Growth in South Korea: An Application of the ARDL Analysis in the Presence of Structural Breaks, 1980-2005", *University of Wollongong Economics Working Paper* 06-17.

International Monetary Fund (2012). *Regional Economic Outlook: Asia and Pacific*.

———. (2013). *World Economic Outlook*, October.

Jadhav, N. (2005). *Industrial Policy in India since 1956. http://www.drnarendrajadhav.info/drnjadhav_web_files/Published%20papers/Indian%20Industrial%20Policy%20Since%201956.pdf*

Kathuria, R. (2012). "Indian Telecom Scandal the Result of Institutional Failure", *East Asia Forum*. March 16.

Kohli, A. (2004). *State-directed Development: Political Power and Industrialization in the Global Periphery*. Cambridge University Press.

Kuznets, S. (1971). *Economic Growth of Nations: Total Output and Production Structure*. Cambridge, MA: Harvard University Press.

Lewis, W.A. (2013). *Theory of Economic Growth*. Vol. 7. Routledge.

Lin, J.Y. (2010). "New Structural Economics", *Policy Research Working Paper* 5197.

Lin, Justin Yifu and Célestin Monga (2010). "Growth Identification and Facilitation: The Role of the State in the Dynamics of Structural Change", *Policy Research Working Paper* 5313, May. The World Bank.

Lloyd, G.R. (1985). *Economic Growth in the Third World, 1850-1980*. New Haven, CT; Yale University Press. pp.413-14.

Maksymenko, S. and M. Rabbani (2011). *Economic Reforms, Human Capital, and Economic Growth in India and South Korea: A Cointegration Analysis*. 1-35. ideas.repec.org/p/pit/wpaper/361.html

Mazumdar, Surajit (2010). "Indian Capitalism: A Case that doesn't Fit?", *MPRA Paper* 28162, November.

McKinsey Global Institute (2014). *From Poverty to Empowerment: India's Imperative for Jobs, Growth and Effective Basic Services*. Mckinsey & Company.

Mohan, R. (2004a). "Infrastructure Development in India: Emerging Challenges", in Francois Bourguignon and Boris Pleskovic (eds.), *Annual World Bank Conference on Development Economics: Accelerating Development*. Oxford University Press and World Bank.

Mohan, Rakesh (2004b). "Industrial Policy and Controls," in Bimal Jalan (ed.), *The Indian Economy: Problems and Prospects*. New Delhi, India: Penguin. p.101.

Nehru, V.E. Swanson and A. Dubey (1995). "A New Database on Human Capital Stock in Developing and Industrial Countries: Sources, Methodology, and Results", *Journal of Development Economics* 46(2): 379-401.

Nolan, P. (2004). *Transforming China: Globalization, Transition and Development*. London: Anthem Press.

Panagariya, A. (2008). "Transforming India. Sustaining India's Growth Miracle", *ASCI Journal of Management* 38(1): 9-45.

Prebisch, Raúl (1950). "The Economic Development of Latin America and its Principal Problems", Reprinted in *Economic Bulletin for Latin America* 7(1) (1962): 1-22.

Rodrik, D. (1995). "Trade Strategy, Exports, and Investment: Another Look at East Asia", *Discussion Paper*. Washington, DC: Institute of Policy Reform.

———. (1996). "Understanding Economic Policy Reform", *Journal of Economic Literature* 34(1): 9-41.

———. (2000). "Institutions for High-quality Growth: What they are and how to Acquire them?", *National Bureau of Economic Research (NBER) Working Paper* 7540 (February).

Sakakibara, M. and Dong-Sung Cho (2002). "Cooperative R&D in Japan and Korea: A Comparison of Industrial Policy", *Research Policy* 31(5): 673-92.

Singer, H.W. (1950). "U.S. Foreign Investment in Underdeveloped Areas: The Distribution of Gains between Investing and Borrowing Countries", *American Economic Review*, Papers and Proceedings 40: 473-85.

Srinivasan, T.N. and S.D. Tendulkar (2002). *Reintegrating India with the World Economy*. Washington, DC: Institute for International Economics.

Subramanian, Arvind (2010). "Why is Inflation in India so Stubbornly High", *rediff.com*; dated: July 28, 2010; *http://business.rediff.com/special/2010/jul/28/spec-why-is-inflation-in-india-so-stubbornly-high.htm*

Subramanian, Arvind (2013). "Why India's Economy is Stumbling", *The New York Times*, August 13.

Timothy, W.C. (1999). *A Comparative Study on the Industrial Policy in Japan and South Korea*. Hong Kong: University of Hong Kong.

UNCTAD (2013). "Global Value Chains: Investment and Trade for Development", *World Investment Report 2013. http://unctad.org/en/PublicationsLibrary/wir2013_en.pdf*

World Bank Database. "Economic Policy and External Debt Indicators", Access date: December 24, 2013.

World Bank Study (1993). *East Asian Miracle*. Washington, DC: World Bank.

World Bank (2004). "Republic of Korea: Four Decades of Equitable Growth", A case study from *Scaling up Poverty Reduction: A Global Learning Process and Conference*. Shanghai. May 25-27.

———. (2006). World Development Indicators. Online database.

———. (2012). World Development Indicators 2012. Washington, DC.

Yergin, D. and J. Stanislaw (1998). *The Commanding Heights: The Battle for the World Economy*. Free Press.

Annexure

Table A-6.1

Development Indicators

Indicators	*India*	*Korea*
Agriculture, value added (% of GDP)	17	3
Services, etc., value added (% of GDP)	57	58
Trade in services (% of GDP)	14.9	19.4
Industry, value added (% of GDP)	26	39
GDP growth (annual %)	3.2	2
GDP per capita (current US$)	1,489	22,590
GDP (current US$)	1,841,709,755,679	1,129,598,273,324
GNI, PPP (current international $)	4,831,971,084,286	1,548,728,614,977
Inflation, consumer prices (annual %)	9.3	2.2
Inflation, GDP deflator (annual %)	8.2	1
Current account balance (BoP, current US$)	-91,471,245,846	43,335,100,000
Gross savings (% of GDP)	34	31
Labour force, total	484,343,281	25,765,234
Mortality rate, under 5 yrs (per 1,000 live births)	56	4
Unemployment, total (% of total labour force)	3.6	3.2
Population ages 15-64 (% of total)	65	73
Mortality rate, infant (per 1,000 live births)	44	3
Population (Total)	1,236,686,732	50,004,000
Population growth (annual %)	1.3	0.5
Population ages 65 and above (% of total)	5	12
Population ages 15-64 (% of total)	65	73
Population ages 0-14 (% of total)	29	15
Unemployment, female (% of female labour force)	4	3
Unemployment, male (% of male labour force)	3.4	3.4
Agricultural land (% of land area)	60.5	18.1
Rural population (% of total population)	68	17

Source: World Bank (2012).

7 Future Tasks for Korea-India Economic Cooperation

Comparative Analysis with Other Asian Countries[1]

Choongjae Cho

Introduction

The global economic slowdown, which began with the 2008 financial crisis in the US and led to a fiscal crisis in Europe, continues until today. Both India and Korea recorded their lowest growth rates in 2012 for the last decade. Korea and India are celebrating the 40th anniversary of the establishment of diplomatic ties in 2013 in an environment of global slowdown. The two countries have raised their relationship to a strategic partnership and launched an free trade agreement (FTA), the Korea-India Comprehensive Economic Partnership Agreement (CEPA). Trade and foreign direct investment (FDI) between the two countries have also increased consistently; consequently, they have become very important partners to each other for economic cooperation. Despite many achievements, however, the two countries are left with more challenges to overcome in the coming 40 years.

In this paper, the two countries' future tasks in the field of economic cooperation have been examined. To achieve this, India-Korea economic relations has been compared with India's economic relations with Japan, Singapore and China in terms of trade, FDI and FTA. Compared to the countries of Europe, America and other Asian countries, the four countries,

1. This contribution was modified, partially changed and translated into English from chapter 5 in the report *Economic Cooperation between India and Selected Asian Countries: Current Status and Policy Implications*, published by the Korean Institute for International Economic Policy in 2012.

Korea, Japan, Singapore and China, have surged ahead in terms of economic cooperation with India, especially since the 2000s.

Comparisons of Economic Cooperation

Political and Diplomatic Relations

In the aspect of politics and diplomacy, the Korea-India relationship is relatively weak compared to the relationship between India and Japan, Singapore or China. First of all, given their geographical contiguity and historical links with India, China's and Singapore's ties with India had been formed much earlier. Both Japan and Korea began to establish ties with India through Buddhism around the same time. In the contemporary era, Korea started to build relations with India much later than other countries did. While China and Japan (both in the beginning of the 1950s), and Singapore (in the middle of the 1960s) had established diplomatic relations with India, Korea did not establish its formal diplomatic relations with India until the end of 1973. It is also worth noting that Korea established diplomatic relations with India more than 20 years after Japan had done so.

Quite apart from the fact that the India-Korea diplomatic relationship was established much later than diplomatic relations with others, the mutual perception of their strategic importance was also late. This may be inferred from the summit-level meetings of the two countries. The first summit meeting between Korea and India had not been held until Prime Minister Rao made a visit to Korea in 1993, 20 years after the establishment of diplomatic relations. Since then, summit meetings became relatively more frequent in the 2000s, although only six meetings in total were held until 2012. In contrast, the first Japan-India summit meeting had been held in 1949 and eight summit meetings were held in the 1980s, at the time of the Cold War. The number of India-Japan summit meetings then seemed to experience a short lull but started to rebound in the 2000s with nine meetings until 2012. Even between China and India, summit meetings were held 17 times despite the severance of their diplomatic relations following the Sino-Indian War of 1962 and subsequent reestablishment in 1979. There were also 10 summit meetings between India and Singapore until recently. In particular, Singapore's former Prime Minister Lee Kuan Yew visited India three times until 1971 and held summit talks after the nation declared its independence in 1965.

However, in spite of the fact that formal diplomatic relations was established and mutual strategic importance perceived quite late, the Korea-India relationship has made relatively fast progress since the 2000s. Japan and India signed a global partnership agreement in 2000 and an upgraded version of this—a global strategic partnership—in 2006; China also has entered into a strategic partnership with India in 2005. Korea signed a long-term co-operative partnership for peace and prosperity with India later than Japan did and upgraded this to a strategic partnership in 2010, later than China.

Korea has not institutionalised its diplomatic cooperation system. No mechanism for regular summit meetings has been set up and the only summit meeting that is predictable for now is the summit meeting at the yearly held East Asia Summits. By contrast, Japan and India have regularised bilateral summit meetings, which have been held every year since 2005; this is apart from the East Asia Summits. China has been holding summit meetings with India every year since the 2000s and from 2011, the Strategic Economic Dialogue, joined by high-level officials of the two countries, has been held on a regular basis. In addition, China has a variety of channels for summit-level diplomatic cooperation with India including the East Asia Summits, BRICS Summits, etc. Table 7.1 provides a comparison of the diplomatic and political relations between India and other countries.

Trade

The establishment of diplomatic relations between Korea and India was followed by a trade agreement in 1974, yet trade between them was miniscule. Through the 1980s, the yearly trade amount could not reach a level beyond US$ 900 million and the growth rate of trade between the two countries in the 1980s was only 11 per cent, which was smaller than the growth rate of 13 per cent in Korea's total trade in the same period. The time when the trade volume between the two countries began exceeding US$ 2 billion was 1993, the year in which Prime Minister Rao visited Korea and had a summit talk for the first time in 20 years. Even after this, trade between the two countries experienced a short slowdown, but in the 1990s in general, its growth rate rose to 14 per cent, higher than Korea's growth rate of total trade of 8 per cent.

Table 7.1

Comparison of Political and Diplomatic Relationship between India and Korea, China, Japan and Singapore

	Japan-India	*Singapore-India*	*China-India*	*Korea-India*
Year of establishment of diplomatic relations	1952	1965	1950 1962 severance 1979 reestablishment	1973
Number of summit meetings (until 2012) -regularisation	19 times From 2005	10 times Not regularised	17 times From 2002	6 times Not regularised
Bilateral relations (year of agreement)	Global partnership (2000) Global strategic partnership (2006)	-	Strategic partnership (2005)	Long-term cooperative partnership for peace and prosperity (2004) Strategic partnership (2010)
System of diplomatic relations (year of commencement)	Bilateral summit meeting (2005) East Asia summit meeting (2005) Strategic dialogue among Japan, US and India (Minister level, 2011) Strategic meeting of foreign affairs ministers (2012)	ASEAN summit meeting (2002) East Asia summit meeting (2005) Joint ministers' conference (2008) Parliamentary friendship group (2012)	Strategic economic dialogue (2011) East Asia summit meeting (2005) BRICS summit meeting (2009)	East Asia summit meeting (2005) Conference of finance ministers (2010) Conference of foreign affair ministers Joint conference of minister level

Source: Cho *et al.* (2012), Table from p.231, partially modified.

The dramatic surge in trade between the two countries started from the 2000s. The trade volume, which had been only about US$ 2.3 billion in 2000, increased to US$ 11.2 billion in 2007, and four years from then, set a record of US$ 20.6 billion in the year 2011. During this period, the annual average growth rate of Korea-India trade was 24 per cent, which was double the annual average growth rate of 12 per cent in Korea's total trade. In 2012, the volume of trade decreased by 8.3 per cent to US$ 18.8 billion, because the two countries' economies slowed down. With the rapid rise in trade, Korea's trade position has moved up from 17th in 2000 to 13th in 2012 (Table 7.2).

Table 7.2

*India's Top 20 Trade Partners in 2012-13**

(Unit: US$ million)

Rank	*Country*	*Export*	*Import*	*Total Trade*	*Trade Balance*
1	UAE	36,316.65	39,138.36	75,455.01	-2,821.72
2	China	13,534.88	52,248.33	65,783.21	-38,713.45
3	USA	36,155.22	25,204.73	61,359.95	10,950.49
4	Saudi Arabia	9,785.78	33,998.11	43,783.89	-24,212.33
5	Switzerland	1,117.28	32,166.54	33,283.82	-31,049.25
6	Germany	7,246.20	14,325.79	21,571.99	-7,079.58
7	Singapore	13,619.24	7,486.38	21,105.63	6,132.86
8	Iraq	1,278.13	19,247.31	20,525.44	-17,969.18
9	Indonesia	5,331.30	14,879.49	20,210.79	-9,548.19
10	Hong Kong	12,279.20	7,907.17	20,186.37	4,372.04
11	Japan	6,100.06	12,412.29	18,512.35	-6,312.24
12	Kuwait	1,061.08	16,588.13	17,649.21	-15,527.05
13	Korea	4,202.25	13,105.12	17,307.37	-8,902.87
14	Qatar	687.18	15,693.08	16,380.26	-15,005.89
15	Belgium	5,507.30	10,046.87	15,554.17	-4,539.57
16	Australia	2,348.65	13,085.70	15,434.34	-10,737.05
17	Iran	3,351.07	11,594.46	14,945.53	-8,243.39
18	UK	8,612.54	6,293.09	14,905.62	2,319.45
19	Nigeria	2,740.04	12,086.11	14,826.15	-9,346.07
20	Malaysia	4,444.07	9,951.06	14,395.13	-5,506.99
Total of Top 20 countries		175,718.13	367,458.11	543,176.24	-191,739.98
India's Total		300,400.67	490,736.64	790,987.00	-190,335.97

Note: * The figures are for the Indian fiscal year, April 1, 2012 to March 30, 2013.
Source: Ministry of Commerce and Industry, India (*http://commerce.nic.in/eidb/iecnttopnq.asp*).

The main factor that led to the rapid increase in trade with India since the 2000s was the rapid growth of the Indian economy. Since 2005, the Indian economy has enjoyed an unprecedented boom, achieving a growth rate of over 9 per cent for three years in a row. Consequently, India's trade volume grew very sharply from US$ 100 billion dollars in 2002 to over US$ 500 billion in 2010. This is much faster than the time taken for Korea and

China to surpass trade volumes of 100 and 500 billion—17 and 13 years respectively.

India's trade increased rapidly, not just with Korea, but with China, Singapore and Japan as well. Looking at the 2011 trade volume as a standard, China, with US$ 473.9 billion, is already India's largest trading partner, with a trade volume that is over 3.5 times than between Korea and India. In the same time period, India-Singapore trade was US$ 28.2 billion, more than 1.3 times the volume of Korea-India trade. Japan has a lower volume than Korea with approximately US$ 17.9 billion. In fact, for the last decade, each country's average growth rate per year in trade with India was 35 per cent, 26 per cent and 25 per cent for China, Singapore and Korea respectively, with Japan having the lowest growth rate of 18 per cent.

All countries, except Singapore, enjoy a large trade surplus with India. In the case of Singapore, despite the consistent growth in trade volume, India has maintained a trade surplus of US$ 2 to US$ 3 billion since 2007. In 2011, the trend reversed into a trade deficit of US$ 100 million.

In terms of export volumes, China takes the lead with exports of approximately US$ 50.5 billion, followed by Singapore (US$ 14.0 billion), Korea (US$ 12.7 billion) and Japan (US$ 11.1 billion). In terms of the growth rate, however, China (30.1%) and Japan (22.4%) outstrip Korea (19.6%) and Singapore (15.3%) during these five years. Japan's export growth rate increased especially since 2007, the year in which there was a dramatic increase in Japanese investment in India.

Consequently, competition for each country's export share in the Indian import market has gradually turned more intense. In particular, there is a high probability that the competition between Japan and Korea will escalate. For the last decade until 2011, the Japanese share in the Indian market decreased gradually from 3.7 per cent to 2.4 per cent. The growth rate of Japan's exports, however, has stayed higher than that of Korea since 2007. Korea's share of exports to India had increased from 2.2 per cent to 2.7 per cent in the same time period, but after hitting a peak of 3.1 per cent in 2009, it decreased continuously and came closer to Japan's share. Meanwhile, Chinese share drastically increased from 4.6 per cent to 12.0 per cent in the same period. The difference between China's share and that of Korea or Japan in the Indian import market is too large for intense direct competition between these countries. Nevertheless, the composition of the main items exported to India or the export similarity index indicates that the competitive relationship is being intensified. First, in the top five items that each country exports to India, Korea's top four items—machinery, electrical equipment, steel and auto-components—are the same as Japan's top four items. Similarly, Korea and China appear to compete in the export of machinery, electrical equipment and plastics. Korea and Singapore also compete in machinery, electrical equipment and plastic products; however, since Signapore's exports consist more of products in transit rather than domestic products, the degree of competition between Korea and Singapore is not so high.

In fact, in the Indian import market, the export similarity index between Korea and Japan and between Korea and China is gradually increasing. The export similarity index between Korea and Japan stayed at 69 in 2002 but rose beyond 70 in 2011, while the export similarity index between Korea and China has increased from 54 in 2002 to 59 in 2011.

With Korea included, the four Asian countries' imports from India have grown at a steady rate. By 2011, the volume of imports by China and Singapore from India was US$ 23.4 billion and US$ 14.1 billion respectively, making them the third and the fourth on the list of countries that India exports to. Korean and Japanese imports from India amount to nearly US$ 7.9 billion and US$6.8 billion respectively. Considering the growth rate of imports from India for the five years between 2007 and 2011, Singapore ranks first with about 28 per cent, and China and Korea are ranked next with about 23 per cent and 22 per cent respectively. Japan ranks the lowest with about 14 per cent.

The share of the top five items as a proportion of total imports from India is the highest for Singapore at about 88 per cent, followed by Korea and China at about 78 per cent and 77 per cent respectively. The share of the top five items in Japan's imports from India is relatively low at about 64 per cent. Naphtha is the largest item of import by Korea, Japan and Singapore. Naphtha accounted for 34 per cent, 77 per cent and 59 per cent of Japanese, Singaporean and Korean imports from India in 2011. China's largest import item, however, is minerals. Minerals account for about 45

Table 7.3

Comparison of Korea, China, Japan and Singapore's Exports to India

	Japan	*Singapore*	*China*	*Korea*
Export volume (US$ billion, 2011)	11.08	14.04	50.53	12.65
Export growth rate (2007-2011, %)	22.4	15.3	30.1	19.6
Export items and shares (2011, %)	Top 5 items 75.3 • Machinery 36.5 • Electrical devices 13.1 • Steel 12.3 • Auto-components 7.8 • Optical instruments 5.6	Top 5 items 77.1 • Machinery 22.2 • Mineral fuels 21.7 • Electrical devices 19.8 • Organic chemical products 8.2 • Plastics 5.2	Top 5 items 66.2 • Machinery 25.2 • Electrical devices 20.5 • Organic chemical products 9.2 • Fertilisers 7.0 • Steel products 4.3	Top 5 items 63 • Machinery 15.4 • Electrical devices 14.6 • Steel 13.7 • Auto-components 12.0 • Plastics 7.3
Market share in Indian import market				
- 2002(%)	3.2	2.6	5.0	3.3
- 2007(%)	2.7	3.2	11.2	2.4
- 2011(%)	2.4	1.7	11.8	2.6

Note: Japan, Singapore and China's data from UN Comtrade, Korea used data from KITA.
Source: Cho *et al.* (2012), Table 5-3 from p.241, partially modified.

per cent of the total imports in 2011. Besides, the four countries import a large amount of iron ore, steel products and organic chemical products.

Foreign Direct Investment

Korea began investing in India after the year 1993, when Prime Minister Narasimha Rao visited Korea. In 1996, when President Young-sam Kim of Korea made a return visit to India, the two countries signed a Bilateral Investment Promotion/Protection Agreement (BIPA). Japan's investment to India had begun in the early 1980s, but except some like Suzuki, most of the Japanese companies experienced a tough time in the mid-1990s. On the other hand, there was an increase in Korean investment

Table 7.4

Comparison of Korea, China, Japan and Singapore's Imports from India

	Japan	*Singapore*	*China*	*Korea*
Import volume ($100 billion, 2011)	6.81	14.14	23.37	7.89
Import growth rate (2007-2011, %)	14.4	28.2	22.5	21.7
Import items and shares (2011, %)	Top 5 items 64.0 • Naphtha 33.6 • Foodstuff 9.3 • Iron ore 8.4 • Jewellery 6.6 • Fish 6.1	Top 5 items 87.8 • Naphtha 75.6 • Jewellery 5.6 • Organic chemical products 2.4 • Machinery 2.1 • Electrical devices 2.1	Top 5 items 76.8 • Minerals 44.6 • Cotton 13.7 • Copper 9.2 • Jewellery 5.1 • Organic chemical products 4.2	Top 5 items 77.9 • Naphtha 59.2 • Steel products 6.1 • Organic chemical products 5.8 • Textiles 4.1 • Food and beverage 2.7

Source: Cho *et al.* (2012), Table 5-4 from p.242-43, partially modified.

led by companies such as Daewoo Motors, Daewoo Electronics, LG Electronics, Samsung Electronics and Hyundai Motors. About 9 per cent of direct investments to India in 1996 were taken up by Korea's large-sized companies. In the same period, the investment share of Japan and Singapore each stayed at 4.1 per cent and 0.9 per cent respectively. In 1999, with an investment share of almost 13 per cent, Korea was among the top five investing countries along with the US and the UK. Large-sized Korean companies, at present, hold the first and second largest shares in the Indian electronics and automobiles market.

Subsequently, Korea's investment in India slowed down rapidly at the turn of 2000s. Until 2011, Korea's share in total direct investment to India was below 1 per cent except once when it went beyond 1.5 per cent in 2005. On the contrary, Singapore and Japan, both of whose investments in India had faltered in the 1990s, are now experiencing a rapid increase in investment in India after the 2000s. Japan, in particular, implemented large-scale investments in the early 2000s with its share in total investment rising dramatically to 11 per cent in 2002. After that, Japan's investment to

India slowed down for a while but soon made a sharp rebound from 2008. In 2011, its share increased to 11.3 per cent. Since Japan agreed to initiate the Comprehensive Economic Partnership (CEP) with India in 2006, Japan's investment in India has increased. Similarly, after the Singapore-India Comprehensive Economic Cooperation Agreement (CECA) and the double tax avoidance agreement came into effect in 2005, investment flows from Singapore to India have been rapidly increasing. Singapore's share of investment in India was only 1.7 per cent in 2004 but increased to 7.3 per cent in 2005 and showed a sharp increase to 15.4 per cent in 2011.

Table 7.5

Cumulative Country-wise FDI Inflows from April 2000 to March 2013

Rank	*Country*	*FDI Inflows (₹ Crore*)*	*FDI Inflows (US$ million)*	*Share in Total FDI Inflows*
1	Mauritius**	341,124	73,666	38.1
2	Singapore	90,182	19,460	10.1
3	UK	80,458	17,548	9.1
4	Japan	70,094	14,550	7.5
5	USA	50,922	11,121	5.8
6	Netherlands	42,378	8,965	4.6
7	Cyprus**	32,328	6,889	3.6
8	Germany	25,512	5,480	2.8
9	France	16,864	3,572	1.9
10	UAE	11,307	2,422	1.3
13	Korea	5,821	1,231	0.6
15	Hong Kong	4,769	1,028	0.5
19	Indonesia	2,825	610	0.3
21	Malaysia	2,730	549	0.3
30	China	1,428	278	0.1
	Sub-total	778,742	167,369	86.6
	Grand Total	896,912	193,403	100.0

Note: * ₹ 10 million, ** a tax haven.

Source: Ministry of Commerce and Industry, India, *http://dipp.nic.in/English/Publications/FDI_Statistics/2013/india_FDI_March2013.pdf.*

The difference is more visible if investment volumes are examined. In 2011, Japan and Singapore each made new investments of US$ 3.1 billion and US$ 4.2 billion while Korea made new investments of only US$ 130 million. From April 2000 until March 2013, Singapore's accumulated investment volume was US$ 19.46 billion and Japan's was US$ 14.55 billion, but Korea's was only US$ 1.23 billion. Singapore had a share of 10 per cent of accumulated investment in this period and ranked second amongst all countries investing in India. Japan has a share of more than 7 per cent and ranked 4th, while Korea has a share of 0.6 per cent and ranked 13th.

The increased gap between the scales of investment by each country in the 2000s led to a disparity between the numbers of each country's companies in India. The number of Japanese companies that had a foothold in the Indian market was approximately 1,800 by October 2012,[2] almost five times the 390 Korean companies that had a presence in the country.[3] Japanese firms are also more widely dispersed than Korean companies. Eighty per cent of Korean companies that have entered India are concentrated in the NCR (national capital region) area, centred at Delhi and the Southern Chennai area. By contrast, only 41 per cent of Japanese companies are in the NCR area.

In terms of the type of businesses that each country has invested in, Korea and Japan appear to have invested in similar businesses while Singapore differs. About 18 per cent of investments by Singapore have been in the manufacturing sector, and the rest consists of IT, finance and insurance, and the wholesale and retail sectors. The IT sector and the finance and insurance sector each take up 48 per cent and 12 per cent of the total investment. Japan and Korea partially differ in how they classify types of business, but they both are concentrated mostly in the manufacturing sector and have a similar structure of investment in that automobiles, electrical and electronic and other machinery comprise a large part of their investment.

When it comes to how much investment each country attracted from India, Singapore is certainly ahead of the others. From 2007 to 2011, more than US$ 29.2 billion was invested in Singapore by India. This, by far,

2. The Japanese embassy in India records and presents the number of Japanese enterprises entering India every year through the regional Japanese Chamber of Commerce in India and Japan's JETRO.

3. As the results of on-site surveys with 531 Korean companies, which were sourced from the Export-Import Bank of Korea's database of 2011, and the list held by KOTRA in India show about 387 companies were identified as in normal category. Refer to Cho *et al.* (2011) for related data.

exceeds the US$ 18.1 billion, that Singapore invested in India until August 2012 since 2000. The reason for this is that India is utilising Singapore not only as a foothold to enter the markets of East Asia, but also to attract investments to India itself. In terms of the amount of investment received from India, Korea stays ahead of Japan as well as China. Korea has received more than US$ 568 million of investment from India until the first half of 2013. Japan has received only a total of US$ 64 million from India until 2011.

Free Trade Agreement

The Korea-India CEPA, for which official negotiations began with President Abdul Kalam's visit to Korea in 2006, came into effect from January 2010, four years after the start of negotiations. The Japan-India CEPA, for which negotiations had started a year later than the Korea-India CEPA, came into effect in August 2011, a year and a half behind the Korea-India CEPA. By contrast, the negotiation on Singapore-India CECA had begun in 2003, much earlier than Korea-India CEPA, and Singapore-India CECA came into effect in August 2005. Not much progress has been made on the FTA between China and India, for which joint research was completed in 2007, until recently in 2013. Considering that China's market share in the Indian import market is rapidly increasing, promoting China-India FTA seems to be a challenge because of opposition from Indian industry.

Singapore has managed to wrest the most in tariff concessions from India as compared to Japan and Korea. Singapore obtained 93 per cent concession until 2015. On the other hand, Korea and Japan obtained 86 per cent and 90 per cent concessions from India respectively. With the two countries' level of concession being lower than Singapore's, the period over which tariffs are to be eliminated is also much longer, lasting until 2019 and 2021 for Korea and Japan respectively.

On the other hand, it is difficult to determine whether Korea's level of tariff concession from India in the commodity sector is higher than Japan's or *vice versa*. The reason is that Japan has a slight advantage in terms of the range of tariff reduction/elimination, but in terms of the speed of tariff reduction, Korea is ahead of Japan. Further, the same rules of origins apply to Korea-India CEPA and Japan-India CEPA. In contrast, Singapore-India

Table 7.6

Comparison of Korea, China, Japan and Singapore's Investment Relations with India

	Japan	*Singapore*	*China*	*Korea*
Investment volume in India (US$ million, 2011)	3,110	4260	50	130
Cumulative investment - Volume (US$ billion, 2011)* - Ratio (%) - Rank	14.55 7.5 4th	19.46 10.1 2nd	0.278 0.14 30th	1.23 0.64 13th
Investment growth rate (2007-2011, %)	160	118.6	665	40
Investment ratio by industry (2011, by the number of businesses, %)	• Transport 53 • Electrical devices 7 • Services 3 • Civil engineering 3 • Others 34	• IT 48 • Manufacturing 18 • Finance/ Insurance 12 • Retail and wholesale 6 • Others 16	• Steel 76 • Chemical 7 • Trade 3 • Machinery 3 • IT 2 • Others 9	• Primary metals 62 • Metal processing 13 • Auto-related 12 • Machinery 5 • Electronic components 2 • Others 6
Investment in India/total investment - Ratio (2011,%) - Rank (2011)	1.8 13th	15 3rd	0.1 42nd	1.7 14th
India's investment - 2007-2011 (million dollar) - Ratio (%, rank)	64 0.1 (48th)	29,225 26.1 (2nd)	192 0.2 (25th)	463 0.4 (13rd)

Note: * From April 2000 to March 2013.

Source: Cho *et al.* (2012), Table 5-5 from p.246, partially modified and updated.

CECA's rules of origins are definitely stricter than in the Korea-India and Japan-India CEPAs.

In the services sector, Singapore and Japan enjoy higher levels of concession than Korea. Korea obtained concessions in 11 fields and 81 sections of the services sector and the condition of favourable consideration about establishing up to 10 Korean bank branches in India within four years of the Korea-India CEPA coming into effect. Japan obtained five more service sections than Korea and also received exemption from the condition of cargo preference for Indian freighters,[4] a long-cherished wish of Korean shipping firms. Singapore did not gain concessions like Korea and Japan, but it was granted a variety of benefits in the area of business service, construction engineering, finance, communication, transport and others. For example, in the finance industry, three Singaporean banks were given the merchant bank status within India, and were allowed to have the condition of favourable consideration about establishing up to 15 branches within 4 years of the Singapore-India CECA coming into force. In fact, these privileges enabled Singapore's DBS and other banks to establish 15 branches by 2009.

The terms for investment flows negotiated in each of the FTAs were similar but for movement of people, in which India has high interest, the terms negotiated differed slightly among the different FTAs. Korea and Singapore opened the doors to India in the case of about 163 and 129 professions respectively as also for existing contractual service suppliers (CSS) and independent professionals (IP). In particular, Korea and India designated 85 among 163 professions to be in the IT area so that they could promote the exchange of IT professionals between the two countries. Japan and India divided all sectors into CSS and IP, and opened doors in the fields that were considered necessary for the two countries. Japan opened up 14 fields including travel, accounting, market research, business consulting, advertisement and exhibition to CSS and 10 fields including computer, architecture, natural science research, engineering and city development to IP from India.

In addition, each FTA included cooperation in various sectors reflecting special features between the contracting parties and in which there were pending issues at the time of the agreement. Japan and India included cooperation in the pharmaceutical and metallurgical technology sector, meaning rare-earth resource development, and Singapore and India included cooperation in infrastructure development and vocational training. Korea and India included cooperation in the joint development of audio-visual content.

4. This is the system in which vessels of Indian nationality must transport at least 40 per cent of liner shipping companies' cargo.

Table 7.7

Comparison of Korea, China, Japan and Singapore's FTA with India

	Japan	*Singapore*	*Korea*
Commencement of negotiation (year)	2007	2003	2006
Agreement concluded (year)	February 2011	June 2005	September 2009
Effective from (year)	August 2011	August 2005	January 2010
Concession in commodity*			
- Total rate of concession (%)	89.7	93	85.5
- Immediate abolition (%)	7.6		38.4
- Abolition and reduction of tariffs (%)	82.1(for 11 years)		47.1 (for 10 years)
- Exempted concession (%)	10.3		14.5
Rules of origins - standard rules	Three HS6 unit changes + regional value content (RVC) above 35%	Three HS4 unit changes + regional value content (RVC) above 40%	Three HS6 unit changes + regional value content (RVC) above 35%
Concession in service sector*	- 11 fields, 86 sections** - Favourable consideration about establishing up to 10 bank branches in 4 years - Exemption from complying with cargo preference condition	- Advantages in 8 fields (business service, construction engineering, finance, communications, transport, etc.)	- 11 fields, 81 sections - Favourable consideration to allow establishment of up to 10 bank branches in 4 years
Concession in investment sector*	National treatment Most-favoured-nation treatment Repatriation of profits Protection of investors	National treatment Expansion of state-owned companies' maximum share Protection of investors	National treatment Most-favoured-nation treatment Repatriation of profits Protection of investors
Manpower movement	Opened independent professionals in 10 fields, contractual service suppliers in 14 fields***	Mutual opening of 129 professions	Mutual opening of 163 professions

contd...

...contd...

	Japan	*Singapore*	*Korea*
Unusual sectors of cooperation	Pharmaceuticals, environment, entertainment information, metallurgical (rare-earth resources), etc.	Infrastructure development, vocational training, skill training, national security, etc.	Audiovisual content, government procurement, pharmaceuticals, renewable energy
Upgrades of agreement	-	- The first negotiation completed in 2007 - The second negotiation in progress since 2010	Agreed in 2011

Note: * Concession by India, by the amount.

** Three areas in communications (electronic information exchange, telex, telegram), two areas in distribution (single-brand retail, single-brand franchise), total five areas.

*** opened sectors in Japan.

Source: Cho *et al.* (2012), Table 5-6, p.251.

The Singapore-India CECA is an exemplary case of upgrading an agreement through a joint committee. By improving the agreement in 2007, 2 years after the 2005 CECA came into effect, the two sides made a considerable increase in the rate of concession in the commodity sector from 75 per cent to 93 per cent. And since 2010, the two countries have been conducting negotiations for a second improvement in the agreement. In contrast, Korea and India decided to process the agreement improvement at their first joint committee in 2011, but their second joint committee was not realised until 2013.

Tasks to Deepen Bilateral Economic Cooperation

Establishment of Enhanced Cooperation System

Regularisation of Bilateral Summit Meetings

As seen from Japan's, China's and Singapore's relationship with India, what is needed first in order to continue strengthening Korea's relationship with India is to hold upgraded high-level discussions on a regular basis. Japan and China already have been holding summit talks with India every year and intensifying bilateral relations. At these summit meetings, not only diplomatic and security cooperation, but also economic cooperation is discussed.

Regularisation of summit talks between two countries signifies the highest-level of bilateral cooperation. If cooperation between Korea and India is established around summit talks held on a regular basis, cooperation between the two countries would intensify and develop more comprehensively and efficiently.

In fact, the cooperation established between Korea and India is relatively vulnerable. Currently, the only high-level talks between the two countries are between the ministers of finance, commerce and foreign affairs and a minister-level joint committee. Even these meetings are not held on a regular basis. Accordingly, cooperation between both the private and public sectors is relatively weak. The Korea-India dialogues, which were held 12 times until 2013, are the only regularised public-private joint policy discussion body so far.[5] In the private sector, the Korea Chamber of Commerce and Industry (KCCI), the Federation of the Korean Industries (FKI) and India's business federations, Confederation of Indian Industry (CII) and Federation of Indian Chambers of Commerce and Industry (FICCI), have been holding meetings of Korea-India private economic cooperation committees; however, these have not been regularised yet. These committees meet only if associated with summit talks or other special events in the two countries, so their durability and effectiveness appear low.

Enhancement of Strategic Partnership and Regularisation of Minister-level Consultations

To upgrade Korea-India cooperation, it is also necessary that minister-level discussion bodies for each major area of cooperation are constituted and regularised. The talks between the ministers of finance, commerce and foreign affairs and the minister-level joint committees, which have no schedule and are sporadic, should be integrated and reorganised. And minister-level discussion bodies for each major area of cooperation—economy and industry, diplomacy and security, education and technology, social and culture sectors, and others—should be systematically formed, and then held on a regular basis. In doing so, the two countries are going to have to explore areas of cooperation actively.

5. Korea's Seoul International Forum and India's renowned research institute, ICRIER coordinate this dialogue every year in India and Korea by turn.

Establishment of a Korean Chamber of Commerce in India and Intensification of Cooperation with Indian State Governments

Even if Korea-India cooperation gets upgraded by summit talks and minister-level cooperation bodies, the two countries' private sector associations/federations ought to be vitalised to intensify cooperation. Regular meetings between private sector associations of the two countries should be scheduled and held to foster stronger ties.

One country whose private sector has been actively cooperating with the Indian private sector is Singapore. There are more bodies for active private cooperation than bodies for cooperation at the government level. Singaporean private organisations hold yearly joint conferences and forums with CII and FICCI; India-Singapore Strategic Dialogue, India-Singapore Business Forum, and the Singapore Indian Chamber of Commerce and Industry (SICCI) are some of the bodies that promote cooperation between the private sectors of the two countries. Korea also has been operating the Indian Chamber of Commerce in Korea (ICCK), established in 2010. However, there is no formal private organisation in India to promote Korean business interests. The Korean government needs to support the establishment of the tentatively named Korean Chamber of Commerce in India (KCCI), to monitor the progress made by the Korean private sector and to promote networking with Indian companies. The KCCI should represent and speak for Korean companies besides vitalising cooperation between the private sectors of the two countries.

In addition, cooperation with India's state governments as well as the central government should be enhanced as Japan and Singapore have done. Because of India's decentralised structure, any business venture would need to interact with state governments to implement their projects. Japan's JETRO and Singaporean state-owned real estate development business, Ascendas, signed MoUs with the Rajasthan, Tamil Nadu and Gujarat state governments. They are now taking the lead in developing industrial complexes. Korea needs to do the same. States whose growth potential and openness are relatively high, for example, Gujarat, Maharashtra, Tamil Nadu and Haryana, will be the preferred targets. Having a clear understanding of the conditions in these preferred target states and establishing a cooperative base pre-emptively will promote the entry of private companies to India.

Improvement of Korea-India CEPA and Maximising its Utilisation

Upgrade of CEPA and Maximising its Utilisation

The most comprehensive and institutionally well-established system, in the aspect of Korea-India economic cooperation, is the Korea-India CEPA, which came into force in 2010. Trade items that satisfy rules of origins already enjoy preferential tax rates, but there are many more to be improved. Even though the two countries agreed to upgrade the Korea-India CEPA at the CEPA joint committee meeting in 2011, there has not been any progress yet.

First, the two countries must resume their joint committee meetings as soon as possible to bring the tariff rate on par with that offered in India's FTAs with other countries. Additionally, it should be noted by India that the more tariff reduction is accelerated, the faster the growth rate of India's exports to Korea and reduction in trade deficit *vis-à-vis* Korea will be.[6]

In commodity trade, it is necessary to use the Korea-India CEPA to greater advantage. Korea also needs to find ways to use India's expertise in the IT sector to a greater extent. In today's IT industry, with the popularisation of smartphones and tablet PCs, etc., the competitiveness of software, rather than hardware, has become more significant than in the past. The movement of independent professionals as well as contractual service suppliers in 163 professions from 2010 is already allowed between the two countries. About 85 professions among 163 are IT related. In particular, the Korean government should reinforce institutional support for Korea's small- and medium-sized IT enterprises to utilise Indian IT professionals more efficiently.[7]

6. Estimates of export increase and welfare improvement when the two countries' most favoured nation (MFN) tariff rate is reduced by 10 per cent, 20 per cent and 50 per cent indicate that India will be more affected than Korea. Shome and Ahn (2012: 176-8).

7. According to a survey of 105 member firms of the Korea IT Venture Business Association in 2008, Korean IT venture and small and medium-sized businesses most preferred Indian IT professionals (India 34%, US 16%, China 13%, etc.) and the level of satisfaction in hiring Indian IT professionals was the highest as well (very satisfactory 27%, satisfactory 66%, average 7%, dissatisfactory 0%). Refer Ministry of Foreign Affairs and Korea Institute for International Economic Policy (2009): 16-17.

Extension of Concession Period for Bank Branch Establishment and Enhancement of Cooperation in Joint Production of Audiovisuals

It is required to extend the period within which Korean banks can set up branches under the Korea-India CEPA. One Korean bank branch was opened in 2012, and while two others are awaiting approval in accordance with the provision stating that there will be favourable consideration about establishing up to 10 branches in India within four years since the CEPA came into force. It seems impossible to establish seven additional branches by the 2013 deadline. The possibility of extending the time available to Korean banks can be considered in the Korea-India CEPA joint committee.

Joint production of audiovisuals and other subordinate agreements are also in need of prompt conclusion. The Korea-India CEPA agreement specifies that audiovisual content produced jointly by the two countries can not only be mutually recognised as domestic products, but also be supported with various benefits, including subsidy, according to the joint production agreement that will be signed afterwards.[8] Subordinate agreements need to be signed immediately to ensure that the two countries have a presence in the global cultural scene. The market for films in Korea has shown a sharp rise with the number of movie watchers rising to over 200 million in 2013. Internationally, India is ranked first in 2011 in terms of movie ticket sales and the number of releases, and ranked sixth (US$ 1.47 billion dollars) in terms of the value of ticket sales.[9] The potential for growth of the cultural contents market is estimated at an annual rate of over 10 per cent until 2016.[10]

Intensification of Supporting Entries by Investment

Aggressive Supporting of Entry by SMEs through M&A and Others

As compared to other countries with which India has economic cooperation, Korea lags far behind in terms of investment volumes. Given the size of the Indian market, it is crucial to increase Korea's investment

8. Audiovisual products in Korea-India CEPA comprise theatre, TV, digital equipment of any kind or all forms of audiovisual content except gambling games.
9. Refer to "A Big Market, But is it a Mature One" from *Business Standard*, June 7, 2012.
10. Refer FICCI-KPMG (2012), *Indian Meaia and Entertainment Industry Report 2012*. p.6 and pp.59-76.

volume and to improve its ranking as an investor in India. The Korean government needs to push for greater investment by Korean businesses, particularly small and medium enterprises (SMEs).

First, it is necessary to formulate policies to support investment by businesses in Greenfield ventures as well as in mergers and acquisitions (M&A). As India rapidly grew at the turn of 2000s, problems related to land acquisition and inadequate infrastructure made investment in Greenfield project difficult. Consequently, many Japanese, Singaporean, American and European companies have used the M&A route to enter the Indian market. Korean companies need to follow suit if they are to establish a presence in the Indian market. The entry of Korean SMEs into India will be facilitated if information about possible M&A deals and M&A consulting services is made available. We may benchmark systems like Trade Match, which arranges trade between the two countries in affiliation with the Singapore Indian Chamber of Commerce and Industry. Positive reviews should be given to implementing a system that arranges partners for M&As, joint investment and trade between SMEs in Korea and India, and provides consulting services.

Strengthening Support for Entry into the Infrastructure Sector

Under the 12th Five Year Plan, which began in 2012, the Indian government plans to invest US$ 1 trillion, which is approximately equal to 53 per cent of India's GDP in 2011, to expand the infrastructure sector. Half of this amount is expected to be funded by the government, while the remaining amount is expected to come from private, including foreign, investments. At summit level meetings with Singapore, China, Korea and Japan, the Indian government has pushed for participation in infrastructural development by partner countries.

Japan and Singapore have aggressively participated in India's infrastructure development business by strategically placing official development assistance (ODA) and state companies in front. Railways in major cities like Delhi, the Delhi-Mumbai industrial corridor and the Chennai-Bangalore industrial corridor are all notable infrastructure projects based on Japanese ODA support to India. Singapore is actively participating in India's IT parks, industrial complexes, ports, communication and others through state enterprises such as Temasek, Ascendas, Singapore Port Authority, SingTel, etc. China has also made use of cheap labour and large-scale financial support from state banks to play an active role in India's infrastructure development. At the China-India Strategic Economic Dialogue, held in November 2012, China agreed to provide support amounting to US$ 3.6 billion and to participate in sectors like renewable energy, power generation, steel manufacturing and other sectors.

Given the limits to mobilising state companies and financial institutions as well as ODA,[11] Korea needs to look at niche strategies. First, Korea should explore ways to participate as subcontractors in individual infrastructure projects. Given that different Indian states have differing regulatory requirements, and consequently, different business environments and investment priorities, the availability of information on these issues would provide an impetus to investment by Korean companies.

In addition, given the emphasis on infrastructure and other development projects, Korean companies need to consider the possibility of setting up consortia to enter these sectors. This would also help Korean companies distribute risk and help them exploit the synergy resulting from working as part of a consortium. And at this point, the chance of receiving government or public financing could be examined, and this will make a significant contribution to reducing the risk of the businesses.

Moreover, there should also be more enhanced financial support to improve Korean companies' competence to receive orders. In this context, the five-year, billion-dollar joint financing by the two countries' export-import banks—promised at the third Korea-India Finance Minister meeting in 2012—was appropriate.[12]

---

11. As the Indian government has declared that it will not receive any ODA support from countries outside of G7 in 2005, there is no way for Korea to provide India with ODA.
12. Export-import banks of the two countries are launching their billion-dollar joint financing support for the next five years in the sector of infrastructure development of India, and to do so Indian export-import bank is supposed to provide the Korean export-import bank with adequate project information for the joint support. Also, the Korean export-import bank has decided to give additional support of US$ 100 million in 2013. Refer to press release on November 2, 2012, from the Ministry of Strategy and Finance, Korea.

Promotion of Industrial Complex for Korean Enterprises

Reviewing of Joint Development with Singapore and Other Countries

One of the biggest concerns of Korean enterprises in India is the challenge they face in acquiring land with well-equipped infrastructure. Korean enterprises prefer to acquire land in industrial clusters. Japan and Singapore have succeeded in developing industrial complexes in India despite the difficulties faced by even large Indian companies in acquiring land. By selling developed sites at cheaper than market prices to companies from their home countries, Japan and Singapore are efficiently providing them support.

The state development firms, JETRO of Japan and Ascendas of Singapore, are some of the business entities involved in developing industrial complexes. Singapore has a strategy of involving its state-owned enterprises to lead the development of industrial complexes in a bid to pre-emptively remove risks that private companies would find difficult to handle. Japan's JETRO does not assume direct risks by investing in shares but it has signed MoUs with Indian state governments or state-government-affiliated corporations for development and promoted businesses to raise public confidence and indirectly reduce development risks.

While it would be infeasible for Korea, which has little experience in building industrial complexes in India, to imitate the strategy adopted by Singapore or Japan at present, it should consider developing industrial complexes jointly with those countries.

Formation of Consortia between India's State Governments and Korea's Large, Small and Medium Enterprises

The Korean government, public institutions and large companies should consider the possibility of tying up with governments of states like Tamil Nadu, Gujarat and Maharashtra, which have experience in the development of industrial complexes and are considered business-friendly. Participation in such development should be broad-based to ensure that risks are distributed over a large number of stakeholders.

In addition, rather than attempt the development of large industrial complexes in the beginning, small- and medium-scale developments with a relatively high success potential should be attempted first. If small- and medium-sized industrial complexes are successfully developed and parcelled out as an industrial complex designated for Korean enterprises, it will act as a stimulant for other state governments to facilitate the development of industrial complexes for Korean enterprises.

Conclusion

The Korea-India relationship has been historically, politically and diplomatically weak from the beginning, yet economic cooperation between the two countries has improved relatively quickly. It is possible that Korea-India relations will continue to develop around their economic cooperation. In the areas of politics, diplomacy and security, Japan and China's relations with India have diverse strengths. Japan and China already treat security and diplomatic cooperation with India on par with economic cooperation. Singapore intensified its security cooperation with India long ago and recently, shifted its attention to economic cooperation. On the other hand, in Korea-India relations, cooperation on diplomatic and security issues does not seem to be as important as in other countries' relations with India. One of the limitations on the extent of cooperation on security issues in the Korea-India relationship is linked to the two countries' individual relationships with China.

Expanded economic relations between Korea and India both offer opportunities and pose risks. The ability to focus on economic cooperation offers opportunity, but if it does not result in significant benefits for both countries, their relationship will weaken because cooperation in the political, diplomatic and security areas is rather limited. It will also call into question the need for cooperation between the two countries. Looked at from this perspective, the entry of Korean businesses into India in the early 1990s and the coming into force of the Korea-India CEPA/FTA earlier than India's partnership agreements with Japan and other countries are very significant.

The problem is that Korea's performance in economic cooperation with India is poorer as compared to that of Japan, Singapore and China towards the end of the 2000 decade. The low volume of Korean investment in India is alarming and needs to be tackled immediately. The rapid advance of Japanese companies in India recently is a threat to Korea. More than a hundred new Japanese firms (about 400 firms, if existing companies' additional establishments are included) have been established in India in 2011 alone. Although Hyundai Motors, LG Electronics and Samsung Electronics hold the largest and second largest market share with high brand awareness in India, Korean companies are dominated by Japanese companies in most industries except the automobile and electrics/ electronics industries. Not only do Japanese enterprises outnumber Korean enterprises in more sectors, they are also more widely spread across the country. While Korean enterprises are concentrated in the northern and southern part of India such as Delhi and Chennai, Japanese enterprises are widely spread out also in the western part, which is an area of high growth, and in the eastern part, where mineral resources and human resources are relatively abundant. This is the task that Korea ought to address as economic cooperation between the two countries develops and intensifies in future.

References

Cho, Choongjae, Young Chul Song, Yoon-Jung Choi, Woong Lee and Hye-won Jung (2012). "Economic Cooperation between India and Selected Asian Countries: Current Status and Policy Implications", *Policy Analysis* 12-22. Korean Institute for International Economic Policy.

Cho, Choongjae, Yoon-Jung Choi and Yong Chul Song (2011). *Management Survey of Korean Firms in India and Performance Analysis*. Korean Institute for International Economic Policy.

Embassy of Japan in India (2012). "Japanese Business Establishment in India".

FICCI-KPMG (2012). *Indian Media and Entertainment Industry Report 2012*.

Ministry of Foreign Affairs and Korea Institute for International Economic Policy (2009). *The Main Contents of Korea-India CEPA*.

Shome, P. and Choongyong Ahn (2012). *Korea-India Deepening Partnership for the 21st Century*. Korean Institute for International Economic Policy.

News Articles:

Business Standard (2012). "A Big Market, But is it a Mature One?", *Business Standard*, June 7.

Database:

CEIC Database.

KITA Database.

UN Comtrade.

Websites:

http://commerce.nic.in/eidb/iecnttopnq.asp

http://dipp.nic.in/English/Publications/FDI_Statistics

8 What does the CEPA Mean for India-Korea Trade?

Ram Upendra Das

Introduction

Given that bilateral and regional trade and economic cooperation have been on the rise in all parts of the world, countries in Asia also have adopted this as a mechanism to scale up economic activities in general and trade integration in particular. Such trade and economic cooperation agreements have made the flow of trade in goods, services and investment more liberal, contributing to higher levels of income and employment generation because of induced investment flows and unleashing a process of economic convergence among participating countries. In other words, these agreements increasingly serve as instruments to address developmental asymmetries, especially in a dynamic setting (Kindleberger, 1966; Panagariya, 2000; Urata, 2002; Negasi, 2009; Das, 2013). The comprehensiveness of these agreements makes them more development-relevant because they recognise the inter-linkages between trade in goods and services, and investment.

It is the economics of regional integration that has driven the proliferation of bilateral and regional economic arrangements. India and South Korea have engaged in such arrangements with their relevant trade partners. Both the countries also embarked upon studying and negotiating a bilateral Comprehensive Economic Partnership Agreement (CEPA) between them including an free trade agreement (FTA) on trade in goods and services along with investment cooperation. Signed in August 2009, it came into effect on January 1, 2010.

This paper analyses the implications of the CEPA for India-Korea trade in goods and services. This is done by analysing the bilateral macro profile of trade in its varied dimensions, followed by an analysis of tariff liberalisation commitments by both countries and the rules of origin formulation in the CEPA. In particular, the paper addresses the oft repeated issues raised in studies by Cho (2013), Kim and Cho (2012), and Lee *et al.* (2011) including the issue of CEPA tariff liberalisation rates being higher than the prevailing most favoured nation (MFN) rates at a given point of time on a few items. Further, the paper briefly analyses the trade in services commitments by both the countries. The last section presents conclusions based on this analysis.

Bilateral Trade: A Macro Profile of Volume, Trends and Mutual Importance

In terms of bilateral trade between India and Korea, some important insights emanate from observing the level or the volume of exports and imports, the mutual importance of India and South Korea in each other's trade basket, and the trends in the movement of bilateral trade in a dynamic setting.

As Table 8.1 shows, India's exports to South Korea increased from a meagre US$ 163 million in 1990 to US$ 457 million in 2000. This increase really accelerated between 2000 and 2012 with the figure touching US$ 4.2 billion in 2012. However, India's exports to Korea as a percentage of India's total exports to the world, while showing a rise, do not show an enormous increase in terms of Korea emerging as a major destination for India's exports during the same period. This is evident from the fact that the share of India's exports increased from 0.92 per cent in 1990 to a marginally higher level of 1.07 per cent in 2000 and further to just 1.42 per cent in 2012. Evidently, South Korea as an export destination for India has become more important by bilateral standards over time but remains low in importance in relative terms *vis-à-vis* India's other export destinations.

India's imports from Korea present a similar picture, although the situation is somewhat better. India's imports from Korea increased from US$ 325 million in 1990 to US$ 988 in 2000 and US$ 13 billion in 2012. The share of India's imports from South Korea in India's total imports from the world increased from 1.36 per cent in 1990 to 1.96 per cent in 2000 and to 2.81 per cent in 2012. This reflects the natural comparative

Table 8.1

India's Trade with Korea

Country	*1990*	*2000*	*2012*
India's exports to South Korea (million US$)	163.60	457.25	4207.77
India's total exports to World (million US$)	17813.10	42627.30	295878.00
India's exports to South Korea as a percentage of India's total exports to World	0.92	1.07	1.42
India's imports from South Korea (million US$)	325.46	988.68	13739.20
India's total imports from World (million US$)	23991.40	50336.40	489257.00
India's imports from South Korea as a percentage of India's total imports from World	1.36	1.96	2.81
South Korea's exports to India (million US$)	435.60	1326.17	11922.00
South Korea's total exports to World (million US$)	67817.10	172692.00	551806.00
South Korea's exports to India as a percentage of South Korea's total exports to World	0.64	0.77	2.16
South Korea's imports from India (million US$)	283.20	984.71	6920.83
South Korea's total imports from World (million US$)	74404.90	160482.00	519711.00
South Korea's imports from India as a percentage of South Korea's total Imports from World	0.38	0.61	1.33

Source: Author's calculations based on IMF DOTS 2013.

Figure 8.1

India-Korea Bilateral Trade

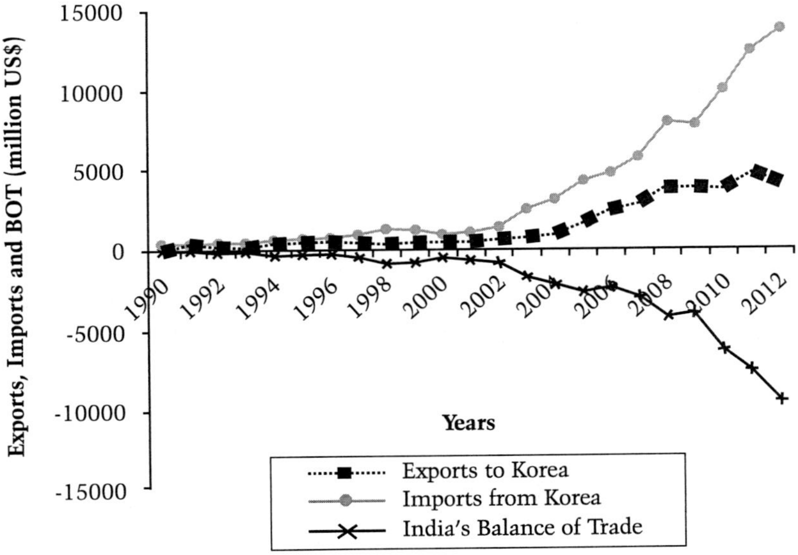

Source: Calculated from IMF DOTS 2013.

advantage that South Korea has enjoyed *vis-à-vis* India because of its being technologically far ahead.

In terms of India's importance in Korea's trade basket, it is interesting to note that Korea's exports to India as a percentage of its total exports to the world increased from a meagre 0.77 per cent in 2000 to a meaningful level of 2.16 per cent in 2012. Thus, in relative terms also, India has emerged as an important destination for Korea in recent years. However, the same is not true for Korean imports from India as a percentage of its total imports from the world, which increased from 0.61 per cent in 2000 to 1.33 per cent in 2012. In a nutshell, Korea has been more an import source for India than a destination for its exports. On the other hand, India now is more an export destination for Korea than an import source.

In terms of the trends in India-Korea bilateral trade, we notice a trajectory shift around the turn of this century (Figure 8.1). Bilateral trade was quite stagnant with small fluctuations between 1990 and 2000. It was only around 2002 that both India's exports and imports started picking up and as the figures show, a dynamic trend set in. India's imports from Korea have risen faster than India's exports and consequently, the trade deficit has widened for India. Here, it may be mentioned that the financial crisis of 2008 had a positive impact on bilateral trade dynamism.

When we turn to the bilateral CEPA from the perspective of trade, the endeavour is to see whether the CEPA has the potential to improve bilateral trade volume as well as to address trade imbalances. We first focus on trade in goods and then trade in services, with the latter being more of a qualitative analysis.

Trade in Goods under CEPA

A detailed empirical exercise was undertaken to probe the nature and extent of tariff liberalisation commitments undertaken by both the countries under the CEPA. The paper uses Harmonized System (HS) six-digit product codes, as the trade data for HS eight-digit product codes was not available on an internationally comparable basis. The country-specific tariff liberalisation schedules of both the countries are given separately with each item placed under a particular category of tariff liberalisation denoting different time frames for duty reduction depth of duty-cuts and the category of country-specific products belonging to the negative list on which no tariff liberalisation is committed or offered. The paper looks at the trade coverage of each country under their respective tariff liberalisation commitments to know whether these commitments have substantial trade coverage or not. These percentages were calculated under different categories of tariff liberalisation commitments and the bilateral average trade data between 2005 and 2009 covered by each category, i.e., before the CEPA came into effect. Aggregation was required of HS 8-digit to HS 6-digit for this exercise, posing significant statistical problems, which were further compounded by the need to match the tariff liberalisation schedules under the CEPA with the trade data available at HS 6-digit level from UN COMTRADE.

India's Tariff Liberalisation

The estimates thus arrived at suggest that India has made tariff liberalisation commitments with substantial trade coverage of 85 per cent. The remaining is kept under the negative list (Table 8.2). It needs to be pointed out that the figures do not add up to 100 per cent because of the discrepancy between trade data and data available on the tariff liberalisation schedule. As the tariff liberalisation schedule shows, on the date of entry of the agreement, India had high import coverage (20%). The maximum trade coverage of 25 per cent is in the category in which goods will be allowed duty free over an eight-year schedule. Around 18 per cent of imports are covered under the category in which duty free entry to imports would be achieved over a five-year period. Approximately 10 per cent trade is covered under the category RED where duty will be reduced to 1-5 per cent over eight years. This is the category for which duties will not become zero. Sensitive goods account for 9 per cent and duties on these are to be reduced by 50 per cent over a period of 10 years. Overall, it appears that India has tried to strike a balance between tariff liberalisation in a substantive manner while at the same time safeguarding sensitive production and trade sectors.

Table 8.2

India's Tariff Reduction Schedule (2005-2009)

(in %)

S. No.	*Categories*	*Average Tariff Liberalised*
1	E-0	20.01
2	E-5	17.87
3	E-8	25.3
4	RED	10.26
5	SEN	9.26
6	On All Imports(Excluding, EXC category)	84.54
7	EXC	13.69

Notes: 1) Duties on originating goods provided for in the items in staging category E-0 in a party's schedule shall be eliminated entirely and such goods shall be duty free on the date this agreement enters into force.

2) Duties on originating goods provided for in the items in staging category E-5 in a party's schedule shall be removed in five equal annual stages beginning on the date this agreement enters into force, and such goods shall be duty free, effective January 1 of year four.

3) Duties on originating goods provided for in the items in staging category E-8 in a party's schedule shall be removed in eight equal annual stages beginning on the date this agreement enters into force, and such goods shall be duty free, effective January 1 of year seven.

4) Duties on originating goods provided for in the items in staging category RED in a party's schedule shall be reduced to one to five per cent from the base rate in eight equal annual stages beginning on the date this agreement enters into force, and such goods shall remain at one to five per cent, effective January 1 of year seven.

5) Duties on originating goods provided for in the items in staging category SEN in a party's schedule shall be reduced:

a) For India, by 50 per cent of the base rate in 10 equal annual stages beginning on the date this agreement enters into force, and such goods shall remain at 50 per cent of the base rate, effective January 1 of year nine.

b) For Korea, by 50 per cent of the base rate in eight equal annual stages beginning on the date this agreement enters into force, and such goods shall remain at 50 per cent of the base rate, effective January 1 of year seven.

6) Duties on originating goods provided for in the items in staging category EXC in a party's schedule are exempt from the obligation of tariff reduction or elimination.

Source: The author's calculations based on UN data.

Korea's Tariff Liberalisation

As seen in Table 8.3, the Korean tariff liberalisation commitment under the CEPA is also substantial and almost 92 per cent of its imports are committed for tariff liberalisation and only around 2 per cent trade is covered under exclusion or the negative list. Once again, it may be pointed out that these figures do not add up to 100 per cent because of the discrepancy between trade data and data available in the tariff liberalisation schedule. In fact, Korean trade coverage is much better than India's trade coverage, making the overall trade coverage under the CEPA quite substantial.

Table 8.3

South Korea's Tariff Reduction Schedule (2005-2009)

(in %)

S. No.	*Categories*	*Average Tariff Liberalised*
1	E-0	27.8
2	E-5	58.63
3	E-8	3.5
4	RED	0.28
5	SEN	1.5
6	On All Imports(Excluding, EXC category)	91.7
7	EXC	1.8

Notes: Same as in Table 8.2.

Source: The author's calculations based on UN data.

Almost 59 per cent of trade is covered under the category in which duty free imports would be allowed from India over a period of five years. This is indeed very substantial. This is followed by 28 per cent of trade covered under the category that allows duty free imports from India on the day of the agreement entered into force. While only 4 per cent trade is covered under the category in which tariff would be brought to 0 over a period of 8 years, a small proportion, i.e., 0.28 per cent, of trade is covered under the category RED and only 1.5 per cent covered under the sensitive category whereby 50 per cent tariff reduction would be achieved over a period of eight years.

It is quite clear that the tariff liberalisation commitment in terms of trade coverage from the Korean side is more liberal and substantial than India's tariff liberalisation commitments. The greater trade coverage of Korea's tariff liberalisation commitment is to be expected given that India faces more daunting developmental challenges than Korea. India's industrial and trade structures are also such that India has to safeguard against various sensitivities pertaining to a marginalised labour force and their livelihoods.

CEPA Tariff Liberalisation and MFN Rates

Concerns have been expressed by the Korean side that the CEPA tariff rates are higher than the corresponding MFN rates in a few products in a given year. Studies like Kim and Cho (2012) and Lee *et al.* (2011) have highlighted this. It may be mentioned that this is not a new phenomenon under any FTA in goods. The bilateral tariff commitments, unless committed to zero duty level, can technically show FTA tariffs being higher in some products than the MFN rates at a given point of time. This is because tariff liberalisation under an FTA is implemented under a mutually agreed schedule and none of the FTA participating countries can predict that, at some point of time, applied MFN rate on a product would be lower. Tariffs are a function of essentiality and availability or the demand and supply balance of a product and until the applied FTA tariff reaches zero, such an anomaly is technically possible.

Two points can be made in the specific context of the India-Korea FTA in goods under the CEPA. First, such anomalies have been observed only in a few products. Secondly, this anomalous situation has been set right to an extent with the number and share of such items getting reduced substantially, as the implementation of CEPA has progressed with tariff reduction in the last four years or so. This is validated by Cho (2013). Therefore, this need not be a major cause of worry regarding trade dynamics under the India-Korea CEPA.

Rules of Origin (ROO) in CEPA

A country would like to allow goods from a partner country on a preferential duty basis under a trade agreement provided the goods have originated in the partner country. Nevertheless, there is always a possibility that third-country goods enter the country's markets through the partner country and that too on a preferential basis. This phenomenon is well known as 'trade deflection' and undermines the country's MFN-customs regime. One of the main objectives of rules of origin is to check trade deflection. It is also important to bear in mind that ROO are not for safeguarding against imports *per se*. Apart from checking trade deflection, ROO also help perform various other trade policy functions such as the imposition of anti-dumping duties, among others. Whether or not a product has originated in a particular country is decided on the basis of whether the product has undergone substantial transformation. In other words, the final product should be distinct from its constituents.

There are broadly three kinds of tests that are applied to determine this. First, there is the change in tariff heading test (at HS four-digit level), which looks at whether the tariff heading of the final product is different from the tariff headings of its components. The second is the percentage test according to which a minimum percentage of total value addition should be achieved with the help of local inputs. Finally, there is the specified process test that requires a product to undergo certain stipulated processes. These together emphasise local value addition, and in turn, employment generation, and hence serves as a development policy tool (Das and Ratna, 2011). The ROO provisions under the India-Korea CEPA have been analysed with this understanding. An attempt is made to examine empirically the trade covered under the ROO provisions of the CEPA.

India's Rules of Origin Commitments

Approximately 45 per cent of India's existing imports are covered under the general rule which stipulates change in tariff sub-heading (CTSH) plus 35 per cent of value addition (Table 8.4). Around 55 per cent of India's imports are covered under product-specific rules (PSRs), of which the maximum, i.e., 30 per cent of imports, are covered under the category of PSR that stipulates CTSH from another heading. Overall, India's ROO formulation is quite balanced as it is neither too stringent in terms of the general rule nor too liberal in PSRs—the latter due to trade deflection sensitivities.

Table 8.4

India's Rules of Origin

S. No.	*Category*	*Percentage*
A.	*Product-specific Rules*	
1	Wholly obtained	0.05
2	CTH from any other heading	1.77
3	CTSH from any other heading	30.00
4	CTSH from any other chapter	0.00
5	CTSH from any other heading plus 25%	1.62
6	CTSH from any other chapter plus 25%	3.41
7	CTSH from any other sub-heading plus 25%	0.01
8	CTH from any other chapter plus 25%	0.02
9	CTH from any other heading plus 25%	0.01
10	CTH from any other sub-heading plus 25%	0.00
11	CTH from any other heading plus 30%	0.01
12	CTSH from any other heading plus 30%	0.57
13	CTH from any other heading plus 35%	0.13
14	CTSH from any other heading plus 35%	0.36
15	CTH from any other chapter plus 40%	N/A
16	CTH from any other heading plus 40%	1.19
17	CTSH from any other heading plus 40%	15.96
18	CTSH from any other chapter plus 40%	N/A
19	CTSH from any other sub-heading plus 40%	0.42
20	CTSH from any other heading plus 50%	N/A
21	CTSH from any other sub-heading plus 50%	0.02
	Total of Product-specific Rules	55.55
B.	*General Rule*	
	RVC is not less than 35% of the FOB value plus CTSH	44.45
	Total of General Rule	44.45
	Total of Product-specific and General Rule (A+B)	100

Source: Author's calculations based on UN data.

Korea's Rules of Origin Commitments

Around 25 per cent of Korea's imports are covered by the general rule (Table 8.5), which means that around three-fourth of its imports are covered by PSRs, which are generally much more stringent than the general rules. The leading example of this is CTSH from any other heading which is a PSR accounting for almost 58 per cent of Korea's imports.

Table 8.5

Korea's Rules of Origin

S. No.	*Category*	*Percentage*
A.	*Product-specific Rules*	
1	Wholly obtained	1.32
2	CTH from any other heading	8.05
3	CTSH from any other heading	58.22
4	CTSH from any other chapter	0.01
5	CTSH from any other heading plus 25%	0.05
6	CTSH from any other chapter plus 25%	0.25
7	CTSH from any other sub-heading plus 25%	0.00
8	CTH from any other chapter plus 25%	0.06
9	CTH from any other heading plus 25%	N/A
10	CTH from any other sub-heading plus 25%	N/A
11	CTH from any other heading plus 30%	N/A
12	CTSH from any other heading plus 30%	0.55
13	CTH from any other heading plus 35%	0.01
14	CTSH from any other heading plus 35%	0.53
15	CTH from any other chapter plus 40%	0.00
16	CTH from any other heading plus 40%	5.22
17	CTSH from any other heading plus 40%	1.50
18	CTSH from any other chapter plus 40%	0.00
19	CTSH from any other sub-heading plus 40%	0.10
20	CTSH from any other heading plus 50%	N/A
21	CTSH from any other sub-heading plus 50%	0.00
	Total of Product-specific Rules	75.86
B.	*General Rule*	
	RVC is not less than 35% of the FOB value plus CTSH	24.14
	Total of General Rule	24.14
	Total of Product-specific and General Rule (A+B)	100

Source: Data extracted from PC-TAS CD-ROM.

With this we may conclude that ROO stipulations are much more stringent in the case of Korea than India as a substantially larger proportion of Korean imports are covered by PSRs.

Trade in Services

There has been little attempt to study the trade in services commitments made by the two countries under the CEPA. This paper categorises sectoral commitments into types, *viz.*, open, regulated and restricted making the comparison of commitments somewhat easier. Broadly, the sectoral coverage in terms of trade in services liberalisation commitments offered by India and Korea is quite similar but not exactly the same. In addition, one observes a marked dissimilarity in respective horizontal commitments.

In terms of India's commitments, for most of the sectors, Modes I, II and III with respect to limitations on market access and national treatment are kept 'open.' However, Mode IV is largely 'unbound,' except as indicated in the horizontal commitments, which is categorised as regulated. This holds true for sectors such as education services, environmental services, construction and related engineering services, for most of the sub-sectors of business services, and tourism and travel-related services. For the remaining sectors, Mode IV under market access and national treatment is mainly regulated but 'open' in transport services such as maritime agency services, maritime freight forwarding services, and maintenance and repairs of sea-going vessels. However, in the other sub-sectors of transport services, Mode IV is restrictive (Table 8.6).

The table on Korean commitments in services is not being given as the provisions are quite similar or in other words, quite standardised across sectors. In Korea's commitments, Mode I has generally been kept open with regard to limitations on market access and national treatment. However, for some sectors, Mode I is both regulated (such as in some sub-sectors of business services, communication services, environmental services) and restrictive (such as in some sub-sectors of transport services, recreational, cultural and sporting services, financial services, educational services, and sub-sectors of business services such as testing, analysis and building cleaning services) with the latter kept as unbound. However, Mode IV is largely 'unbound,' except as indicated in the horizontal commitments, which is categorised as regulated.

Bilateral trade in services statistics is hard to get and therefore, it is difficult to assess the impact of CEPA on trade in services between the two countries. One of the areas in which India has been able to export services to Korea is tourism. Over 100,000 Koreans visited India, in 2013, attracted not only by the main tourist attractions like Taj Mahal and Jaipur, but

Table 8.6

Schedule of Services' Trade Commitments of India

Sector or Sub-sector	*Limitations on Market Access*	*Limitations on National Treatment*
	I. Horizontal Commitments	
All Sectors included in this Schedule	3) FIPB approval will be required in sectors where the provision of Press Note 1 (2005 Series) issued by the Government of India 3) A foreign company can set up operations in India under the following routes: a) As a incorporated entity by incorporating a company under the Companies Act 1956 through a joint ventures or wholly owned subsidiaries. These entities can undertake activities permitted as per FEMA (transfer or issue of securities by a person resident outside India) Regulation, 2000 (FDI Scheme) b) As an office of a foreign entity through liaison office/representative office, project office and branch office. Such offices can undertake activities permitted under the Foreign Exchange Management Act (Establishment in India of Branch Office or other place) 4) Unbound except as per commitments in Chapter 8 on Movement of Natural Persons.	3) In the case of collaboration with public sector enterprises or government undertakings as joint venture partners, preference in access will be given to Korean service suppliers/entities which offer the best terms for transfer of technology. 3) Taxation laws for domestic and Korean service suppliers, as per the provisions of the Income tax Act, 1961, shall apply. 3) Subsidies, where granted, shall be available only to domestic service suppliers. 4) None, except for requirement of requisite visa and the conditions attached to entry and temporary stay under such a visa for each of the categories specified in the Market Access column including: For all categories: fulfilment of specific requirements regarding information in support of the application and required documentation For categories (c) and (d): • Proof of Contract • Possession of requisite educational and professional qualifications relevant to the service to be provided including work experience

contd...

...contd...

Sector or Sub-sector	*Limitations on Market Access*	*Limitations on National Treatment*
	II. Some Sector Specific Commitments	
Transport Services: (a) International Transport (Freight and Passengers)	1) 3) Regulated 2) Open 4) Restrictive	1) Regulated 2) Open 3) Open 4) Restrictive
Maritime Auxiliary Services : Maritime Cargo Handling Services	1) Restrictive 2) Open 3) Regulated 4) Restrictive	1) Restrictive 2) Open 3) Regulated 4) Restrictive
Storage and Warehousing Services in Ports	1) Restrictive 2) Open 3) Regulated 4) Restrictive	1) Restrictive 2) Open 3) Regulated 4) Restrictive
Customs Clearance Services	1) Restrictive 2) Open 3) 4) Restrictive	1) Restrictive 2) Open 3) 4) Restrictive
Container Station and Depot Services	1) Restrictive 2) Open 3) Regulated 4) Restrictive	1) Restrictive 2) Open 3) Regulated 4) Restrictive
Maritime Agency Services	1) 2) Open 3) Regulated 4) Open	1) 2) Open 3) Regulated 4) Open
Maritime Freight Forwarding Services	1) 2) Open 3) Regulated 4) Open	1) 2) Open 3) Regulated 4) Open
Maintenance and Repairs of Sca Going Vessels	1) 2) Open 3) Regulated 4) Open	1) 2) Open 3) Regulated 4) Open
Ship Broking Service (CPC 748)		1) Restrictive 2) Open 3) 4) Regulated
Air Transport Services	1) Restrictive 2) Open 3) 4) Regulated	1) 2) 3)Open 4) Regulated
(d) Maintenance and Repair of Aircraft (CPC 8868)	1) 2) 3) Open 4) Regulated	

Note: 1) Mode I, 2) Mode II, 3) Mode III and 4) Mode IV.

Source: Extracted from Schedule of Commitments under CEPA.

also by the Buddhist sites (Embassy of India, Seoul, 2014). It is not clear whether the CEPA has had any effect of this; one may expect that due to the CEPA, there is increased flow of information and more people-to-people contact in general and greater business-to-business contact in particular, which could have had some impact.

One of the positive implications of the trade in services agreement under the CEPA is that India's trade imbalance with Korea can be corrected by greater services exports from India, as suggested by some reports whereby India has sought greater market access in Korea for India's exports of information technology (IT) and related services (*Indian Express*, September 8, 2013). This is expected to further enhance India's exports to Korea as the latter has reportedly not opened its market access in IT to India as much it has under Korea-EU FTA.

The liberalisation commitments made suggest that trade in services could be scaled up between the two countries. However, it may also be highlighted that unless adequate progress is made with regard to mutual recognition agreements (MRAs) and visa and work permits, this is unlikely to translate into actual trade flows in several sectors.

Broad Conclusions

Korea as an export destination for India has become more important by bilateral standards over time but remains low in importance in relative terms *vis-à-vis* India's other export destinations. The same is true of India's imports from Korea, although the situation is somewhat better in this regard. This situation is reflective of the natural comparative advantage that Korea has enjoyed *vis-à-vis* India due to its technological superiority that helped strengthen the Korean industrialisation process in earlier decades and helped diversify its industrial base. India has emerged as an important export destination in relative terms for Korea over the years. However, the same is not true in terms of Korean imports from India.

In terms of the trends in India-Korea bilateral trade, we notice a trajectory shift around the turn of this century. It was only around 2002, that both India's exports and imports started picking up and a dynamic trend set in. It is also evident that India's imports from Korea have risen faster than India's exports. Consequently, the trade deficit has widened for

India. It may be mentioned that the financial crisis of 2008 had a positive impact on bilateral trade dynamism.

On probing the nature and extent of tariff liberalisation commitments undertaken by the two countries under the CEPA, it is seen that India has tried to strike a balance between tariff liberalisation in a substantive manner while at the same time safeguarding the sensitive production and trade sectors. The Korean trade coverage is much better than India's trade coverage, making the overall trade coverage under the CEPA quite substantial. This is expected and quite natural given the fact that in comparison India faces much more daunting developmental challenges than Korea. India's industrial and trade structures are also such that India has to safeguard against various sensitivities pertaining to a marginalised labour force and their livelihoods.

With regard to the concerns expressed by the Korean side that the CEPA tariff rates are higher than the corresponding MFN rates in a few products in a given year, the paper explains why such an anomaly is technically possible and that the problem is not as pronounced as believed. The ROO stipulations are much more stringent in the case of Korea than India as a substantially larger proportion of Korean imports are covered by PSRs that are largely more stringent than the general rules.

There has been little attempt to study the trade in services commitments made by both the countries under the CEPA. This paper categorises sectoral commitments made into types, *viz.*, open, regulated and restricted. Broadly, the sectoral coverage in terms of trade in services liberalisation commitments offered by India and Korea is quite similar but not exactly the same. In addition, one observes a marked dissimilarity in the respective horizontal commitments. The liberalisation commitments made do suggest that trade in services could be scaled up between the two countries. However, unless adequate progress is made with regard to MRAs and work permits/visa issues, this potential is unlikely to be converted into actual trade flows in several sectors.

Overall, the India-Korea CEPA has covered vast ground in terms of tariff liberalisation and rules of origin formulation, in a manner that is contrary to popular expectations of low trade coverage and complexities in Indian rules of origin. In trade in services too, the CEPA provides a good base to be built upon further through MRAs and more effective market access in sectors and modes of mutual export interests, such as IT and Mode IV.

References

Cho, Choong-jae (2013). "Four Years under Korea-India CEPA, Concessions Require for Improvement", *POSRI Chindia Quarterly*, Spring.

Das, Ram Upendra (2013). "Regional Economic Integration: New Context and Analytical Constructs", in Byasdeb Dasgupta (ed.), *External Dimensions of an Emerging Economy, India: Essays in Honour of Sunanda Sen*. London and New York: Routledge.

Das, Ram Upendra and R.S. Ratna (2011). *Perspectives on Rules of Origin*. UK: Palgrave-Macmillan.

Kim, Misu and C. Cho (2012). "A Relationship between Trade and Investment: A Case Study of Korea and India", Presented at *ARTNeT Conference on Empirical and Policy Issues on Integration in Asia and the Pacific*, November 2.

Kindleberger, C.P. (1966). "European Integration and the Intranational Corporation", *Columbia Journal of World Business* (1): 65-73.

Lee, Woong, Y. C. Song and C.J. Cho (2011). "Two Years On: Achievements and Challenges in Trade Sector of Korea-India CEPA", *KIEP World Economy Update* 1(3). December.

Negasi, M.Y. (2009). *Trade Effects of Regional Economic Integration in Africa: The Case of SADC*. Services Sector Development Thematic Working Group.

Panagariya, A. (2000). "Preferential Trade Liberalization: The Traditional Theory and New Developments", *Journal of Economic Literature* XXXVIII: 287-331.

Urata, S. (2002). "Globalization and Growth in Free Trade Agreements", *Asia-Pacific Review* 9(1): 20-32.

9 Opportunities and Challenges in FDI Relationship between Korea and India after CEPA

Changho Kwag and Daewoo Lee

Introduction

Since Korea and India began a diplomatic relationship 40 years ago, the two countries have consistently endeavoured to enhance bilateral cooperation. Their efforts have borne fruit, particularly in terms of economic relations. The economic gap between the two nations has narrowed. During those four decades, bilateral trade and investment relations have steadily and remarkably improved. The bilateral trade volume, which was a mere US$ 14.3 million in 1973, went up to US$ 18.8 billion in 2012. The cumulative sum of Korean direct investment in India amounted to US$ 1.8 billion and that of Indian investment into Korea reached US$ 467 million in 2013.

Their economic relationship culminated in the Comprehensive Economic Partnership Agreement (CEPA), a wider version of free trade agreement (FTA), in August 2009. After this agreement, trade between the two countries has increased substantially. The bilateral trade volume, which was US$ 12.1 billion in 2009, soared by 50 per cent to US$ 18.8 billion in 2012. However, the increase in bilateral investment has not been as significant as expected. In 2010, foreign direct investment (FDI) fell to US$ 131 million, 21 per cent lower than in the previous year. After rising to US$ 245 million in 2011 (may be due to the halo effect of the CEPA), it showed a down turn again and decreased to US$ 215 million in 2012.

In addition, the importance of India as a destination for outgoing Korean FDI remains very low as India ranked 12th in the list in 2011. India ranked lower than Brazil, Vietnam, Singapore and Thailand, which ranked

8th through 11th, respectively (The Export and Import Bank of Korea, n.d.). Considering the size of its economy and its growth potential, India should have received more Korean FDI.

FDI plays a very important role in host country economic development because it provides a channel to garner resources for economic development. First, FDI brings capital to the host country and affects its economic growth. Second, FDI can bring in modern technology, which increases productivity that boosts economic growth. Third, FDI can provide access to unexplored export markets because multinational companies, which bring in FDI, have their own very large intra-firm markets to which only their own affiliates have access.

Thus, it is necessary to analyse whether the CEPA has had a real long-term effect on bilateral trade and investment relations. Besides analysing the long-term effect on bilateral investment, this study also looks at whether the performance of Korea and India in drawing FDI has been good enough, and if it has not, what needs to be done to attract FDI.

This paper is organised as follows. Previous literature and empirical findings will be reviewed in the second section to find out key determinants of FDI and the extent to which a bilateral agreement affects FDI flows. The third section deals with case studies of the comprehensive bilateral economic agreements between India and three countries, *viz.*, Singapore, Japan and Korea. The fourth section looks at the performance of Korea and India in attracting FDI in general and evaluates the bilateral FDI relations. The fifth section explains why India and Korea need to intensify bilateral cooperation given the huge potential room for the two to cooperate and create great synergy. Lastly, in the sixth section, conclusions and policy implications are presented.

Literature Review

FDI Determinants

There are a number of studies on FDI determinants. Liu (2008) argued there are four FDI determinants: home country factors, host country factors, bilateral linkage factors and regional integration factors.

(1) *Home Country Factors*: The amount of FDI depends on the size of the home country economy. Nankani (1979) explains that FDI usually flows from developed countries into developing countries and that there is a strong correlation between FDI flows and the size of a home country's economy.

(2) *Host Country Factors*: United Nations Conference on Trade and Development (UNCTAD) (2009) developed a conceptual framework for host country determinants, using three major factors: economic determinants, policy framework and business facilitation. Economic determinants, in turn, are composed of three factors: market-seeking, efficiency-seeking and resource-seeking. The policy framework for FDI refers to economic, political and social stability; rules regarding entry and operations; international agreements on FDI, etc. Business facilitation refers to investment facilitation services and social amenities (Appendix Table A-9.1)

(3) *Bilateral Linkage Factors*: Distance and openness determine FDI inflows. The farther a host country is away from a home country, the less FDI inflows are expected from the home country to the host country. In addition, the more open the host country is in terms of rules and regulations, the more FDI inflows are expected.

(4) *Regional Integration Factors*: BITs (bilateral investment treaties) and FTAs enhance FDI to host countries. There are three effects of BITs on FDI: commitment effect, signalling effect and the effect of its being taken as a proxy for the quality of institutions in the host country (UNCTAD, 1998).

The commitment effect refers to a binding international commitment to investment protection and treatment of foreign investors to reduce risks and increase FDI from home countries. The signalling effect arises from a general improvement in the enforcement of property rights, thus stimulating FDI from all countries, not just from BIT contracting parties. BITs may also be considered as a proxy for improved institutional quality, thus stimulating FDI inflows from all countries.

Over the years, literature on this topic has confirmed that the economic determinants of FDI are the primary factors in influencing FDI flows. UNCTAD (2009) and Nunnenkamp and Spatz (2002) showed that the recent global FDI boom has largely taken place in the non-tradable services sector, which is, by definition, a market-seeking sector. Thus, the host country's market-size variables have been the dominant factors in attracting FDI, and market-seeking FDI has been the main type of FDI. The determinants of efficiency-seeking FDI constitute the second most important economic determinant of inward FDI, particularly in developing countries.

But for these economic determinants to be fully effective, they have to work in combination with the policy framework or business facilitation measures, which are, by nature, supportive and necessary but not sufficient conditions. Apart from economic determinants, macroeconomic conditions and political stability have been found to be among the most important FDI determinants (UNCTAD, 2007).

The effects of regional or bilateral investment agreements are limited. BITs do not change key economic determinants such as market size instead they stimulate FDI only through the improvement of policy and institutional frameworks. The effect of regional and bilateral investment agreement also depend upon whether FDI is vertical or horizontal. A bilateral investment agreement can have a positive impact on vertical FDI rather than horizontal FDI (Moon, 2009). Horizontal FDI refers to investment aimed at seeking entry into the big market of the host country. When the FTA is signed and comes into effect, companies in the home country prefer export to FDI as they are able to exploit lower tariffs. Vertical FDI refers to investment that helps investors take advantage of low-cost operations in the host country. When the FTA becomes effective, investing companies prefer FDI to export as they can import parts and intermediate goods produced in the home country at a lower price exploiting lower tariffs, which further reduce manufacturing cost in the host country.

Table 9.1

The Impact of the BIT on Horizontal FDI and Vertical FDI

	Horizontal FDI	*Vertical FDI*
Purpose	Market entry (Similar to market-seeking)	Low-cost operation (Similar to efficiency-seeking)
FTA effect	Negative effect on FDI (Lower tariff enhances export rather than FDI)	Positive effect on FDI (Lower tariff on imported parts may enhance FDI on parts manufacturing)

Sources: Moon (2009).

Empirical Studies and Investor Surveys

Previous empirical findings were somewhat ambiguous since results varied on a case-by-case basis. However, many recent studies have shown that BITs have a positive effect on FDI inflows into developing countries. According to FIA (Foreign Investment Agency) of the Vietnamese government, since Vietnam and the United States (US) signed an agreement on bilateral trade in 2001, US investment in Vietnam has increased by 27 per cent annually during 2002-2004, whereas the annual growth rate for the period 1996-2001 was just 3 per cent. The FIA report attributed increased FDI to several clauses in the agreement, which helped improve Vietnam's investment environment and increased the degree of transparency in the investment process. With improved rules and regulations, US companies have more confidence in investing in Vietnam.

Studies by Reilly *et al.* (2007) and Waldkirch (2010) also indicate the positive effect of BITs on FDI after examining the North American Free Trade Agreement (NAFTA). According to Reilly *et al.* (2007), since 1994, when NAFTA became effective, US companies' FDI in Canada has increased significantly. Waldkirch (2010) examined the trend of the US's outward FDI into Mexico after 1994. He found that NAFTA had a positive effect on FDI from the US to Mexico.

A number of surveys on investors also deal with the impact of BITs on FDI. UNCTAD surveyed 602 transnational companies (TNCs) in 2007 and found that BITs are important to TNCs in terms of investment protection and enhancing stability and predictability of FDI projects. The survey also found that BITs are often taken into account when investors choose their investment destinations.

Case Studies

In the past, countries have engaged in bilateral/regional economic relationships with other countries through FTAs and/or regional trade agreements (RTAs). However, FTAs did not have a great impact on investment flows because investment-related clauses were not fully specified in the FTAs. However, in recent years, the coverage of FTAs is wider and includes services trade and investment relationships, as Korea and India did when they finalised the CEPA.

In this study, we have examined three cases of the wider version of the FTAs between India and other countries to identify the effect on FDI flows. India has signed comprehensive economic cooperation/partnership agreements with Singapore, Japan and Korea.

Comprehensive Economic Cooperation Agreement between Singapore and India

Since India and Singapore signed the Comprehensive Economic Cooperation Agreement (CECA) in 2005, trade volume and investment flows between the two countries have increased significantly. The bilateral trade volume reached US$ 21.3 billion in FY 2012, a 145 per cent increase from US$ 8.7 billion in 2005. Singapore's FDI in India during 2000-2005 was only US$ 500 million; this increased to US$ 3 billion in 2007 and US$ 5.2 billion in 2011 as shown in Figure 9.1. There is a huge difference between the periods before and after the CECA. The CECA definitely had an effect on the FDI increase.

Figure 9.1

Singapore's FDI in India

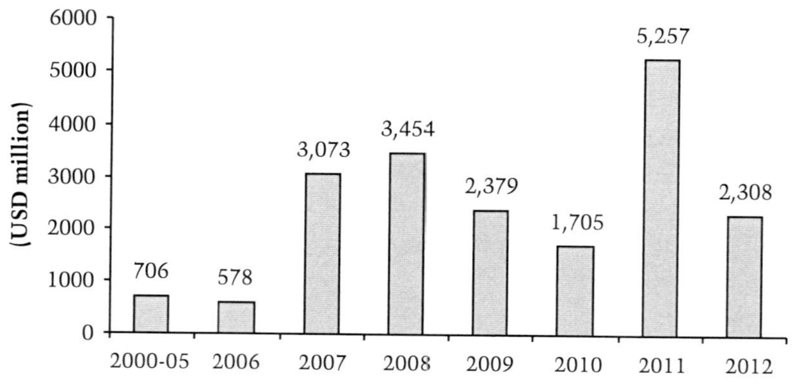

Source: DIPP, 2013a.

Regarding sector-wise FDI inflows into India, the services sector ranked first according to the Department of Investment Policy & Promotion (DIPP) report in 2010, accounting for 28.1 per cent of total investment as shown in Table 9.2. Telecommunication, petroleum and natural gas, computer software and hardware, and the construction sector ranked second through fifth, respectively. Singapore did not invest much in India's manufacturing sector.

Since the CECA was inked in 2005, Singapore has become one of the most important FDI origins. Singapore invested US$ 21.3 billion from April 2000 to June 2013 and ranked second in terms of total FDI as shown in Appendix Table A-9.2. It ranked first in terms of India's overseas investment destination as shown in Appendix Table A-9.3.

The reasons for this close relationship between the two countries are as follows. First, the CECA includes favourable investment clauses such as a double taxation avoidance agreement (DTAA). Indeed, the CECA is definitely different from traditional FTAs, particularly the one India signed with Thailand in 2003. Under the DTAA, India and Singapore have agreed to lower the withholding tax on royalties and fees for technical services while Singapore has agreed to exempt foreign institutional investors (FIIs) from capital gains tax on income from sales of shares in India, which is a great incentive for Indian investors.

Table 9.2

Singapore's FDI in India by Sector (From January 2000 to December 2010)

(US$ million)

Rank	*Sector*	*FDI Amount (Equity)*	*Percentage of FDI Inflows*
1	Service Sector	3,268	28.1
2	Telecommunication	1,451	12.5
3	Petroleum and Natural Gas	1,251	10.7
4	Computer Software and Hardware	1,012	8.7
5	Construction Activities	738	6.3
	Total	7,721	66.3

Source: DIPP, 2010.

Second, Singapore has many commonalities with India in terms of culture, human network and history. It is said that Indians account for approximately 9 per cent of Singapore's total population and is the third largest ethnic group after the Chinese and Malays. Therefore, it may not be difficult for Indian companies to start business and build a business network in Singapore. The CECA between Singapore and India has boosted not only trade but also investment in both directions. This remarkably successful CECA gave confidence to the Indian government and enabled it to move forward to conclude the CEPAs with Korea and Japan.

CEPA between Japan and India

The Japan-India CEPA was signed in February 2011. India tried to attract more investment from Japan and accelerate the Delhi-Mumbai Industrial Corridor project through the CEPA with Japan. In terms of market openness, India will remove tariffs on 94 per cent of goods over the next 10 years while Japan will remove 97 per cent of them. The Japan-India CEPA has shown more market openness than the CEPA between Korea and India in which India agreed to eliminate tariffs on 74.5 per cent of goods and Korea agreed to remove tariffs on 84.7 per cent of imported products. However, the progress of the Japan-India CEPA will be slower than that of the Korea-India CEPA, which will eliminate tariffs within 8 years.

One of the key features of the India-Japan CEPA is that India is the first CEPA partner of Japan. Japan has agreed to approve India's application for the release of generic medicines in Japan. Japan will provide 'national treatment' to Indian companies applying for approvals for the release of generic medicines, and complete the procedures within a reasonable time period. India is expected to exploit the huge Japanese pharmaceutical market. Japan is the world's second largest buyer of prescription drugs after the US.

Figure 9.2 shows Japan's FDI in India. It is a bit difficult to interpret this figure because there is an outlier, the year 2008. In 2008, Japanese FDI inflow into India recorded US$ 4.4 billion as Daiichi Sankyo, a Japanese pharmaceutical company, acquired Ranbaxy Laboratory for US$ 3.3 billion. Without Daiichi Sankyo's acquisition, Japan's FDI into India would have been around US$ 1.1 billion in 2008.

The year 2011 in which the CEPA was signed witnessed sharp increases in FDI between the two countries while the next year saw a decrease. If we exclude the Daiichi Sankyo's exceptional investment case in 2008, it seems that after the CEPA came into effect, slightly more Japanese FDI flowed into India in 2011 and 2012. However, it is too premature to confirm whether the CEPA has had any impact on bilateral investment flows.

Figure 9.2

Japan's FDI in India

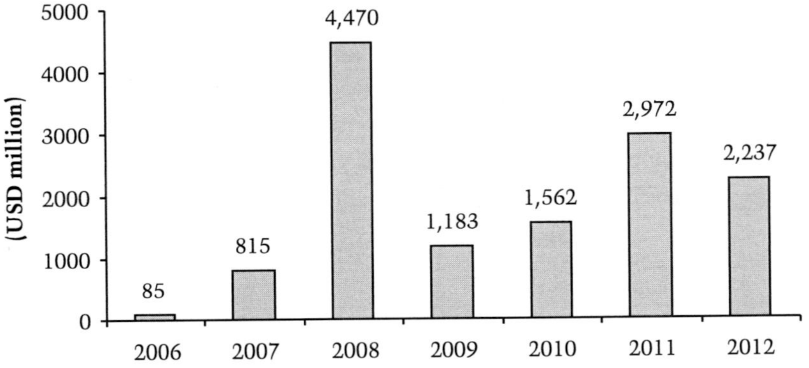

Note: Equity investment only.
Source: DIPP, 2013b.

Table 9.3 indicates Japan's FDI in India by sector from April 2000 to February 2013. Drugs and pharmaceuticals ranked first, accounting for 29.3 per cent of total FDI inflows, followed by the automobile industry (16.2%), and the services sector (14.4%). A large portion of the FDI from Japan flowed into the manufacturing sector, while the services sector made up 14.4 per cent, a non-negligible portion of the total FDI. What is interesting is that it is the drug and pharmaceutical sector that attracted the most FDI from Japan within the manufacturing sector, thanks to Daiichi Sankyo's acquisition.

Table 9.3

Japan's FDI in India by Sector (From April 2000 to February 2013)

(US$ million)

Rank	*Sector*	*FDI Amount (Equity)*	*Percentage of FDI Inflows*
1	Drugs and Pharmaceuticals	4,230	29.3
2	Automobile Industry	2,339	16.2
3	Services Sector	2,077	14.4
4	Metallurgical Industries	1,334	9.2
5	Electrical Equipment	651	4.5
	Total	10,632	73.7

Source: DIPP, 2013b.

Appendix Table A-9.4 indicates top 10 Japanese investments that flowed into India. Daiichi Sankyo ranked first, followed by JFE Steel, Nippon Life Insurance and Nissan Motors. As mentioned above, the services sector industries, such as life insurance, is one of the main areas of Japanese investments. Nippon Life Insurance and Sumitomo Mitsui Banking Corporation are also included in the list. Considering the fact that most Korean FDI flowed into the Indian manufacturing sector, this indicates that Japan is tapping an opportunity of investing in sectors, apart from the manufacturing sector, in which it has an advantage over other countries.

CEPA between Korea and India

The CEPA between Korea and India was signed in August 2009 and came into effect on January 1, 2010. Since 2010, both countries witnessed a significant increase in bilateral trade volume as mentioned in the introduction of this study. As far as bilateral investment relations are concerned, Korea's FDI in India, which stood at US$ 167 million during FY 2009-10, has risen to US$ 215 million in 2012, up 34 per cent (DIPP, 2013c). In the meantime, India's FDI in Korea, which was US$ 3.3 million in 2009, increased by 230 per cent to US$ 10.9 million in 2012 (Ministry of Trade, Industry and Energy, the Korean Government).

Figure 9.3

Korea's FDI in India

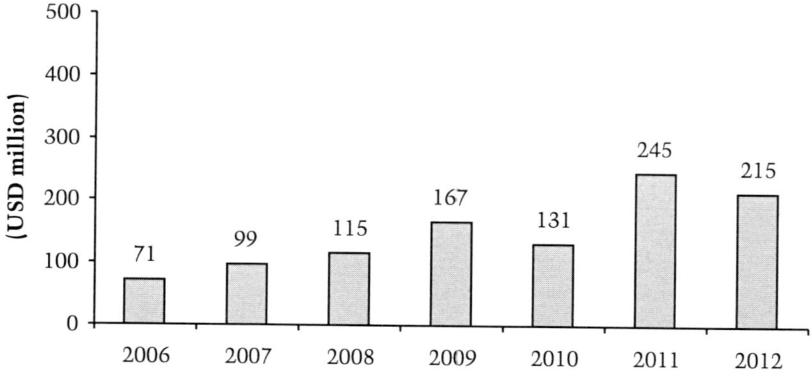

Note: 2012 figures are accumulated data from April 2012 to February 2013. All the figures are equity investment only.

Source: DIPP, 2013c.

The key issue regarding Korea's FDI in India is that the amount of FDI lags far behind that of other countries such as Japan and Singapore. The cumulative sum of Korean FDI inflows into India from April 2000 to June 2013 amounts to less than one-tenth the Japanese FDI into India (Table 9.5).

As for sector-wise investment in India, the metallurgical industry ranks the highest, making up 25.9 per cent of total FDI inflow, followed by prime movers, machine tools, automobiles and electronics. The top five sectors take a total of 56.7 per cent and all of the top five sectors are associated with manufacturing industry (Table 9.4). According to the Export and Import Bank of Korea, 84.8 per cent of Korean FDI inflows into India from 1980 to June 2013 went into the manufacturing sector; FDI inflows into the services sector are not substantial.[1]

Table 9.4

Korea's FDI in India by Sector (From April 2000 to February 2013)

(US$ million)

Rank	*Sector*	*FDI Amount (Equity)*	*Percentage of FDI Inflows*
1	Metallurgical Industries	317.0	25.9
2	Prime Movers (other than electrical generators)	125.2	10.2
3	Machine Tools	99.4	8.1
4	Automobile Industry	79.7	6.5
5	Electronics	72.2	5.9
	Total	6,936.6	56.7

Source: DIPP, 2013c.

Bilateral FDI inflows from India to Korea indicate that India's FDI in Korea has been intermittent from 2000 to 2012 with a cumulative investment amount of US$ 467 million. In 2004, India invested US$ 53 million in FDI through measures such as Tata's acquisition of Daewoo Commercial Vehicles. In 2010, the FDI stood at US$ 371 million, thanks to Mahindra & Mahindra's acquisition of Ssangyong Motors.

1. The details of top FDI inflows from Korea (remittance-wise) is shown in Appendix Table A-9.5 in which POSCO, a global steel major, has invested a total of US$ 433.7 million from April 2000 to February 2013.

Figure 9.4

Trends of India's Outward FDI into Korea (From 2000 to 2012)

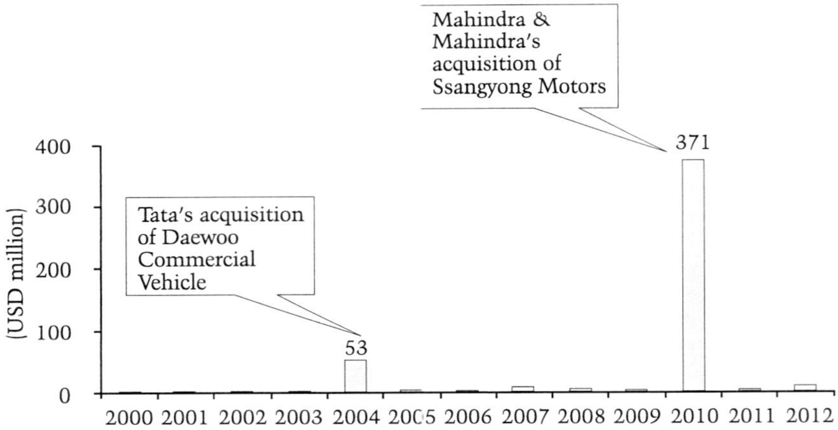

Source: The Ministry of Trade, Industry, and Energy, Korea.

Performance of Korea and India in Attracting FDI

Being one of the BRIC (Brazil, Russia, India and China) countries, India has been recognised as one of the most fascinating investment destinations. India achieved very high GDP growth (which peaked at 9.6 per cent in 2006-07) during the 2000s, indicating that India had the potential to become an economic powerhouse. Its high economic performance and a domestic market with the world's second largest population made India a desirable FDI destination.

Figure 9.5 shows FDI inflows into India, Korea and China. Until 1991, the FDI inflows into China, India and Korea had not been noteworthy. However, from 1991, FDI inflow into China picked up. In recent years, China has received more than US$ 100 billion of FDI each year. By contrast, India and Korea failed to draw substantial amounts of FDI until 1995. It was only after 1996 that India and Korea began to attract significant amounts of foreign investment. From 1996 to 2005, each country managed to draw FDI of between US$ 5 and 6 billion on average per year. However, since 2006, FDI inflow into India has increased to reach approximately US$ 47 billion in 2008, while inflows into Korea have remained stagnant at around US$ 8 billion. In 2012, even under the global economic crisis, India attracted US$ 26 billion of FDI while Korea drew only US$ 9.9 billion

Figure 9.5

FDI Inflows into Korea, India and China

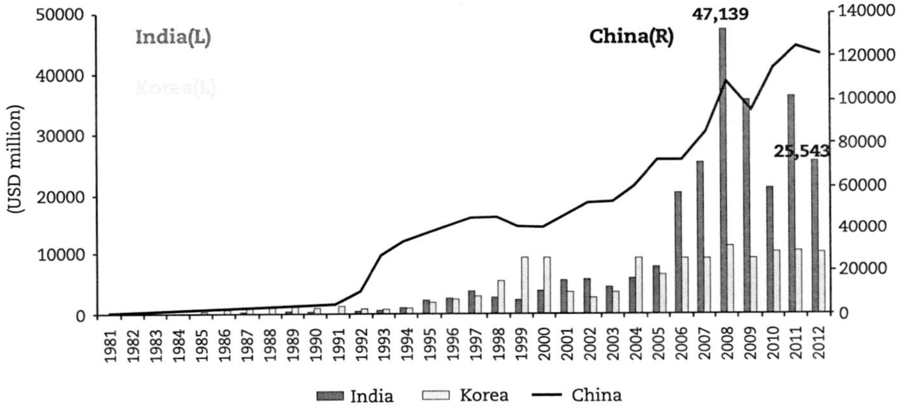

Source: UNCTAD, UNCTAD stat, Foreign Direct Investment.

The performance gap in drawing FDI in recent years has led to a huge difference in the FDI stock in the two countries. Until 2007, the level of FDI stock in Korea had always been higher than that in India. For instance, the Korea's FDI stock was US$ 122 billion while that of India's was only US$ 105.8 billion in 2007. However, since then, FDI stocks in India have accumulated very fast, surpassing that of Korea in 2008 and touched US$ 226.3 billion in 2012 as shown in Figure 9.6. The FDI stock in Korea reached a mere US$ 147.2 billion in the same period. The gap in FDI stock is expected to widen further.

Another indicator, which enables us to compare the FDI performance of countries, is the ratio of FDI inflows over gross capital formation (GCF). This ratio shows the contribution of foreign direct investment to domestic capital formation. Figure 9.7 indicates that the ratio of FDI inflows over GCF in India has been on the rise, while that of Korea has been on the decline after its peak at 7.5 per cent in 1999. The ratio for India has increased continuously to reach 9.7 per cent in 2008. In 2011, amid the global economic recession, India's FDI over GCF ratio was 5.4 per cent, while that of Korea remained at 3.1 per cent. Globally, the ratio has shown

Figure 9.6

FDI Stocks in India and Korea, 1991-2002

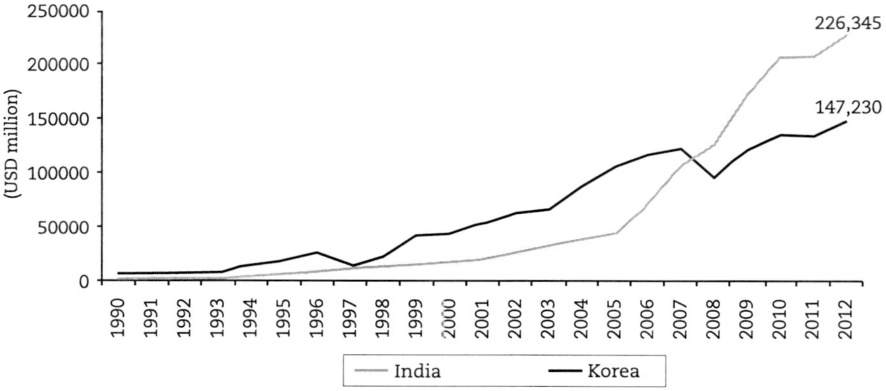

Source: UNCTAD, UNCTAD stat, Foreign Direct Investment.

a fluctuating trajectory after reaching its peak at 19.5 per cent in 2000. The figure fell to 10.1 per cent in 2011 due to the recent economic recession. This means both countries have not depended heavily on FDI for GCF, and FDI has not played an active role so far.

Figure 9.7

FDI Inflows as a Percentage of Gross Capital Formation

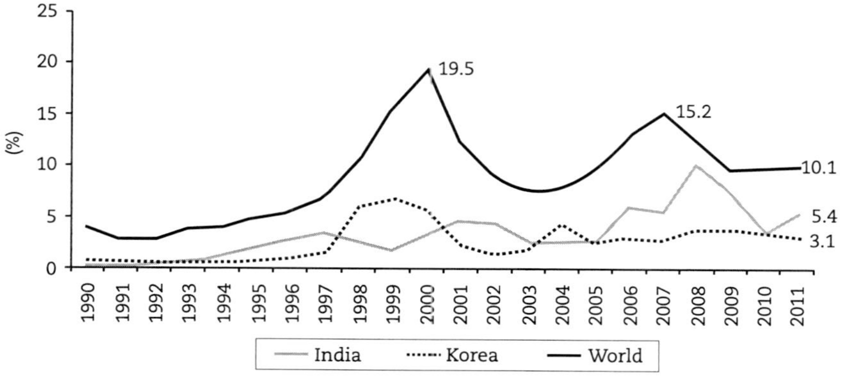

Source: UNCTAD, UNCTAD stat.

All the three findings point to the fact that the recent global economic crisis had a great impact on international FDI flows, and India and Korea have not been able to avoid the impact. As FDI inflows into both countries decreased, graphs of FDI stocks and FDI/GCF flattened. However, China seems to have been an exception. More and more FDI is flowing into China even under the current global economic crisis.

To figure out the bilateral relationship between Korea and India, we need to look at the country of origin of FDI inflows. In the case of India, the Indian government has released recent FDI inflow data from April 2000. Korea ranks 13th with its FDI in India reaching US$ 1.2 billion during the April 2000 to June 2013 period as shown in Table 9.5. The percentage of Korea's FDI to total inflows into India was just 0.6 per cent. However, counting FDI inflows into India from April 2000 may underestimate the contribution of Korean investment because the first round of Korean FDI flowed into India during the 1990s. During that decade, Korea invested US$ 563 million in India and ranked fourth after the US, Mauritius and the UK. Korea's renowned conglomerates including Samsung Electronics, LG Electronics and Hyundai Motors took their first steps in entering the Indian market during that decade.

However, in the first decade of the new century, the inflow of Korean FDI into India has not been as large as those of other countries even though there was another wave of Korean FDI during the second half of the decade.

In 2005, POSCO and the state of Odisha signed an MoU for investment worth US$ 12 billion, the largest ever FDI for India. However, for several reasons, such as environmental clearance and land acquisition, POSCO has not yet made tangible progress in the project. POSCO is carrying out several other projects to establish downstream mills in the state of Maharashtra and runs three processing centres in India. FDI inflows from Korea to India are expected to increase significantly when POSCO begins full-fledged investments in Odisha. Even without counting the Odisha project, POSCO has already invested US$ 433.7 million in India in several small and big projects.

Table 9.5

Country-wise FDI Inflows into India (From April 2000 to June 2013)

(US$ million)

Rank	*Country*	*FDI Amount (Equity)*	*Percentage of FDI Inflows*
1	Mauritius	74,765	37.6
2	Singapore	21,312	10.7
3	UK	17,599	8.9
4	Japan	14,749	7.4
5	US	11,436	5.8
6	Netherlands	9,373	4.7
7	Cyprus	6,993	3.5
8	Germany	5,990	3.0
9	France	3,672	1.8
10	UAE	2,472	1.2
13	South Korea	1,259	0.6
	Total	198,800	

Source: DIPP, 2013a.

India's FDI inflow into Korea is shown in Table 9.6. Korea has not been an attractive investment destination for Indian investors. As shown in Appendix Table A-9.3, the three most favourable destinations for Indian investors are Singapore, Mauritius and the Netherlands, and Korea is not included in the top 10 list. India ranked 27th among the countries that invested in Korea and the total cumulative sum of Indian FDI inflows into Korea was just US$ 467 million from 2000 to 2012. Nankani's (1979) argument that FDI flows from a developed country to a developing country may partly explain why Indian FDI into Korea has not been substantial.

Indian firms that have established their presence in the Korean market include Tata Motors, L&T Infotech, Mahindra Satyam, Indian Overseas Bank, Tata Consultancy Services, Jindal Stainless Steel, Nucleus Software Solutions and Wipro Technologies. It may be noteworthy that Indian automobile firms acquired Korean firms through M&A deals in 2004 and 2010. India's investment into Korea significantly increased in 2004 and 2010, as shown in Figure 9.4.

Table 9.6

Country-wise FDI Inflows into Korea (From 2000 to 2012)

(US$ million)

Rank	*Country*	*FDI Amount*	*Percentage of FDI Inflows*
1	US	34,814	22.5
2	Japan	24,691	16.0
3	Netherlands	14,783	9.6
4	UK	10,654	6.9
5	Germany	8,257	5.3
6	Singapore	6,851	4.4
7	Hong Kong	5,137	3.3
8	Canada	4,916	3.2
9	France	4,446	2.9
10	China	4,388	2.8
27	India	467	0.3
	Total	154,468	

Source: The Ministry of Trade, Industry and Energy, Korea.

All these findings suggest that the two countries have not been very active in their bilateral direct investment relationship. However, the effect of the CEPA on the bilateral investment relationship has to be quantitatively analysed to confirm such a conclusion.

To do so, we use the concept of bilateral FDI intensity, which is a ratio that compares the actual value of the FDI stock of country *'i'* in country *'j'* with what might be expected, given the world position of each of them as a home or host economy, respectively. Thus, bilateral FDI intensity from country *'i'* to country *'j'* can be denoted as:

FDI intensity ratio (R) = FDI_{ij} / $ExpFDI_{ij}$

FDI_{ij} = Actual amount of FDI stock from country i to country j.

$ExpFDI_{ij}$ = Expected value of FDI stock from country i to country j.

$$\frac{FDI_{wj}}{FDI_{ww}} \star \frac{FDI_{iw}}{FDI_{ww}} \star FDI_{ww} \quad (1)$$

where, FDI_{wj} = total inward stock in the j country; FDI_{iw} = total outward FDI stock of country i in the world; and FDI_{ww} = Worldwide inward or outward *FDI* stock.

If the intensity ratio is greater than 1, the FDI relationship is stronger than expected based on the relative importance of the two economies as home and host; if it is less than 1, it is weaker than expected.

To calculate bilateral intensity, we first need to evaluate both countries' positions in the global FDI market. For India, inward FDI stock has always been higher than outward stock during 2007-2012. Inward FDI stock increased from US$ 105.8 billion in 2007 to US$ 226.3 billion in 2012. During the same period, the outward FDI stock of India increased from US$ 44.1 billion to US$ 118.2 billion. In 2012, the gap between inward and outward stock exceeded US$108 billion, implying that India received more FDI than it invested in other countries.

Data on Korea tell a different story. Up to 2007, inward FDI stock had been greater than outward stock. However, from 2008, outward FDI stock became larger than inward stock, as outgoing Korean FDI exceeded FDI coming into Korea. In 2012, the inward FDI stock was US$ 147.2 billion while outward Korean FDI stock was US$ 196.4 billion. Thus, considering their positions in the global FDI market, the expected Korean FDI stock in India was calculated as US$ 438 million in 2007 and US$ 1,949 billion in 2012, while the expected Indian FDI stock in Korea was US$ 69 and US$ 471 million, respectively.

Since the actual data were not available, the cumulative sum of FDI inflows and outflows was used as proxies for those stock variables. In doing so, the starting year of counting the cumulative sum of FDI flows was important. However, as the Indian government suddenly switched the starting year from 1991 to 2000 in 2007, it was not an easy task to get consistent Korean FDI flow data in US$ from 1991. However, we managed to develop a consistent Korean FDI data series with three fact sheets on FDI in 2007 and a recent special report on Korean FDI flows into India (DIPP, 2013c).

The results of the bilateral FDI intensity calculations were very similar to what was expected. The intensity of FDI from India to Korea was 0.23 in 2007 and went up to 0.71 in 2010 and then stayed almost flat at 0.62 in 2012. In contrast, the intensity of FDI from Korea to India was 2.08 in 2007. It showed a downward trend until it reached 0.92 in 2010 and stayed flat at 0.92 in 2012.

First, this implies that Korea's investment in India had been greater than the supposed-to-be level until 2009, even though it has shown a downward trend. However, from 2010, the intensity went down below one and stayed there, indicating that Korea's FDI into India has not reached the expected levels. In the case of India's investment in Korea, the intensity has been much less than the supposed-to-be level, even though it has shown an upward trend. It has gone up to 0.71 in 2010 but has since remained at that level.[2]

Second, it is worth noting that both intensities have remained almost flat below one level since 2010 when the CEPA between two countries came into effect. We have seen that bilateral FDI inflows between the two countries increase once a CEPA comes into effect, albeit not very substantially. This implies that the CEPA might not have played an important role in promoting bilateral investment between Korea and India.

Figure 9.8

Bilateral FDI Intensity between India and Korea

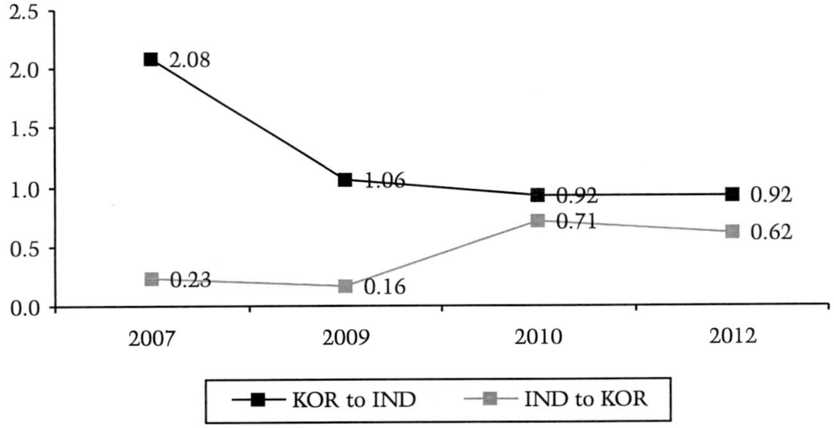

Note: FDI_{ij}: cumulative sum of FDI inflow is used as a proxy for FDI stock variable (Korean FDI into India: Aug 1991 to Feb 2013, Indian FDI into Korea: 1986-2012).

Source: The bilateral FDI data sourced from DIPP, Ministry of Trade, Industry and Energy.

2. In the previous study conducted in 2012 (Kwag, 2012), the bilateral intensities for both India and Korea were miscalculated due to data collection errors.

Why India and Korea Need to Strengthen Bilateral Cooperation

Two main challenges facing the Indian government are the fiscal and current account deficits. India has experienced chronic CADs as the trade deficit has increased to such an extent that it cannot be covered by the surplus in invisible net as shown in Figure 9.9. The fundamental cause for the rising CAD is that India lacks competitiveness in the manufacturing sector due to lack of adequate infrastructure, strict labour regulations, lack of financial aid to manufacturing companies, etc. This lack of competitiveness in the manufacturing sector has significant implications for the job market. In emerging countries, a large number of jobs are created in the manufacturing sector. A big factory usually generates thousands of decent jobs. In India, however, the services sector has driven economic growth without creating enough jobs to hire all entrants to the job market. So even when India enjoyed high growth in the mid-2000s, many people called for 'growth with justice.'

Figure 9.9

India's Trade Balance and Current Account (unit: US$ million)

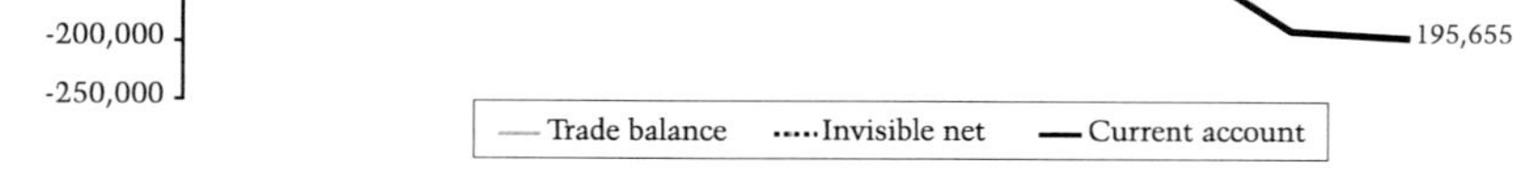

Source: The Reserve Bank of India, Database on Indian Economy.

The Indian government has made efforts to improve the competitiveness of its manufacturing sector. However, the outcome has not been satisfactory. To tackle this issue, India needs to learn a lesson from China's experience. China has attracted a huge amount of FDI and transformed its economy into a global manufacturing base through appropriate investment policies.

India has been very successful in drawing a huge amount of FDI in recent years. However, most of the FDI inflows have gone to India's services sector and infrastructure development projects while not much flowed into the manufacturing sector. Figure 9.10 indicates sector-wise FDI inflows into India. Thirty-eight per cent of FDI flowed into the services sector, 22 per cent into construction development, 13 per cent into telecommunications and 12 per cent into computer software, leaving about 15 per cent which went to the manufacturing industries such as drug and pharmaceuticals, chemicals, automobiles, electricity and steel.

This may imply that India's business environment is not attractive enough to draw FDI in the manufacturing sector and some urgent measures must be taken to enhance India's competitiveness as a manufacturing base.

On the other hand, Korea has a saturated market and is losing growth momentum due to its aging population. It needs a new catalyst for growth as well as a new market with huge potential purchasing power. In addition, the country also needs manufacturing bases for exporting its products to the EU, the Middle East and African markets. As much as 84.8 per cent of total Korean FDI inflows into India have been in the manufacturing sector. Therefore, if India and Korea cooperate with each other, they might find huge win-win opportunities to create synergy.

Conclusion and Policy Implications

The literature review and empirical findings given above indicate that bilateral or regional investment agreements have a positive but not significant effect in attracting FDI. Economic determinants are the most significant factors in determining FDI inflows. .

The case studies of the CECA between India and Singapore, the CEPA between India and Japan, and the CEPA between India and Korea showed mixed results. The CECA between Singapore and India had a significantly positive effect on FDI inflows to India, but the CEPA between India and Korea turned out to have a negligible effect on bilateral FDI flows, implying that some follow-up measures should be taken to boost bilateral investment activities.

The success of the CECA may be associated with policies. The CECA included tax clauses favouring Indian companies. However, the CEPAs with

Figure 9.10

Sector-wise FDI Inflows into India (From April 2000 to July 2013)

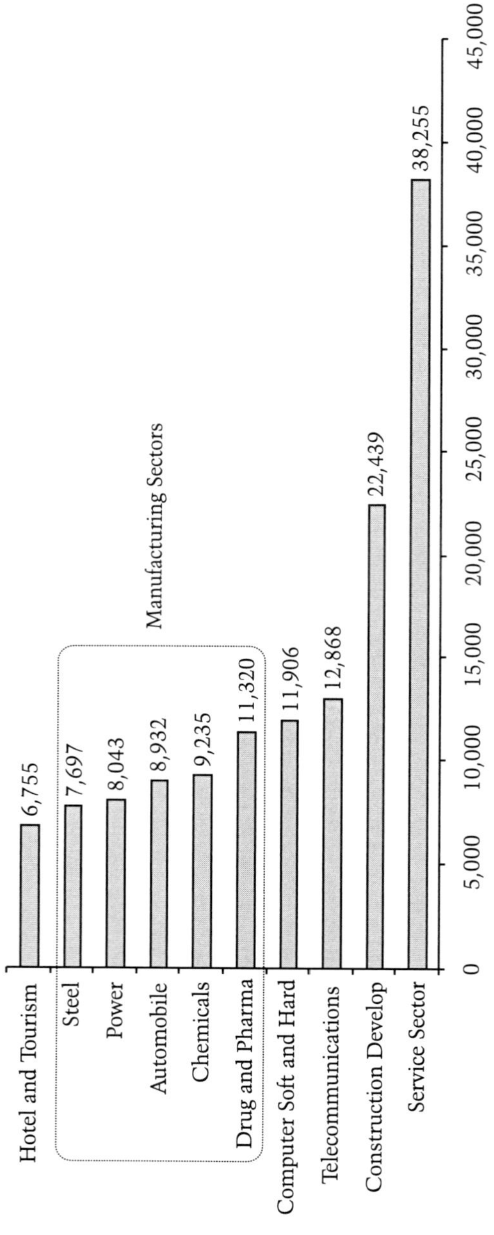

Source: DIPP, 2013a.

Japan and Korea did not include clear changes in policies regarding FDI. Therefore, to enhance more FDI inflows to India, India's policy framework must be examined further.

Third, India's performance in attracting FDI in recent years has been quite satisfactory. However, considering the world average, the Indian government has to work hard to draw more FDI, particularly in the underdeveloped manufacturing sector. The Korean government also has a long way to go to reach the world average level in attracting FDI.

Fourth, Korea and India can find great opportunities to set up win-win strategies through FDI. Should India draw a huge amount of Korean FDI in the manufacturing sector, thus creating massive employment, it would be able to become another manufacturing base for the global market.

However, for that dream to come true, India needs to carry out radical reforms. The World Bank releases "Doing Business Index (DBI)" each year. It surveys 183 countries and ranks them based on measures in 10 regulatory areas. The DBI in Table 9.7 shows how bad India's business environment is and the areas where reforms are required.

Singapore ranked at the top with the world's most favourable business environment for FDI. In the DBI 2013, Korea and India ranked 8th and 132nd, respectively. These figures show that Korea provides a fairly good business environment while India's remains substandard. India ranked low in categories such as starting a business, paying taxes and enforcing contracts. This indicates that India has too many procedures and it costs too much for investors to get a licence from the Indian government. In India, it takes nearly five years on average to resolve business conflicts in court, implying that the country needs to reform its legal system to make it more business friendly. Appendix Table A-9.6 indicates in detail which areas should be improved and where policy reforms need to be focused to increase FDI inflows into India.

However, one may be misled by data about Korea. In the DBI 2010, Korea ranked 19th. It jumped to one of the top eight countries in 2013. Does this mean Korea worked hard to improve its business environment? One of the notable features of Korea's business environment is that it has a bad reputation as a labour market. In the DBI 2010, Korea ranked 150th in the 'hire and fire' category, indicating the rigidity of the Korean job market.

Table 9.7

Business Environments of India

Economy	*Rank*	*Start biz*	*Deal licence*	*Electricity*	*Property*	*Get Credit*	*Protect Invest*	*Paying Taxes*	*Export Import*	*Contracts*	*Close biz*
Singapore	1	4	2	5	36	12	2	5	1	12	2
Korea	8	24	26	3	75	12	49	30	3	2	14
Malaysia	12	54	96	28	33	1	4	15	11	33	49
Thailand	18	85	16	10	26	70	13	96	20	23	58
Japan	24	114	72	27	64	23	19	127	19	35	1
China	91	151	181	114	44	70	100	122	68	19	82
Vietnam	99	108	28	155	48	40	169	138	74	44	149
Indonesia	128	166	75	147	98	129	49	131	37	144	148
Bangladesh	129	95	83	185	175	83	25	97	119	182	119
India	132	173	182	105	94	23	49	152	127	184	116

Note: Indicators on business regulations and the protection of property rights across 183 economies.

Source: "Doing Business 2013", World Bank, *www.doingbusiness.org/rankings.*

According to the 2010 survey, when a company lays off a worker in Korea, it must pay 91 weeks of salary on average.

The World Bank has replaced 'hire and fire' with 'getting electricity' for unknown reasons. Korea is well-known as a country that provides good-quality electricity at low prices. Therefore, the change drove up Korea's ranking in the 2013 survey. However, Korea still has to solve the problem of labour market rigidity.

To enhance bilateral FDI, Korea must keep in mind the following facts. First, Korea should make its labour market more flexible. Many foreign companies consider the rigid labour market a major obstacle to investing in Korea. Violent labour unions have tarnished the image of 'Corporate Korea.' Reasonable and flexible labour-management relations must be established in Korea.

Second, India needs to develop more industrial parks and SEZs (special economic zones). In India, as private developers must purchase land on their own, they have to deal with issues such as getting licences, ownership investigation and transferring ownership, which are almost impossible tasks for them. In China, to develop an SEZ, state governments purchase land from local people and construct infrastructure in advance and then allocate the land to individual investors. Such a process enables investing companies to focus on production, marketing and other businesses. Some state governments in China operate a single window system to handle all issues related to FDI at one place. A few states in India have adopted the same approach, but actual implementation will not be easy. In addition, China operates incentive systems for its government officials in charge of FDI in which some state governments offer them 0.6-1.0 per cent of total investment as incentives only when the project makes a profit.

Third, in order to make full use of the CEPA, both governments should cooperate with each other in promoting FDI flows through an exchange of government officials and help them work together to understand each other, exchange information and remove obstacles. This will pave the way for a better relationship between the two nations and result in larger FDI flows.

As mentioned above, there are many areas in which India and Korea can cooperate, and both countries have the potential to create synergy. To exploit the full potential, the two countries should make efforts to develop appropriate policies, and if necessary, to carry out radical reforms. Above all, they must keep in mind that the key to success is not to plan but to implement projects.

References

Department of Investment Policy and Promotion (DIPP) (2010). *FDI Synopsis on Country Singapore as on 31.12.2010*. Ministry of Commerce and Industry of India.

———. (2013a). *Fact Sheet on Foreign Direct Investment, from April, 2000 to June, 2013*.

———. (2013b). *FDI Synopsis on Country Japan as on 28.02.2013*.

———. (2013c). "FDI Synopsis on Country Korea as on 28.02.2013."

Export and Import Bank of Korea (n.d.). *The Statistics of Foreign Investment*. Available at *http:// www.koreaexim.go.kr/kr/work/check/oversea/use.jsp*

FIA (Foreign Investment Agency), Ministry of Planning and Investment of Vietnam (2005). *The Impact of the U.S.-Vietnam Bilateral Trade Agreement on Overall and U.S. Foreign Direct Investment in Vietnam*. Hanoi: National Political Publisher.

Kevin Reilly, Peter J. Buckley, Jeremy Clegg and Nicolas Forsans (2007). "A Simple and Flexible Dynamic Approach to Foreign Direct Investment Growth: The Canada-United States Relationship in the Context of Free Trade", *The World Economy* 30(2): 267–91, February.

Kwag, Chang-ho (2012). "The Trends of FDI Flows into India and Korea", in Parthasarathi Shome and Choong Yong Ahn (eds.), *Korea-India: Deepening Partnership for the 21st Century.* Korea Institute for International Economic Policy. pp.185-213.

Liu, Tianshu (2008). "Impact of Regional Trade Agreements on Chinese Foreign Direct Investment", *The Chinese Economy* 41(5): 68-102.

Ministry of Trade, Industry and Energy, Government of Korea. *http://www.motie.go.kr*

Moon, Jongchol (2009). "A Study of the Effects of Free Trade Agreements on Foreign Direct Investment." A Dissertation submitted for the degree Doctor of Philosophy in Economics, University of California, Los Angeles.

Nankani, G.T. (1979). *The Intercountry Distribution of Direct Foreign Investment in Manufacturing*. New York and London: Garland Publishing.

Nunnenkamp, Peter and Julius Spatz (2002). "Determinants of FDI in Developing Countries: Has Globalization Changed the Rules of the Game?", *Transnational Corporations* 11(2): 1-34.

Reserve Bank of India. *http://www.RBI.org.in*.

UNCTAD (1998). *World Investment Report 1998: Trends and Determinants*.

———. (2007). "Worldwide Survey of Foreign Affiliates", *Occasional Note*. Geneva.

———. (2009). *Report on The Role of International Investment Agreements in Attracting Foreign Direct Investment to Developing Countries*.

Waldkirch, Andreas (2010). "The Effects of Foreign Direct Investment in Mexico since NAFTA", *The World Economy*. Blackwell Publishing Ltd., pp.710-45.

World Bank (2013). *Doing Business 2013. http://www.doingbusiness.org/rankings*

Appendix Table A-9.1

Host Country FDI Determinants

Host Country FDI Determinants		*Explanation*
I. Economic Determinants	A. Market-seeking	- market size and per capita income
		- market growth
		- access to regional and global markets
		- country-specific consumer preferences
		- market structure
	B. Efficiency-seeking	- cost difference (of resources and assets)
		- the quality of infrastructure
		- the ease of doing business
		- the availability of skill
		- the availability of complementary local factors for production
	C. Resource-seeking	- raw materials
II. Policy Framework for FDI		- economic, political and social stability
		- rule regarding entry and operations
		- standards of treatment of foreign affiliates
		- policies on functioning and structure of markets
		- international agreements of FDI
		- privatisation, trade and tax policy
III. Business Facilitation		- investment promotion including image-building and investment-generating activities and investment-facilitation services
		- investment incentives
		- hassle costs related to corruption, administrative inefficiency and etc.
		- social amenities (bilingual schools, quality of life, etc.)
		- after-investment services

Source: UNCTAD 1998. *World Investment Report 1998*.

Appendix Table A-9.2

Country-wise FDI Equity Inflows into India (From April 2000 to June 2013)

(US$ million)

Rank	*Country*	*FDI Amount (Equity)*	*Percentage of FDI Inflows*
1	Mauritius	74,765	37.6
2	Singapore	21,312	10.7
3	United Kingdom	17,599	8.9
4	Japan	14,749	7.4
5	US	11,436	5.8
6	Netherlands	9,373	4.7
7	Cyprus	6,993	3.5
8	Germany	5,990	3.0
9	France	3,672	1.8
10	UAE	2,472	1.2
	Total	198,800	100.0

Source: DIPP, 2013a.

Appendix Table A-9.3

Top 10 Country-wise Overseas Investments by India

(US$ million)

Rank	*Country*	*2008-09*	*2009-10*	*2010-11*	*2011-12**	*Total*
1	Singapore	4,060	4,200	3,990	1,860	14,110
2	Mauritius	2,080	2,150	5,080	2,270	11,570
3	Netherlands	2,790	1,530	1,520	700	6,540
4	US	1,020	870	1,210	870	3,970
5	UAE	630	640	860	380	2,510
6	British Virgin Islands	0	750	280	520	1,550
7	United Kingdom	350	340	400	440	1,530
8	Cayman Islands	0	40	440	140	620
9	Hong Kong	0	0	160	310	460
10	Switzerland	0	0	250	160	410
	Other countries	7,650	3,190	2,650	1,230	14,710
	Total	18,580	13,710	16,840	8,860	

Note: * April 2011 to February 2012.

Source: Reserve Bank of India, Foreign Investment Statistics.

Appendix Table A-9.4

Top 10 FDI Cases from Japan to India (From April 2000 to February 2013)

(US$ million)

Rank	*Investing Company*	*Name of Indian Companies Invested*	*Sector*	*FDI Amount*
1	Daiichi Sankyo	Ranbaxy	Pharmaceuticals	3,363
2	JFE Steel	JSW Steel	Metallurgical Industry	1,060
3	Nippon Life Insurance	Reliance Life Insurance	Life Insurance	543
4	Nissan Motors	Renault Nissan Auto India Pvt. Ltd.	Automobile	275
5	Nippon Life Insurance	Reliance Capital Asset Management	Life Insurance	261
6	Matsushita Electric Works Ltd.	Anchor Electricals Pvt. Ltd.	Electrical Equipment	342
7	Sumitomo Mitsui Banking Corporation	Kotak Mahindra Bank	Bank	303
8	Honda Motors	Honda Siel Cars India Ltd.	Automobile	216
9	HITACHI	TELCO	Construction Equipment	260
10	Suzuki Motors	Maruti Udyog Ltd.	Automobile	208

Source: DIPP, 2013b.

Appendix Table A-9.5

Details of Top FDI Inflows Received from Korea (Remittance-wise) (From April 2000 to February 2013)

(US$ million)

Rank	*Investing Company*	*Name of Indian Companies Invested*	*Sector*	*FDI Amount*
1	POSCO	POSCO Maharashtra POSCO India POSCO Chennai	Steel products	433.7
2	Samsung Electronics	Samsung Elec. India	Electronics	46.6
3	Mirae Asset	Mirae Asset Global Inv.	Real Estate	45.3
4	Doosan Heavy Industries	Doosan Chennai Works	Boiler, Prime mover	38.6
5	Mobis	Mobis India	Automobile parts	34.7
6	Hyundai Heavy Ind.	Hyundai Construction Equipment India	Construction machinery	30.4
7	Korea Western Power	Pioneer Gas Power	Power Plants	20.0
8	Lotte	Parry Confectionery	Confectionery Sales	14.0
9	Lanco Infratech	Lanco	Power Generator	9.8
	Total of Above			673.1

Sources: DIPP, 2013c.

Appendix Table A-9.6

Areas to Reform: India/Korea

	Indicators	*India*	*Korea*	*OECD*
Starting Biz (173/24)	Procedures (number)	12	5	5
	Time (days)	27	7	11.8
	Cost (% of income/capita)	49.8	14	4
	Min capital (% income/capita)	140.1	0.0	13.3
Dealing with Licences (182/26)	Procedures (number)	34	11	14
	Time (days)	196	29	143.5
	Cost (% of income/capita)	1,528	127.2	78.7
Enforcing Contracts (to resolve a dispute) (184/2)	Procedures (number)	46	33	31.4
	Time (days)	1420	230	510.5
	Cost (% of claim)	39.6	10.3	20.1

Sources: "Doing Business 2013", World Bank.

10

India-Korea CEPA

Harnessing the Potential in Services

Saon Ray, Nisha Taneja
and Neetika Kaushal Nagpal

Introduction

The services sector is a major contributor to GDP, international trade and employment in not just developed economies but also in emerging economies. With rapid expansion of the services sector in most countries, any trade liberalisation is considered incomplete without liberalisation of the services sector. Realising this, the World Trade Organization (WTO) broadened the scope of negotiation during the Uruguay Round in 1995 to include trade in services by establishing the General Agreement on Trade in Services (GATS).[1] However, the limited success of the Uruguay Round and sluggish progress of the Doha Development Agenda (launched in November 2001) in multilateral trade negotiations spurred the process of bilateral and regional trade agreements (RTAs). Many WTO members embraced RTAs as "trade policy instruments and as complimentary to MFN" (Crawford and Fiorentino, 2005).

A distinct feature of these agreements, also called the 'New Age FTAs,' is that they extend beyond merchandise trade to include services, investment, government procurement and a range of other cooperation issues apart from trade in goods. The purpose of these comprehensive trade agreements is not only to enhance bilateral trade flows but also to strengthen strategic ties or overcome historic animosities (Fink and

1. GATS established the rules and discipline governing trade in services in a multilateral framework. It aims to create a credible and reliable system of international trade rules, ensuring fair and equitable treatment of all participants (principle of non-discrimination), stimulating economic activity through guaranteed policy bindings, and promoting trade and development through progressive liberalisation.

Molinuevo, 2007a). Fink and Molinuevo (Ibid.) note that although services were previously considered non-tradable, technological progress and the trend towards private and competitive provision of infrastructure services have enabled trade in a wide range of service activities. The services sector has come to account for the fastest growing segment of international commerce (World Bank, 2002).

In line with this pattern of bilateralism/regionalism, India and Korea have been signing a number of Comprehensive Economic Partnership Agreements (CEPA) with several countries and regions. Some of these agreements are with neighbours while others are in the inter-regional framework of economic cooperation ranging from bilateralism to sub-regionalism to regionalism.

The feasibility of signing a CEPA between India and Korea was examined by a Joint Study Group in 2005. The Indo-Korea CEPA was concluded in 2009 and implemented in 2010. The agreement covers goods, services, investment, bilateral cooperation, intellectual property rights and competition.

With the objective of identifying the areas that hold potential for harnessing services trade between India and Korea, this paper attempts to describe the performance and composition of the services sector in both countries, assess liberalisation commitments under CEPA and examine the extent to which these are more liberal than unilateral commitments. In the sectors selected for qualitative examination, the paper assesses trade possibilities and analyses the exisitng market access barriers.

Approach to the Paper

The comparison of commitments that India and Korea have undertaken under the WTO and the India-Korea CEPA is examined using the GATS framework, which provides member countries with a structure for negotiating the removal of external and domestic barriers. GATS categorises services trade into four modes of supply, depending on the location of supplier and consumer. Mode 1 (cross-border supply) is the delivery of services across countries without the physical movement of the supplier or buyer of the service. Mode 2 (consumption abroad) refers to the physical movement of the service consumer to the territory of the service provider for consumption. Mode 3 (commercial presence) pertains to the establishment of foreign affiliates and subsidiaries of foreign service companies, joint ventures, partnerships, representative offices and branches, and Mode 4 (presence of natural persons) refers to natural persons who themselves are service suppliers, as well as natural persons who are employees of service suppliers temporarily present in another member's market to provide the service.

Unlike goods, barriers to trade in services are not in the form of import tariffs. Instead, service trade barriers take the form of restrictions, prohibitions, government regulations, etc. Service trade liberalisation is dependent on the removal and relaxation of these non-tariff barriers. GATS identifies two broad categories of barriers: market access (MA) and national treatment (NT). Market access barriers exist when a country does not allow (or partially allows with some restriction) foreign service providers to enter and operate in its markets. Restrictions in market access include barriers such as limitations on the number of foreign service providers, the total quantity of service output, valuation of transactions and assets, the number of persons to be employed, etc. A country is said to have imposed a national treatment barrier if it accords a treatment less favourable to service providers from other countries than to its domestic service providers. These barriers include discriminatory taxes, residency requirements, registration and licensing, etc. (Tanjea *et al.*, 2004).

Based on this framework, member countries can offer commitments for each of the four modes of supply of services across all sectors (horizontal commitments) or in specific sectors/sub-sectors (sectoral commitments). For each sector under each mode, member country can impose market access and/or national treatment barriers. If the country imposes no barriers in a particular mode, it is said to have 'full' commitment. If the county imposes some restrictions in a mode, then it is said to have offered 'partial' commitments. If a country does not make any commitment to liberalise the sector in a mode and reserves the rights to impose restrictions in the future, the country is said to have kept the sector 'unbound.' On the basis of this categorisation, countries offer liberalisation commitments on service trade sectors using the services sectoral classification list by GATS (MTN.GNS/W/120—July 1991). This list, with 12 broad sectors, has been drawn from the United Nations Central Product Classification (UNCPC), which provides a comprehensive coverage of all services sectors.

Estimates and data for trade in commercial services in Modes 1, 2 and 4 are derived from a country's balance of payment (BoP) account and for Mode 3 using the Foreign Affiliates Trade in Services (FATS) statistics.[2] However, export and import of commercial services is classified and recorded using the concepts, definitions and classifications under the fifth edition of the International Monetary Fund (IMF) *Balance of Payment Manual* (1993). Under this classification, the current account of BoP is sub-divided into goods, services (including government services not included elsewhere), income (investment income and compensation of employees), and current transfers.

Commercial services are defined as all services minus government services not included elsewhere. It is further sub-divided into three categories: transportation, travel and other commercial services. Transportation services cover air, maritime, rail, road and pipeline transport services that involves freight, passenger and other auxiliary services such as warehousing, cargo handling, etc. Travel consists of hotels and restaurants, travel agencies, tour operators and tourist guides. Unlike other services, travel is not a specific type of service but is an assortment of goods and services consumed by travellers. Other commercial services comprises nine sub-sectors: insurance, financial services, computer and information, construction, communications, royalty and licence fees, other business services, and personal, cultural and recreational services.

The data on trade in services are available only at the country level and not at the bilateral level. For the period under study (2000-2011), data are available for almost all categories and sub-categories with a few exceptions. The data for secondary analysis are extracted from WTO, United Nations Conference on Trade and Development (UNCTAD) and World Bank at the aggregate level.

WTO *versus* CEPA: A Comparative Analysis

The process of services trade liberalisation began with the formulation of GATS, which was a landmark achievement under the Uruguay Round

2. Metadata, WTO International Trade Statistics.

(1995).[3] In this round, member countries submitted a schedule of commitments for selected service sectors. This was followed by the Doha Round (which commenced in 2001) that marked the beginning of the first round of negotiations under the Council for Trade in Services. Its objective was to lower trade barriers around the world in order to facilitate trade in services. As a part of this round, member countries submitted a revised offer for negotiations, which is still under discussion.

In both rounds of trade negotiations, India and Korea have actively participated in the liberalisation process. Compared to the Uruguay Round, both countries have submitted a schedule of commitments under the Doha Round that is much wider in its coverage and includes commitments in market access as well as national treatment under all modes.

In the Doha Round, India offered commitments in 12 sectors and 161 sub-sectors.[4] It extended full commitment under market access and national treatments in many sub-sectors such as architectural, engineering, management consulting, general construction services, etc., and undertook most favoured nation (MFN) exemptions[5] for communications (audio-visual and telecommunications), construction, recreational and transport services.[6] Korea, an otherwise more open economy than India, submitted an offer including all 12 sectors and 98 sub-sectors. Compared to the Uruguay Round (UR) offer, Korea made considerable improvements in sectors such as business services, construction, distribution, education, financial and transportation services. It also allowed complete market access and national treatment in several sectors such as legal, wholesale trade, retailing services, etc., under Modes 2, 3 and 4. Moreover, it

3. Uruguay Round was the 8th round of multilateral trade negotiations conducted within the framework of the General Agreement on Trade and Tariff (GATT) that was spread over the period 1986 to 1994, in which 123 countries participated as 'contracting parties.' It transformed the GATT into the WTO. It came into effect in 1995 and has been implemented over the period up to 2000 (2004 in the case of developing country contracting parties) (*Source*: Wikipedia and WTO).

4. WTO Service Sectoral Classification List: MTN/GNS/W/120.

5. An MFN exemption was a once-only opportunity for WTO member countries to take an exemption from the MFN principle of non-discrimination between a member's trading partners. The measure for which the exemption was taken is described in a member's MFN exemption list, indicating to which member the more favourable treatment applies, and specifying its duration (*Source*: WTO).

6. India's Revised Offer submitted to WTO—TN/S/O/IND/Rev.1 submitted on August 24, 2005.

participated in the extended GATS negotiations on financial services and telecommunications and became a member and observer, respectively, of the plurilateral Agreements on Government Procuremen (GPA)[7] and Trade in Civil Aircraft.[8]

Under the CEPA, both countries have offered liberal commitments in services trade. They have offered commitments in all sectors classified under the GATS according to the MTN.GNS/W/120[9] document. The schedule of commitments under the CEPA has the same framework as GATS. The commitments on 11 sectors cover national treatment, market access, domestic obligations, exceptions, definitions and scope but it does not venture into safeguards, subsidies and procurement. In terms of sub-sectors, the Indian schedule includes 28 sub-sectors and the Korean schedule includes 31 sub-sectors. In addition, it also has separate chapters on telecommunications, financial services, audio-visual services and movement of natural persons (Mode 4) enlisting additional commitments and terms for trade.

Comparative Analysis

This section draws a comparison between commitments offered under the Doha Round and under the CEPA for each sub-sector. The focus is on assessing the possible additional gains that the two countries can have in each other's markets under the CEPA and the extent of liberalisation in the bilateral agreement *vis-à-vis* the multilateral agreement.

Mode 1: As compared to Doha Round the revised offer, India has not made many changes to its commitments under the CEPA for cross-border services. It has offered to give full commitments in research and development (R&D) in natural sciences and biotechnology, hotels and other

---

7. The GPA is the only legally binding agreement in the WTO focusing on the subject of government procurement. It is a plurilateral treaty administered by a Committee on Government Procurement, which includes the WTO members that are parties to the GPA, and thus have rights and obligations under the agreement (*Source*: WTO)

8. Plurilateral Agreement on Trade in Civil Aircraft entered into force on January 1, 1980, and has 31 signatories. It eliminates import duties on all aircraft, other than military aircraft, as well as on all other products covered by the agreement—civil aircraft engines and their parts and components, all components and sub-assemblies of civil aircraft, and flight simulators and their parts and components (*Source*: WTO).

9. *www.wto.org/english/tratop_e/serv_e/mtn_gns_w_120_e.doc*

lodging services, and travel agency and tour operator services, and partial commitment in advertising services. Korea, on the other hand, offered more liberal commitments for cross-border services under its revised offer (submitted in 2003) than under the CEPA. In the former, it fully liberalised sub-sectors like engineering, urban planning, advertising, environmental testing, audio-visual services, etc. It also gave partial commitments in courier, adult education, life insurance non-life insurance and reinsurance services. However, under the CEPA, Korea has added the requirement of 'local presence' in all these services as a condition for foreign individuals or juridical persons wishing to provide services within the territory. This requirement is often made in case of services that require close supervision to guarantee consumer protection (Hoekman *et al.*, 2002). However, it may hinder international trade because it is likely to impose a financial cost on foreign service providers. This requirement has made Korea's commitments under the CEPA more restrictive than the multilateral agreement.

Mode 2: Trade through consumption abroad primarily takes place in education, travel and tourism, and healthcare services. In both the revised offer as well as in the CEPA, India has offered liberal commitments for trade in these services. Korea, on the other hand, has offered liberal commitments in only two out of these three services: education, and travel and tourism. It has not included healthcare services in either schedule, implying that market access is restricted in this sector.

Mode 3: India offered liberal commitments in Mode 3 under the Doha Round revised offer. It included sub-sectors such as engineering, computer and related services, rental and leasing, construction services, etc. Under the CEPA, it offerred further liberalised trade commitments in all of these sub-sectors. In addition, it included some other sub-sectors such as R&D on natural sciences, advertising, internet, factoring and services incidental to mining. Korea has offered liberal commitments in the revised offer as well as under the CEPA. In the revised offer, it allowed conditional access to foreign investors in 18 sub-sectors and full access in the remaining sub-sectors. However, it limited investment in stocks to companies listed under the Korea Stock Exchange with an upper ceiling of 6 per cent of the company's total stock by individual foreign investors and an aggregate 23 per cent of foreign investment per company. Under the CEPA, it offered more liberal commitments in comparison to the revised offer by including sub-sectors such as building, cleaning, technical and analysis services of physical properties, and sporting and other recreational services (only for national treatment). Moreover, both countries have agreed to give preference to applications from the partner country's banks for establishment of branches if they meet industry requirements.

Mode 4: Under the revised offer, both India and Korea have specified their commitments in the movement of natural persons in the horizontal commitments section. In the revised offer, India has included four categories of persons: business visitors (BV), intra-corporate transferees (ICT), contractual service suppliers (CSS) and independent professionals (IP). In the latter two categories, it specifies a list of sub-sectors in which a CSS or an IP can obtain a service contract. The Korean revised offer allowed ICT, BV and services salespersons (SS) to stay temporarily in Korea with a visa but has imposed restrictions on CSS. Under the CEPA, however, movement of natural persons is covered in a separate chapter. It covers four categories of natural persons—ICT, BV, CSS and IP, as defined under WTO/GATS. For the latter two categories, the countries have prepared a positive list of 163 professions that professionals from the two countries can engage in, provided the person complies with applicable immigration measures. In the case of ICT, India has agreed to grant visa for temporary stay for an initial period of up to one year as against Korea, which has agreed for a visa for up to two years. For BVs, India has agreed to grant temporary stay for a period of not more than 180 days, while Korea has agreed to temporary stay for a period of only 90 days. The commitments also cover employment of spouse and dependents, regulatory transparency, resolution of problems, dispute settlement and reservations.

Overall, both India and Korea have offered more liberal commitments under the bilateral agreement than the revised offer by covering a larger number of sectors and sub-sectors in the respective schedules. However, Korea's requirement of local presence in Mode 1 is restrictive. It has similar requirements in other FTAs as well such as the Korea-EU FTA but not under the Korea-US and Korea-Singapore FTA.

Performance and Composition

In recent years, both the Indian and Korean economies have undergone major economic and structural changes, which have resulted in the emergence of services as a leading sector contributing significantly to GDP and international trade. Earlier, the services sector in both economies was subject to substantial trade and investment barriers. Liberalisation was adopted to lower prices, improve quality, increase competitiveness and reduce the loss of consumer surplus. Services accounted for 56 per cent of GDP in India and 58 per cent of GDP in Korea in 2011. The size of the sector increased almost five times from US$ 241 billion[10] in 2000 to US$ 1041 billion in 2011 in India, and more than doubled from US$ 306 billion in 2000 to US$ 650 billion in 2011 in Korea.

The share of the sector in total trade of goods and services has also accelerated in both countries. During 2000-2010, it contributed around 28-30 per cent of India's and 16-17 per cent of Korea's total trade in goods and services. In 2010, services trade for India was US$ 240 billion accounting for 14 per cent of GDP while that of Korea was US$ 183 billion accounting for 17 per cent of GDP. Exports of services also increased more than six times in India from US$ 16 billion to US$ 124 billion and tripled in Korea from US$ 30 billion in 2000 to US$ 95 billion in 2010. While India has been a net exporter of services since 2004, Korea's trade deficit has worsened from US$ 2.4 billion in 2000 to US$ 8.6 billion in 2010.

The lag in the growth of services trade in Korea as compared to India is explained by its economic policy and structure. After putting an end to the inward-looking policy in 1990's, India adopted a service-export led development policy, primarily driven by IT-ITeS services. Korea, on the other hand, has concentrated more on a manufacturing sector-led export policy over the last 40 years. However, the Korean services sector has now gained a strong foothold in merchandise exports by providing cost-efficient solutions through inventory control, sales, marketing, etc. This has created

10. All monetary figures are in US dollar.

Table 10.1

Service Sector Overview

	India					Korea				
	2002	*2004*	*2006*	*2008*	*2011*	*2002*	*2004*	*2006*	*2008*	*2011*
GDP (US$ billion at current prices)	522.80	721.59	949.12	1224.10	1872.84	575.93	721.98	951.77	931.40	1116.25
Services as per cent of GDP	53.0	53.0	52.9	53.9	55.7	59.8	58.1	59.7	60.8	58.11
Annual Growth of Services (in %)	7.0	8.1	10.1	10.0	8.2	7.7	2.5	4.4	2.7	2.7
Trade in Services as per cent of GDP	7.7	10.2	13.5	16.0	14.0	11.7	13.1	13.3	20.1	17.4
Trade in Services as per cent of Trade in Goods and Services	27.7	29.9	30.7	28.5	25.8	17.7	16.5	16.5	17.8	15.3

Source: Compiled from *World Development Indicators* (2012), World Bank.

Figure 10.1

Export of Services (US$ billions)

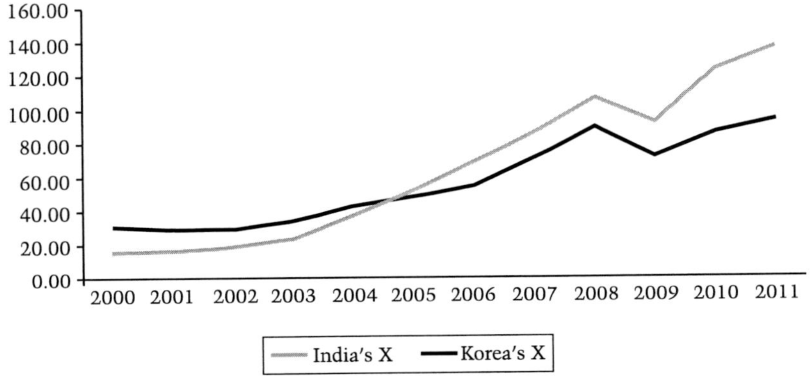

Source: Compiled from WTO.

a 'manufacturing-services continuum,' a phenomenon particularly evident in South Korea.[11]

Unlike the schedule of commitments that use the service sector classification list by GATS (MTN.GNS/W/120—July 1991), export and import of services trade is based on classification under the fifth edition of IMF *Balance of Payment Manual* (1993). Under this classification, commercial services are sub-divided into three categories: transportation, travel and other commercial services. If one looks at the composition of services trade, other commercial services (OCS) accounts for the maximum share of India's trade basket followed by travel and transportation (Table 10.2). During 2000-2011, the share of OCS in India's total commercial services export increased substantially from 71 per cent in 2000 to 74 per cent in 2011. On the other hand, the share of travel declined from 16 per cent in 2000 to 13 per cent in 2011. The share of transportation has remained unchanged at around 12 per cent during the period. Within the nine sub-sectors of OCS, computer and information and other business

11. See Macdonald (2006), Korea Investment Forum (*http://ncta.osu.edu/lessons/korea/econ/Koreanpercent20 Economicpercent20Developmentpercent20Flaig.pdf*)

services together accounted for about 70 per cent of total services export. This indicates that India's trade in OCS is not very diversified.

Table 10.2

Structure of Export

(US$ billions)

Service Category	*India*			*Korea*		
	2000	*2006*	*2011*	*2000*	*2006*	*2011*
A. Transportation	2.5 (12.9)	7.6 (10.9)	17.5 (12.8)	13.2 (44.8)	25.8 (46.6)	37.0 (39.5)
B. Travel	3.1 (16.2)	8.6 (12.4)	17.5 (12.8)	5.9 (20.1)	5.8 (10.5)	12.3 (13.1)
C. Other Commercial Services	13.5 (70.8)	53.3 (76.7)	101.5 (74.4)	10.4 (35.1)	23.7 (42.9)	44.4 (47.4)
Total	16.0 (100)	69.5 (100)	136.5 (100)	29.7 (100)	55.3 (100)	93.9 (100)

Note: * Figures in parenthesis indicate share of category export in total commercial service export.

Source: *World Development Indicator (WDI)*, World Bank.

Unlike India, the Korean trade basket has changed in the last decade. In 2000, transportation accounted for the largest share followed by OCS and travel. The share of transport services has declined to 39.5 per cent in 2011 while that of OCS has risen to 47.4 per cent, led by an increase in the export of construction and other business services. Thus, while OCS accounts for the largest share in total commercial services export in India as well as Korea, the sub-sectors within OCS leading exports are different for both countries.

Trade Possibilities

Most studies conducted to assess bilateral trade possibilities between the two countries use two conventional tools: revealed comparative advantage (RCA) index (Balassa, 1965) and trade complementarity index (TCI) (Michaely, 1994). The prospects of trade expansion are likely to be strong for countries that have either comparative advantage for dissimilar products, or trade structures that exhibit high complementarity. Such indices, although widely used in the goods context, have not been used often in the context of trade in services primarily due to shortcomings in available data (Tanjea *et al.*, 2004).

The RCA index is a ratio of the share of a product in a country's export to the share of the product in world exports. A value of more (less) than unity indicates that a country has a revealed comparative advantage (disadvantage) in that product. The TCI measures trade complementarity at the bilateral level in terms of the overall export-import structure of the trading partners. While the RCA index is a measure of comparative advantage that a particular country has *vis-à-vis* the rest of the world, the TCI is a bilateral measure in the context of bilateral trade. Hence, the TCI may be more appropriate to analyse trade possibilities between the two countries. However, lack of data on bilateral trade flows in services explains why this index is not used very often. In the context of the present study also, data are available on trade carried out by India and Korea with the rest of the world but not bilaterally, making it possible to compute the RCA index but not the TCI.

But the use of RCA index to identify trade possibilities in services has a limitation. Being a market share index, RCA can be an indicator of true competitiveness only under conditions of free trade. Since trade in services is governed by a plethora of non-tariff barriers, this indicator becomes weak. Hence, in the context of the present study, the RCA index will be applied only to identify service sectors with potential trade possibilities. This will be for sectors where one of the two countries is competitive and will be supplemented with a qualitative survey, which could help identify trade possibilities and barriers.

There are various ways of constructing the RCA indices but the one most commonly used is the Balassa index (Balassa, 1965; 1977; 1979; 1986). Balassa's definition of RCA pertains to the relative trade performance of individual countries in particular commodities (Batra and Khan, 2005). It is based on the assumption that the trade pattern reflects differences in relative costs and non-price factors at the country level, and hence, reveals the comparative advantage of the trading partners. The factors that contribute to changes in RCA are economic: structural change, improved world demand and trade specialisation.

Hoekman (1995) uses RCA for trade in services and concludes that developed economies specialise in commercial services that are capital intensive while developing countries specialise in labour-intensive commercial activities. Wickramasinghe (2000) examines the RCA coefficient for South Asian countries both at an aggregate and disaggregated level of trade in services. A study by Batra and Khan (2005) points out that the advantage of using the revealed comparative advantage index is that it takes into account the inherent advantage of exporting a particular commodity/service and is consistent with changes in the relative factor endowment and productivity of an economy. The limitation of the index is that it is unable to differentiate between improvements in factor endowments and implementation of appropriate trade policies by a country.

Balassa's (1965) RCA index is calculated as follows:

$$RCA_{ij} = (x_{ij}/X_{it}) / (x_{wj}/X_{wt})$$

where x_{ij} = country i's export of service j, x_{wj} = world exports of service j, X_{it} = total services exports of country i, and X_{wt} = total services exports of world.

Table 10.3 shows the RCAs of India and Korea for services for four years. The year 2000 has been chosen to examine the competitiveness of the two countries at the beginning of structural reforms, the year 2006 keeping in mind its proximity to the year the Joint Study Group to examine the feasibility of the India-Korea CEPA was set up, the year 2008 to examine the impact of the recent global financial crisis on the competitiveness of the two economies and the year 2011 to study the competitiveness after their recovery from the crisis.

An examination of the computed RCA indices indicates that India has a comparative advantage (RCA>1) while Korea does not have a comparative advantage (RCA<1) in commercial services (see Table 10.3). At a disaggregated level, India specialises in computer and information technology while Korea specialises in transportation and construction services. This is in conformity with the export structure of the two countries analysed in the previous section.

Three sectors have been taken up for in-depth analysis: computer and information, construction, and transportation. While computer and information will be examined from India's export and Korea's import point of view, construction and transportation will be examined from Korea's export and India's import point of view. In addition, the audio-visual sector is also covered. It has received a special mention under the CEPA as a separate chapter under which both countries have agreed to enter into a co-

Table 10.3

RCA Comparison for Service Sectors

Service Category	*India*				*Korea*			
	2002	*2006*	*2008*	*2011*	*2002*	*2006*	*2008*	*2011*
A. Transportation	0.5	0.5	0.5	0.6	2.0	2.1	2.2	1.9
B. Travel	0.7	0.5	0.4	0.5	0.6	0.4	0.4	0.5
C. Other Commercial Services	1.5	1.5	1.5	1.4	0.7	0.8	0.7	0.9
C.1 Insurance	0.6	0.7	0.7	0.9	0.0	0.2	0.2	0.2
C.2 Financial	0.5	0.4	0.5	0.6	0.3	0.6	0.5	0.5
C.3 Computer and Information	12.5	9.1	8.8	NA	0.0	0.10	0.0	0.1
C.4 Communication	1.8	1.3	0.9	0.5	0.6	0.5	0.3	0.3
C.5 Construction	0.5	0.4	0.3	0.2*	3.4	5.3	5.4	6.6
C.6 Royalty and Licence Fee	0.0	0.0	0.0	0.0*	0.5	0.7	0.4	0.7
C.7 Other Business	0.6	1.0	0.8	0.6	0.9	0.8	0.6	0.8
C.8 Personal, Cultural and Recreational		0.3	0.6	0.2*	0.4	0.5	0.5	0.7
Total Commercial Services	1.4	1.9	1.9	1.6	0.8	0.8	0.9	0.8

Note: * Figure for 2010. Data for 2011 is not available.

Source: The authors' calculations based on data from WTO Database.

production agreement for national treatment and better market access for joint products.

Sectoral Trade Possibilities and Regulatory Barriers

This section provides a qualitative examination of the four shortlisted sectors. The analysis discusses the potential areas of collaboration and engagement between the two countries.

Computer and Information Services (C&I)

In the last decade, India has emerged as a significant player in the world C&I market on account of software, information technology (IT) and information technology enabled services (ITeS).[12] The total revenue of the sector has grown from US$ 8 billion in 2000-01 to US$ 101 billion in 2012 [National Association of Software and Services Companies (NASSCOM), 2013] and it is expected to generate a revenue of US$ 225 billion by 2020 (NASSCOM, 2012). The share of IT/ITeS sector in GDP increased from less than 2 per cent in 2000-01 to 8 per cent in 2012-13 (NASSCOM, 2013). The export of C&I services has come to occupy a major share of 65 per cent of India's total commercial service exports in 2009 from a share of 44 per cent in 2000, indicating the country's growing competitive advantage in the delivery of such services. This phenomenal growth has come about with India's rise as a major outsourcing hub on account of its proficient, technically skilled and cost-effective human capital base (Ghibutiu and Dumitriu, 2008) and the technological development, globalisation and liberalisation of domestic markets (Satija and Mukherjee, 2013). The software and IT services sector is also gaining momentum in Korea with an average annual growth rate of 36.5 per cent.[13] The sector contributed

12. IT services are those services that are directly related to computer software/hardware. For example, providing custom software will be classified as an IT service. An ITeS is one that uses computers/telecommunications systems to provide the service for a non-IT field such as banking, finance, etc. Some of the examples of ITeS are medical transcription, back-office accounting, processing of insurance claims, credit card processing. Business process outsourcing (BPO) involves the contracting of operations and responsibilities of specific business functions (or processes) to a third-party service provider. It can be back office outsourcing (such as accounting) or front office outsourcing (customer-related services). BPO services are often termed as ITeS-BPO services because it indicates the provision of BPO services using IT services.

13. Korea Software Industry Association (KOSA).

around 8-8.5 per cent to GDP during 2003-2009. The IT sector's exports increased from US$ 284 billion in 2005 to US$ 364 billion in 2009 (National Information Technology Promotions Agency, 2010). Embedded software industry holds the largest share of 88.3 per cent (Electronics and Telecommunications Research Institute, Korea, 2010), followed by IT service and packaged software with a share of 10.1 per cent and 1.6 per cent respectively.

The availability of a skilled labour force, a large unsaturated market and government support in the form of export promotion schemes and incentives have had a positive impact on foreign direct investment (FDI) inflow into the IT/ITeS sector in India. Cumulative FDI inflows in computer services (including hardware and software) from April 2000 to February 2012 were US$ 12.6 billion, which accounted for 7 per cent of the total FDI inflows.[14] In order to bolster the growth of the industry and attract more investments, India allowed 100 per cent FDI through the automatic route[15] in various segments of the industry in 2008 with the implementation of the Information Technology Act (Amendments) 2008. The FDI statistics (DIPP, n.d.) show that Samsung India Software Operations is one of the Korean companies, which has made investment worth US$ 8 million in data processing and software development services. Samsung has set up its R&D centre in India and has employed about 3,000 engineers and experts (Confederation of Indian Industry, 2011) LG has also gained a presence in electronic services and has set up an R&D centre in India.

Given the importance of the IT/ITeS industry and its growth trends in both India and Korea, there exist numerous possibilities for cooperation. The IT/ITeS sector is highly skill intensive. India has a huge pool of English-speaking skilled labour while Korea has a shortage of English-speaking professionals. The expansion of knowledge-based industries, especially ICT, in Korea has led to an increase in the demand for English-speaking highly skilled IT professionals. As a result, a majority of Korean companies are turning to foreign talent to meet their

14. Department of Industrial Policy and Promotion (DIPP) Factsheet on Foreign Direct Investment for April 2000 to March 2012.

15. FDI is allowed through two routes in India: automatic route under which foreign investors are not required to take any approvals from the government and the Foreign Investment Promotion Board (FIPB) route, under which the foreign investor is required to take an approval.

staffing requirements in the IT industry. India with a young and qualified manpower complements the increasing skill requirements of the Korean IT industry. This complementarity can be synergised by allowing easy cross-border movement of IT/ITeS professionals. The CEPA allows for the movement of business visitors as well as intra-corporate transferees. The positive list of professionals under CEPA for movement of independent professionals and contractual service suppliers also includes IT consultants, computer system designers and analysts, database consultants, and many more IT-related professions under which people from both countries can move across borders to render their services.

Over a period, Indian companies has moved up the value chain from being mere application development and maintenance units to becoming strategic partners providing testing, infrastructure, and consulting and system integration services to their customers, enabling customers to expand their operations across different geographies (Satija and Mukherjee, 2013). The Indian IT/ITeS sector has become the country's premier growth engine, crossing significant milestones in terms of revenue growth, employment generation and value creation. At the same time, Korean software firms are also engaged in providing sophisticated and innovative IT products and solutions such as gaming and smart-phone applications, defence robotics control platforms and 'green' energy software applications to their clients. This difference in product segments can be another area of partnership where companies can set up operations in the partner country for service delivery. India can provide a platform to Korean firms for catering to third world countries and Korea can provide a platform to Indian firms to cater to the innovative solution requirements of Asian, European and American technology companies. Korean firms can invest in India and set up operations to cater to the surging domestic demand for services like government, banking, retail, travel, transportation, etc. Satija and Mukherjee (Ibid.) note that with the evolution of the Indian domestic market from a captive dominated market structure to third party transformational outsourcing relationships, there is an increase in domestic demand for software services. With the India-EU Broad-based Trade and Investments Agreement (BTIA) and India-Taiwan Economic Co-operation Agreement (ECA) negotiations in process, Korea needs to act fast in its engagements with the Indian IT industry to avoid competitive pressure and gain a major share of the market.

The government of Korea is also investing in digitising its services and adopting cloud computing. For instance, the Ministry of Public Administration and Security is investing in cloud technologies for national computing resources and the Ministry of Knowledge Economy has launched a study on how to combine green IT with cloud platforms. Korea has put in place a successful e-governance project that has enabled it to gain the top position on the E-Government Development Index,[16] conducted under the UN Global E-Government Survey (2010). Its exports of e-government solutions surpassed US$ 200 million on the basis of its leading position in the evaluation of e-governments by the UN. On the other hand, although there is an increase in the use of IT in the delivery of Indian government services, the process is still at a nascent stage of digitisation. Indian government departments and agencies have not yet resorted to usage of advanced technologies like cloud computing. The Indian and Korean government can collaborate to adopt best digitised practices and software programmes in the delivery of their services.

There are also complementarities between the Indian software industry and the Korean hardware and manufacturing industry.[17] Korea has a comparative advantage in microelectronics and semiconductor production. This expertise can be leveraged with Indian software development with a specific focus on applications like telecom software, broadband networking solutions, banking and insurance, multimedia and system integration, etc. Furthermore, Korea can also take advantage of India's advanced and developed BPO services. Korean software industry is engaged in providing specialised vertical-specific application packages for industries such as autos, pharmaceuticals, healthcare and financial services. Part of this process can be outsourced to India. India can also benefit from Korean IT

16. E-Government Development Index, compiled by the United Nations, is a measure of the capacity and willingness of a country to use e-government for ICT-led development. Along with an assessment of the website development patterns in a country, the E-Government Development Index incorporates the access characteristics, such as the infrastructure and educational levels, to reflect how a country is using information technologies to promote access and inclusion of its people. E-Government Development Index is a composite index comprising the web measure index, the Telecommunication Infrastructure index and the Human Capital index (*http://www.un.org/en/development/desa/publications/connecting-governments-to-citizens.html*).

17. *http://www.kdcstaffs.com/it/main_view.php?mode=view&nNum=5126&parts=Country*

services such as cloud computing, mobile computing and social networking. As new cloud computing offerings increase demand from companies, the need for investments in data centres will also rise. This can be another opportunity for Indian investors. In a geographical context, while India can serve as a regional hub for Korean companies targeting the South Asian market, Korea can serve as a hub for Indian companies targeting the North and North-Eastern Asian market.

While trade possibilities appear to be immense, the requirement of local presence by Korea for trade in Mode 1 can be a possible barrier. It can hinder businesses as the financial cost of enterprises providing only cross-border services will increase if they are mandatorily required to establish office and hire staff in Korea. Another significant barrier for Indian software and BPO entities interested in doing business in Korea will be language.

Transportation

In this section, transportation and logistics are used interchangeably based on the definition of 'transportation' services in the *IMF BoP Manual* (1993). Transportation forms part of the larger logistics sector. The demand for transportation and logistics sector[18] services is derived from its synergy with other economic activities that expand as a country moves up the growth trajectory. With an increase in goods trade, India invested heavily in developing its logistics and transportation sector. It was ranked 8th in the WTO list of top 15 leading exporters of transportation services in 2011 (International Trade Statistics 2012, WTO). At present, the transport sector contributes significantly to India's GDP (around 6.4% in 2007-08) and accounts for a substantial part of FDI inflow (around US$ 16 billion in 2000-10).[19] In 2010, the industry was estimated at US$ 80 billion; it is expected to grow at a compound annual growth rate (CAGR) of approximately 15-20 per cent over the next three to five years *vis-à-vis* the average world logistics industry growth of 10 per cent, reaching revenues of

18. Logistics services include integration of information, transportation, inventory, warehousing, material handling and packaging. However, the *IMF BoP Manual* (fifth edition) and WTO service sector classifications list logistics services such as warehousing and cargo handling as auxiliary services under transportation services. For the purpose of the paper, we have used the larger definition of logistics, which encompasses transportation and thus, the two terms have been used interchangeably.

19. FDI Statistics, DIPP, Ministry of Commerce, Government of India.

about US$ 385 billion by 2015 (Fitch Ratings, 2012). This growth is likely to increase when new reform measures such as FDI in multi-brand retail and implementation of goods and services tax (GST) are introduced.

Korea has a well-developed transportation and logistics infrastructure, comparable to that of many other OECD (Organisation for Economic Cooperation and Development) countries.[20] Huge investment inflows and attractive government incentives have contributed greatly to this. Korea was ranked 5th in the WTO list of top 15 leading exporters of transportation services in 2011 (International Trade Statistics 2012, WTO). Valued at US$ 84 billion, the sector accounts for 6.1 per cent of GDP and is expected to reach 10 per cent of GDP by 2015. The Korean transportation sector is equipped with world-class airports and seaports, a well-organised highway network, multi-modal cargo terminals and logistics complexes. Korea had a high index value of 101.7 in 2012 on the UNCTAD Liner Connectivity Index, indicating its excellent connectivity with the global shipping network, and was ranked 23rd in the World Bank Logistics Performance Index.

In India, despite the inflow of huge investments from both domestic as well as international sources, demand is still unmatched by an equivalent supply of logistics services. It had a low index value of 41.3 in 2012 on the UNCTAD Liner Connectivity Index[21] and was ranked 47th by the World Bank Logistics Performance Index[22] (2010), indicating a huge

20. India is not a member of the OECD countries.

21. UNCTAD Liner Shipping Connectivity Index captures how well countries are connected to global shipping networks. Its computation is based on five components of the maritime transport sector: number of ships, their container-carrying capacity, maximum vessel size, number of services, and number of companies that deploy container ships in a country's ports. For each component, a country's value is divided by the maximum value of each component in 2004, the five components are averaged for each country, and the average is divided by the maximum average for 2004 and multiplied by 100. The index generates a value of 100 for the country with the highest average index in 2004.

22. World Bank Logistics Performance Index (LPI) is an interactive benchmarking tool created to help countries identify the challenges and opportunities they face in their performance on trade logistics and what they can do to improve their performance. It is based on a worldwide survey of operators on the ground (global freight forwarders and express carriers), providing feedback on the logistics 'friendliness' of the countries in which they operate and those with which they trade. They combine in-depth knowledge of the countries in which they operate with informed qualitative assessments of other countries with which they trade, and experience of the global logistics environment.

demand-supply gap in logistics services. Indian logistics costs are among the highest in the world at about 10-20 per cent of GDP and 14 per cent of the total value of goods. Since India is not a single market, there are several impediments to intra-state movement of goods. These high costs are attributable to infrastructure bottlenecks, a multi-layered tax regime, delays in processing documents and other inefficiencies that are a part of doing business in the economy (Deloitte, n.d.).

Given India's increasing demand for integrated logistics infrastructure and Korea's expertise in supplying it, there is a strong possibility of expansion in trade and investment between the two countries.

The Indian government has been actively pursuing proactive policies and providing tax incentives over the last decade to boost the industry and attract investments. Under the automatic route, 100 per cent FDI is allowed in services such as ports and harbour services, storage and warehousing services, and transport and transport services. Currently, over 70 per cent of the world's top 50 logistics firms have a presence in India and are providing freight forwarding services, having entered the market through a variety of modes including acquisitions, joint ventures (JVs), and the establishment of local subsidiaries (KPMG, 2011). However, Indian FDI statistics show that the transportation and logistics sector is not amongst the top five sectors attracting investments from Korea.[23] There are very few Korean logistics and cargo firms with presence across India providing services such as freight forwarding, customs clearance, warehousing, domestic air freight, cargo marking, door-to-door delivery, etc.[24] According to a recent survey on the management of domestic logistics businesses in foreign markets conducted by the Korean Chamber of Commerce and Investment,[25] a majority of firms select and base their businesses in foreign logistics markets based on its growth potential. Given that India is likely to invest a cumulative amount of US$ 1 trillion under the ongoing Twelfth Five Year Plan (2012-2017) to develop an organised logistics market and

23. The DIPP note "FDI Synopsis on South Korea" dated February 28, 2011, shows that the top five sectors attracting FDI from South Korea are metallurgy, automobile, industrial machinery, electronics and electrical equipment.

24. The Korea Desk webpage on DIPP.

25. *http://english.korcham.net/sub02/report_view.asp?nKey=1424&searchfield=&searchtext=*

meet the demand for integrated logistics infrastructure solutions, India can prove to be a strong potential market for Korean logistics and freight firms.

The significant presence of various other Korean businesses such as Hyundai, Samsung, etc., in Indian destinations, especially Chennai, has also led to an increase in demand for direct flights between the two countries. Currently, India's international carriers—Air India and Jet Airways—have direct flights to Seoul. Air India also signed a code-sharing agreement[26] with Asiana Airways[27] in 2012 which allows both airlines to share flight codes by each other on the India-South Korea (Seoul) and *vice versa* sectors, on a free flow basis.[28] This development is indicative of the facilitation of trade relations between India and Korea as it ensures direct connectivity of different Indian destinations with Seoul.

With CEPA in place, Indian businesses can also take advantage of Korea's well-connected logistics network. Korea operates as an international logistics hub for north-eastern Asia and offers frequent sea and air transport services to and from some of the key regions of the world such as north-eastern China, the western coastal areas of Japan and the far eastern region of Russia. The world's major marine transportation channels i.e., the European, American, Southeast Asian, Korea-China and Korea-Japan routes are directly connected to Korea's seaports. Its Incheon International Airport[29] (handling the world's second largest international air cargo volume) and Busan Port[30] (world's fifth busiest container port) are amongst the world's leading international trade gateways. Indian businesses can use Korea's airports and seaports to participate in efficient supply chains that connect a large number of cities within Northeast Asia.

26. Code-share is a business arrangement where two or more airlines share the same flight. A seat can be purchased on one airline but the flight is actually operated by a co-operating airline under a different flight number or code.

27. Asiana Airways is a major South Korean airline.

28. *http://www.airindia.com/SBCMS/Webpages/air_india_and_asiana_airways_April_29_2012.aspx*

29. Incheon airport provides an extensive network connecting 172 cities in 53 countries *via* 67 airlines.

30. Busan Port is the largest trans-shipment port in northeast Asia. Located on the world's main marine transportation route, the port handles more than 13 million TEU (Twenty Feet Equivalent Unit which represents a unit for containers) annually through an active exchange with 500 ports in 100 countries. It handles a massive volume of transhipment to China and Japan.

Korea has come to be known for its competent customs clearance system. According to the World Bank's evaluation of customs-related administrative services for 2009, South Korea was ranked 8th among 183 countries. India, on the other hand, has a complicated and corrupt customs clearance system, which raises the cost of doing business considerably. India can counter this problem by collaborating with Korea to put in place a customs clearance system similar to Korea's UNI-PASS, which is the world's best one-stop logistics information and customs clearance system enabling export clearance within 2 minutes, import clearance within 2.5 minutes, customs drawbacks within 5.2 hours and tax payment within 10 hours.[31] Through the pre-declaration system in UNI-PASS, importers can obtain complete clearance before entry into the port. If India implements a similar system, it will ease customs procedures, increase the capacity of ports and airports to handle cargo, and stop evasion of duty considerably, decreasing the loss to the exchequer.

Once new reform measures such as FDI in multi-brand retail and GST are implemented, the demand for third party logistics (3PL) is likely to surge. According to industry estimates, 3PL solutions are slated to grow at a CAGR of over 20 per cent in India by 2015. Aiming to develop strong supply chain networks, companies are readily looking to outsource their logistics requirements to improve efficiency and delivery of services to the end customers (Deloitte, n.d.). The Korean logistics industry has a fast-growing 3PL logistics business. Its logistics companies provide 3PL services solutions to businesses all over the world. India can be another potential market for such Korean companies, which can get the first mover advantage by engaging in partnership with Indian logistics firms. Further, the Korean firms can go beyond the conventional supply chain perspective of ensuring movement of goods to providing reverse logistics[32] as well. As a part of their regular goods supply chain, Indian manufacturers are also looking to outsource their entire reverse logistics flow to a 3PL.

---

31. Korea Trade and Investment Promotion Agency.

32. Reverse logistics includes failed components repaired to serve as spare parts, unsold stock being recovered, old products improved to meet latest standards, reusable material returned and refilled/re-developed along with response to customer query, a suitable system to collect old products from a customer and if possible, to replace it with a new product, etc. Reverse product flows may generate value on a product, component or material level.

Korea can also gain from India in this sector. By 2020, the Korean government aims to strengthen the domestic software-oriented logistics system to promote the efficiency of the national logistics system. This could be another area of collaboration, where Korea can engage with Indian IT-services firms. Thus, Korean logistics and transportation companies can outsource their IT-related operations to India, while India can allow Korean logistics companies to set up operations in India to support the growing need for infrastructure.

Although the Indian logistic industry is in its infancy and there is potential for growth, it is plagued by significant regulatory barriers that make it unattractive for investments. Given the high-cost low-margin nature of the business, the problem for organised players in the industry is compounded by the existence of unfair competition from unorganised players. These unorganised players are often able to provide services at competitive prices by getting away without paying taxes and without following operating norms under the Motor Vehicles Act. The high cost of operations and delays caused by cumbersome documentation requirements of different states make the business unattractive (Mishra, n.d.). Poor physical and communications infrastructure is another deterrent to attracting investments. There is also lack of IT penetration in the sector, which restricts seamless flow of information. Lack of transparency in the cost structure and poor service delivery are other problems in this sector. These issues need attention to encourage more public-private partnerships in the sector.

Construction Services

Given its contribution to infrastructure, transfer of technology and attaining socioeconomic development objectives, the construction service sector is considered vital to development. In India and Korea, this sector accounted for 8.2 per cent and 11 per cent of GDP respectively in 2008-09 and contributed significantly to employment and foreign exchange earnings.

In India, the construction industry is the second largest contributor to GDP after the agriculture sector. It employs a workforce of nearly 32 million, half of which are women, and its market size is worth about US$ 45 billion.[33] The sector has been growing between 9 and 11 per

33. Construction Industry Development Council, Government of India.

cent year-on-year because of heightened industrialisation, urbanisation and economic development. The DIPP[34] data show that the construction industry is the second largest sector in terms of FDI inflows with a cumulative FDI inflow of 12 per cent during 2000-2012.[35] A report by EC Harris Research (2011) estimates that the growth rates for the construction industry is likely to exceed overall GDP growth over the next 2 years, underlying a continued strong demand.

In the global construction market, India is ranked 12th and accounts for 17.5 per cent of the US$ 3.4 trillion global market. According to a global economic survey, India is ranked the sixth fastest growing country in terms of construction (Ministry of Commerce, Government of India).[36] Overseas construction occupied an important position in India's export portfolio after the early 1970s with the spurt in construction activity in the oil-exporting region of the Middle East. The thrust of India's project export bids has exhibited a significant shift towards cash-terms projects, and multilaterally funded overseas projects (MFPO).[37] There is growing emphasis on competitive pricing and aggressive strategic marketing by Indian construction companies for securing contracts. Contracts secured in recent years have been quite diverse in nature, indicating the growing versatility and technological capabilities of Indian project exporters. Regions that continue to be potential markets for the Indian construction sector include Asia (South, West and East), Africa, Middle East, Russia, the CIS (Commonwealth of Independent States) and Latin America.

The Korean overseas construction industry has grown rapidly in the last four decades and in particular, in the last five years. According to the Ministry of Land, Transportation, and Maritime Affairs and the Korea Institute of Construction Technology, the Korean construction industry was ranked 7th in 2012 among 23 national construction industries in terms of global competitiveness compiled by them. This rise in the ranking of the

---

34. DIPP uses NIC definition, which means that construction sector includes goods and services pertaining to the real estate sector.
35. DIPP FDI Factsheet from April 2000 to December 2012, available at *http://dipp.nic.in/English/Publications/FDI_Statistics/2012/india_FDI_December2012.pdf*. The data use DIPP FDI data base and considers equity capital components only.
36. *http://commerce.nic.in/annual2004-05/englishhtml/lesson-11.htm* accessed on October 13, 2013.
37. Ministry of Commerce.

Korean construction industry can be attributed to the continuous increase in overseas construction. By region, the Middle East accounts for the largest share of 60 per cent followed by the Asian market with a share of 30 per cent. By construction type, plant construction orders account for the largest share of 54 per cent of cumulative overseas orders.

However, growth in this sector has been volatile and has seen a slump in recent years in both countries due to a rise in material costs, higher interests outgo and declining profit margins.[38] But given infrastructure and real estate needs, trade in this sector has soared as government and private sector companies collaborate through public-private partnership (PPP) models to bridge the gap.

Trade in this sector takes place mostly under Mode 3 (commercial presence in the form of FDI, joint ventures, etc.) and Mode 4 (movement of natural persons). With the advancement in IT and communication, cross-border supply of services (Mode 1) has become an important component of trade in this sector. But given the capital-intensive nature of the service, the requirement of specific skills and technical know-how, and the strong client-oriented focus of these services, the bulk of trade in this sector continues to take place through commercial presence and movement of natural persons (Mukherjee, 2001).

Data for India's inward FDI show that construction is not amongst the leading sectors attracting FDI from Korea. Investments by Korean firms in construction activities in India are limited when compared to investment in other industries (such as automobiles, metallurgical industry, electronics, etc). As India prepares to bridge the demand and supply gap in infrastructure by investing a cumulative amount of US$ 1 trillion under the ongoing Twelfth Five Year Plan (2012-2017), it presents opportunities for Korean firms to make investments in the construction sector and collaborate with Indian construction firms. While India has an abundance of unskilled and semi-skilled workers, Korea has experience in exporting construction services in developing countries.

Construction was accorded 'industry' status in 2000 in India, following which a number of initiatives in infrastructure related projects on PPP basis were undertaken. This resulted in an increase in private ownership

38. *Economic Survey of India*, 2011-12.

of build-operate-transfer (BOT), build-operate-own-transfer (BOOT) and build-operate-lease-transfer (BOLT) projects. Indian private construction majors have been engaging with foreign construction and real estate companies for project financing, technical assistance and management support. Korea, with its rich experience in overseas construction projects, can play an active role by participating in these projects. The potential for this collaboration is particularly large in urban infrastructure, mass rapid transport system (MRTS) and water management. Moreover, FDI up to 100 per cent is allowed under the automatic route for townships, housing, built-up infrastructure and construction of development projects. Many Indian states such as Haryana and Gujarat are also taking significant steps towards industrial development.

Statistics show that apart from large Korean enterprises, even small and medium Korean construction firms are engaged in overseas construction activity. To bolster the overseas construction industry, the Korean government has provided initiatives to ease financing of projects and the entry of SMEs into foreign construction markets. With the Korean government aiming to make Korea one of the five powerhouses in the overseas construction industry by 2014, the Ministry of Land, Transport and Maritime Affairs (MLTM) is likely to reinforce its support and policies (Choi, 2012). It is planning to expand the number of professional workers it fosters and to allocate 150 billion won for the water industry to support companies advancing into developing countries. This is in addition to the 400 billion won global infrastructure fund formed in 2010. MLTM has also listed India in its priority list of core partners for the upcoming financial year where it will focus on providing financial and diplomatic assistance to companies bidding for overseas projects in these countries (Ibid.). This effort will strategically push forward Korea's plans to boost overseas construction projects in India.

International trade in construction is subject to a plethora of regulatory barriers and institutional constraints which are applied not only at the national but also at regional and local levels (Mukherjee, 2001). World Bank's *Doing Business Report 2012* shows that while India is among the top countries in terms of housing and work space needs, it is ranked 181st in construction permission processes. There are 34 procedures and the average time taken is 227 days. Therefore, in order to make most of its prospective collaboration with Korea in construction sector, India will have to ease some of its regulatory barriers pertaining to land acquisition that require approvals from multiple agencies (such as central and state government ministries), high stamp duty and cumbersome paper procedures. While India has eased some of the barriers related to land acquisition through the recent Land Acquisition Bill, the cumbersome procedures that construction companies will have to undergo to acquire land from farmers can pose a problem and make investments unattractive in the sector. Despite the existence of these challenges, India can still prove to be a huge investment opportunity to Korean construction firms to set up projects and engage in collaborations for infrastructure development. Both countries signed a Civil Cooperation Agreement on July 26, 2011, after which Korea has already asked India to allot land for its nuclear industry to build power plants in which it specialises (Roche, 2012). Korean firms have also shown interest in building the Dighi port and in the Delhi-Mumbai Industrial Corridor (DMIC).

Audio-Visual Services

Audio-visual services include services and fees related to the production of motion pictures, radio and television programmes, and musical recordings. The *IMF BoP Manual* (1993) categorises audio-visual services under personal, cultural and recreational services, but the WTO Services Sectoral Classification List (MTN.GNS/W/120) based on the UNCPC, which is used for the purpose of making commitments, lists audio-visual services as a sub-sector of communication services. Since this paper uses the former classification to compute the RCA index, we assume that the audio-visual service is a sub-category of personal, cultural and recreational services.

Neither India nor Korea has a comparative advantage in personal, cultural and recreational services. The CEPA, however, focuses on audio-visual services through a separate chapter in which the two countries have agreed to sign a co-production agreement. According to the agreement, India and Korea will collaborate to produce films and audio, animation, TV programmes, etc., to strengthen cultural ties. The co-production agreement accords national treatment with concomitant national benefits (including government support) to products of the partner country. The agreement enables not just easy access to finance but also ensures transfer of technology, investment in infrastructure and increased market access.

Films, music and entertainment programmes produced in India and Korea have gained huge popularity and appreciation from audiences around the globe. The industry is expanding and engaging in providing a variety of services to international production studios. Even during the 2008 financial crisis, the Indian media and entertainment (M&E) industry managed to grow at a rate of 11 per cent from US$ 12.9 billion in 2009 to US$ 14.4 billion in 2010.[39] A recent report by the Federation of Indian Chambers of Commerce and Industry (FICCI) and KPMG states that with the increase in per capita consumption of entertainment, the industry is slated to grow at CAGR of 14 per cent to reach US$ 28.1 billion in 2015.[40] Factors such as high demand for India-specific products (both domestically and from non-resident Indians (NRIs), and other South Asian markets) increase in the export of television content and films and availability of high-skilled labour at competitive prices have contributed to the growth of the sector.

For Korea, the sector gained significance with the beginning of its flagship 'Korean Wave,' an initiative to promote South Korean culture across Asia by way of export. The country was the ninth largest exporter and importer of audio-visual services in 2008.[41] Its export of audio-visual and related services increased from US$ 13 million in 2000 to US$ 208 million in 2008. Imports during the same period increased from US$ 79 million to US$ 346 million. The country has the fifth largest film industry and is a pioneer of TV *via* mobile devices and the internet.

While the Indian audio-visual sector has prospered mainly through the efforts of private entrepreneurs with the government playing the role of only a facilitator, the Korean Government has played a pivotal role in promoting its entertainment industry by way of a wide range of funding and protectionist policies. For instance, to promote the film industry, the

39. *http://www.indiainbusiness.nic.in/industry-infrastructure/service-sectors/media-entertainment.htm*
40. *http://www.ficci.com/PressRelease/755/press-21mar-entertainment.pdf*
41. Table III.40, WTO (2010).

Korean Film Council maintains a film development fund of approximately US$ 430 million, of which the government contributes US$ 172 million.[42]

Mukherjee *et al.* (2007) point out that other than providing access to subsidised finance, a co-production treaty signed with one country permits both parties to avail of the advantages of co-production treaties with other countries that the respective countries may have. India presently has a co-production agreement with France, Brazil, Germany, New Zealand, Italy, UK, Poland and Spain. Korea has a co-production agreement with New Zealand, EU and France, under which it grants benefits such as screen quota and selective financial support for production and distribution to co-produced products. While Korea can avail of the benefits of other co-production agreements signed by India, India already has a co-production treaty with Korea's co-production treaty partners. Moreover, India is one of the few countries to take MFN exemption under GATS that allows it to offer preferential treatment to motion pictures and television programmes from countries with which it has a co-production agreement (Ibid.). This move was driven by the objective to promote cultural exchange and was applicable for an unspecified period of time.

Once the terms and conditions of a co-production agreement between India and Korea are negotiated, both the countries will be able to benefit through cooperation in different streams and production stages (pre-production, production and post-production) of the entertainment industry. India and Korea have a huge audience with exposure to international channels and movies. The conclusion of negotiation between the two countries would entitle the joint product for national treatment and will facilitate temporary migration and import of equipment within existing regulations.

Sub-sectors such as animation, films and television are likely to benefit the most from this collaboration. Korea has a vast (valued at US$ 0.9 billion in 2008 with more than US$ 80 million worth of exports) and technological advanced animation industry producing original cartoons and animations. The Indian animation industry, though close to the Korean industry in terms of market size (valued at US$ 0.5 billion in 2009), is primarily engaged in catering to the demands of domestic

42. Korean Film Council (KOFIC): *http://www.koreanfilm.or.kr/jsp/kofic/intro.jsp*

end-user segments (such as feature films, television programmes, advertisements and commercials, and computer games), and processing outsourced work of various international studios (especially from the US) and gaming companies. A co-production agreement between the two countries will enable Indian and Korean companies to collaborate and engage in all activities from pre-production to post-production. While Korean animators can work on innovation and content, Indian animators can provide production and post-production services. At the same time, the collaboration can provide Indian companies with both human and financial capital to venture into high-quality animations such as 3D, 4D and other new animation types for the new age.

The film industry in both India (the second largest in the world) and Korea (fifth largest in the world) is well developed across the value chain, from development to exhibition. While domestic films have been a prime source of entertainment in both countries, the emergence of multiplexes has increased the demand for foreign cinema including films, documentaries and short movies. The India-Korea co-production agreement entitles co-produced products to avail of the benefits provided to local firms such as financing and screen space in movie theatres in accordance with screen quotas. Korea has given similar benefits under its co-production agreements with New Zealand and France. The Korean government recently launched a support and incentive programme for both domestic and international film-makers filming in Korea.This will benefit the Indian company participating in the co-production agreement[43] who can partner with Korean companies to select, get permissions and shoot in Korean locations.

The television broadcasting sector is of high importance to both India and Korea, contributing significantly to the entertainment and media industry. There has been a rapid development of this sector in both the countries following changes in regulatory regimes and the adoption of liberal policies. With the co-production agreement in place, broadcasters from both the countries can showcase programmes in each other's language

43. Recently, Indian film distribution house Eros International Plc. signed a multi-film agreement with Korea's second largest mobile carrier KT Corp. to showcase 50 of its film titles on multiple digital platforms. Under the arrangement, KT Corp through its Olleh TV will showcase 50 films from Eros's library on a revenue sharing basis. With a strong slate of film titles under its banner, Eros recently listed its unit Eros International Media Ltd. on the Bombay Stock Exchange (BSE).

to promote cultural ties. As India is becoming a content exporter, many Indian broadcasters are now catering to the requirements of local audiences around the world. By producing programmes for the local Korean audience, Indian enterprises can utilise the development fund and improve the exisitng production facilities. Korea maintains a comprehensive system of providing information to 47 countries on overseas broadcasting and communication business activities to companies intending to engage in such activities. The Indian advertising industry can also enter Korea as regulations in advertising have been eased. Similarly, Koreans can export some of their popular dramas to be telecast in India. Korea can continue to provide India with technical consulting services to encourage import of Korean technologies and services. Further, Indian agencies and authorities can learn from Korean broadcasting and communications policies that have made Korea a broadcasting and communications powerhouse. Korea has bigger industries than any other nation in the communications technology segments like digital multimedia broadcasting, digital TV, etc.

To enhance cooperation in this sector, the FICCI and Korea Creative Content Agency (KOCCA)[44] signed a Memorandum of Understanding (MoU) in 2011. The agreement specified that the two countries would cooperate on overseas marketing of Indian and Korean content in each country and exchange information, statistical data and expertise about the Indian and Korean content market. Further, the two would collaborate in educating and training professionals of the content industry and organise events such as seminars, conferences, stakeholder consultations, etc. This MoU is valid for five years and at the end of the period, the organisations will discuss and extend it further if required.

However, to promote the Korean animation industry, the Korean Government has put in place a broadcasting quota (under the Korean Broadcasting Act) for domestic animation to provide the industry with opportunities to promote domestic animation through the TV network. Foreign animation is restricted to only 55 per cent and 65 per cent of

44. KOCCA under the Ministry of Culture, Sports and Tourism, Government of Korea, is an agency dedicated to promoting all areas of media and entertainment including broadcasting, film, gaming and animation. It is responsible for providing a comprehensive support system to nurture the industry along with conducting various support businesses to help M&E corporations and aims to make Korea one of the top five content powerhouses in the world.

all animation content for terrestrial and cable and satellite broadcasts respectively. This is an area of contention, which has not been discussed in the MoU signed between FICCI and KCCA in 2011. The quota can prove to be a hindrance for an Indian company that wishes to broadcast its products in Korea.

Way Forward and Conclusion

With the opening of the global economy and advancement in IT, the significance of the service sector has increased in almost all economies, including India and Korea. This has resulted in the inclusion of this sector in many recent trade liberalisation agreements, including the India-Korea CEPA. In services, both India and Korea have undertaken liberalisation commitments in 11 service sectors along with additional commitments in audio-visual, financial and telecommunication services, and in the movement of natural persons. An analysis of the services sector in the above sections shows that there are strong complementarities in services such as IT, transportation, construction and audio-visual, which can be accentuated by further liberalising trade and movement of natural persons.

Often, the commitments made under these comprehensive trade agreements (CEPA, CECA, FTA and PTA) are more liberal than those made under GATS or the Doha Round. Under the India-Korea CEPA, bilateral commitments have gone beyond the revised offers in the Doha Round with both countries offering more liberal commitments. However, both countries have also imposed some restrictions that hinder trade. Korea has imposed the restriction of local presence in Mode 1 in a number of sub-sectors. India, while being more liberal in its bilateral commitments under the CEPA than in its multilateral commitments under the revised offer, has put some restrictions on foreign participation (Mode 3). These areas of contention must be addressed in the near future to allow free trade.

Nevertheless, the potential benefits that the India-Korea CEPA offers can be increased if issues relating to market barriers are addressed. With the objective of identifying the areas that hold potential for harnessing services trade between India and Korea, this paper attempts to describe the performance and composition of the services sector in both countries, assess liberalisation commitments under CEPA and examine the extent to which these are more liberal than unilateral commitments. In the four sectors selected for qualitative examination, the paper assesses trade possibilities and analyses the exisitng market access barriers. India has a competitive advantage in IT and can provide sophisticated testing, consulting and system solutions to Korean clients. Korea is one of the leading exporters of transportation services with a highly advanced logistics network. India, with a huge demand-supply gap, can synergise with Korean logistics service providers to meet its shortfall. India can also prove to be a huge investment opportunity for Korean construction firms who have garnered rich experience in overseas construction services. With the CEPA in place, the two countries can develop inter-industry linkages to collaborate rather than compete in the future. For instance, Korean logistics and transportation companies can outsource their IT-related operations to India, while India can allow these companies to set up operations in its territory to meet the growing need for infrastructure. Both countries can also promote their culture and heritage through audio-visual services.

Governments, agencies and consulates are taking a number of steps to take advantage of the CEPA and boost trade. To ease movement of people, both countries signed an agreement on visa simplification in March 2012 in the presence of the Indian PM and the Korean President. Korea has also established business centres of Korea Trade and Investment Agency (KOTRA) in New Delhi, Mumbai and Chennai to render support to existing and prospective Korean businesses in India. A number of MoUs and agreements have been signed since 2009 to improve relations in different aspects, including a strategic partnership agreement. An MoU was signed between Defence Research and Development Organisation (DRDO) of India and Defence Acquisition Programme Administration (DAPA) of Korea for cooperation in R&D. To create awareness of Indian culture among Koreans, an Indian Cultural Centre (ICC) was also established in 2011. ICC holds special programmes, yoga classes, cookery lessons and traditional dance training in Korea, catering to popular demand among people.

To realise trade possibilities, both countries will have to address some urgent issues restricting trade. They must work together on expanding the positive list of professionals to include more professions that require greater movement of people. At present, the Indian community in Korea is estimated at only 7500, which includes businessmen, IT professionals, scientists, research fellows, students and workers (Ministry of External Affairs, Government of India).[45] This is much smaller when compared to other countries such as the USA, the UK, Australia and Canada where Indians are present in large numbers.

Another possible barrier in services trade, especially Mode 1, is language. Indians are well versed in English but will have to learn Korean to render services to and in Korea. Similarly, Koreans will have to learn English to do business in India. This barrier will hold for all services requiring communication directly between parties of the two countries.

By pursuing the task of deepening mutual cooperation in areas of mutual interest and taking measures to provide more effective market access by removing substantial barriers to bilateral trade in services, both the countries will benefit by gaining a competitive advantage in the global supply chain. The India-Korea CEPA can go a long way in increasing bilateral flow of services between the two countries.

References

Balassa, B. (1965). "Trade Liberalisation and Revealed Comparative Advantage", *The Manchester School of Economic and Social Studies* 33(2): 99-123.

———. (1977). "Revealed Comparative Advantage Revisited: An Analysis of Relative Export Shares of Industrial Countries, 1953-1971", *The Manchester School of Economic and Social Studies* 45 (4): 327-44.

———. (1979). "The Changing Pattern of Comparative Advantage in Manufactured Goods", *The Review of Economics and Statistics* 61 (2): 259-66.

———. (1986). "Comparative Advantage in Manufactured Goods", *The Review of Economics and Statistics* 68(2): 315-19.

Bank of Korea (2012). "Current Economic and Financial Movements", *Quarterly Bulletin*, Chapter 1, March.

Batra, A. and Z. Khan (2005). "Revealed Comparative Advantage—An Analysis for India and China", *ICRIER Working Paper* 168.

Chanda, R. (2002). *Globalisation of Services—India's Opportunities & Constraints*. New Delhi: Oxford University Press.

Chandra, P. and N. Jain, N. (2007). "The Logistics Sector in India: Overview and Challenges", Indian Institute of Management, *Working Paper* No. 2007-03-07.

Choi J. (2012). "Korea's Overseas Construction Orders Exceed US$ 500 Billion", published on July 10, in Korea.net, *http://www.korea.net/NewsFocus/Business/view?articleId=101184*

45. *http://www.mea.gov.in/Portal/ForeignRelation/India-Korea_ROK__Relations.pdf*, accessed on October 21, 2013.

CMM-I (n.d.), "Trade in Audio Visuals Market: China, Mongolia and South Korea", *Report*, UNESCO.

Confederation of Indian Industry (2011). *South Korea Looks at Punjab as Preferred Investment Destination*.

Crawford, J. and R. Fiorentino, (2005). "The Changing Landscape of Regional Trade Agreements", *Discussion Paper* No. 8. World Trade Organisation,

Deloitte (n.d.) "Logistics and Infrastructure—Exploring Opportunities", last accessed on January 13, 2012, available at *http://www.deloitte.com/assets/Dcom India/Local%20Assets/Documents/aLogistics%20and%20infrastructure%206%20Aug.pdf*

Department of Industrial Policy and Promotion (DIPP) (n.d.), "FDI Synopsis of South Korea", Ministry of Commerce, Government of India, available at *http://dipp.gov.in/English/Investor/Korea_Desk/FDI_Synopsis_KoreaSouth_31August2012.pdf*

———. (2012). "Factsheet on Foreign Direct Investment (FDI) (April 2000 to March 2012)", Department of Industrial Policy and Promotion, Ministry of Commerce, Government of India, last accessed on December 1, 2012, available, at *http://dipp.nic.in/English/Publications/FDI_Statistics/2012/india_FDI_March2012.pdf*

Department of Information Technology (2011). *Annual Report 2010-11*. Ministry of Communication and Information Technology, Government of India.

Dewan P.N. Chopra Consultants Private Limited (n.d.). "The Indian Logistics Industry: An Overview", available at *http://www.dpncindia.com/news/Logistics.pdf*

EC Harris Research (2011). *International Bulletin*. Summer.

FICCI-KPMG (2011). "India Media & Entertainment Industry to Touch US$28 Billion by 2015", *Report*. Available at *http://www.kpmg.com/IN/en/Press%20Release/FICCI_KPMG_M_E.pdf*

Findlay, C. and T. Warren (2000). *Impediments to Trade in Services: Measurement and Policy Implications*. London and New York: Routledge.

Fink, C. and M. Molinuevo (2007a). *Liberalisation of Trade in Services*, World Bank.

———. (2007b). "East Asian Free Trade Agreements in Services: Roaring Tigers or Timid Pandas?", *East Asia and Pacific Region Poverty Reduction and Economic Management Report*, World Bank.

Fitch Ratings (2012).. "2012 Outlook: Indian Logistics Industry", *Report*.

Ghibutiu, A. and I. Dumitriu (2008). "The Effects of Offshoring on Trade in Services—Evidence from Romania", *Working Paper*, European Trade Study Group, available at *http://www.etsg.org/ETSG2007/papers/dumitriu.pdf.*

Hoekman, B. (1995). "An Assessment of the General Agreement on Trade in Services", in Will Martin and L. Alan Winters (eds.), *The Uruguay Round and the Developing Economies*, The World Bank, Cambridge, UK: Cambridge University Press.

Hoekman, B., A. Mattoo and P. English (2002). *Development, Trade and the WTO—A Handbook*. World Bank.

Hufbauer, G. and T. Warren (1999). "The Globalisation of Services: What has happened? What are the Implications?", Peterson Institute for International Economics, *Working Paper*, available at *http://www.piie.com/publications/wp/99-12.pdf*

Hulme-Jones, L. (2011). *South Korea-Telecoms, Mobile, Broadband and Forecasts*, 17th edition. Paul Budde Communication Pty Ltd.

International Monetary Fund (1993). *Balance of Payments Manual*. Last accessed on October 15, 2012, available at *http://www.imf.org/external/pubs/ft/bopman/bopman.pdf*

Interview of Ambassador Nagesh R. Parthasarathi (2008). "Ambassador Explains India's IT Policy", Country Report, *Korea IT Times*.

Invest Korea (2009). *Promising Investment Opportunities—Logistics*.

Investment Technology Promotion Division (2007). "Dynamic Business Partner: Investor Friendly Destination—Media and Entertainment Industry", Ministry of External Affairs, Government of India available, at *http://www.indiainbusiness.nic.in/Book.pdf*

Kathuria, R. (2008). "Prospects for the Telecommunication Sector under the India-EU Trade and Investment Agreement", *Final Report for India-EU BTIA*, Indian Council for Research in International Economic Relations (ICRIER)

Kathuria, R. and M. Kedia (2012). "India: Evolution of Telecommunications and Information Technology since Independence", *Yojna* 56. Publication of Ministry of Information and Broadcasting,

Kim, H. (2001). "The Audiovisual Sector in another Part of the World", *Audiovisual Industry Seminar*, WTO.

Kim, J. and J. Kim (2003). *Liberalisation of Trade in Services and Productivity Growth in Korea*. Conference Volume-NBER, University of Chicago Press, Chapter 6, pp.179-207.

Korea Chamber of Commerce and Industry (2012). "Survey on Management of Domestic Logistics Businesses in Foreign Markets".

Korea Communication Commission (2008 and 2010), *Annual Report*.

———. "KCC Plan for 2011".

KPMG (2011). "Logistics in India", Part 1, 2 and 3, available at *http://storenmove.com/links/news/Logistics-in-India-Part-1.pdf*

Kwak, K. (2009). "Broadcasting Deregulation in Korea", *Academia Paper Series*, available at *http://keia.org/publication/broadcasting-deregulation-south-korea*

Lee, N. and H. Lie (2003). *Korea's Telecom Services Reform through Trade Negotiations*, Conference Volume – NBER, University of Chicago Press, pp.243-281, available at *http://www.nber.org/chapters/c10161.pdf*

Macdonald, S. (2006). "South Korea Braves the Knowledge Economy", *Korea Investment Forum*, available at *http://www.atimes.com/atimes/Korea/HF28Dg03.html*

Michaely, M. (1994). *Trade Preferential Agreements in Latin America: Ex-ante Assessment*. Washington, D.C.: The World Bank Latin America and Caribbean Region, available at *http://www-wds.worldbank.org/servlet/WDSContentServer/WDSP/IB/1996/03/01/000009265_3961019193227/Rendered/PDF/multi0page.pdf*

Ministry of Commerce, Industry and Energy (MOCIE), Korea Trade Investment Promotion Agency (KOTRA) and Deloitte & Touche Corporate Finance (n.d.). *A Guide to Investment in Korea*.

Mishra, S. (n.d.). "Logistics Industry: Global and Indian Perspective", European Business and Technology Centre.

Mukherjee, A. (2001). "Trade in Construction and Consultancy Services: India and the GATS", *ICRIER Working Paper* No. 75.

———. (2003). "Audio-visual Policies and International Trade: The Case of India", *HWWA Report*, Hamburg Institute of International Economics, available at *http://ec.europa.eu/culture/media/media-content/media-mundus/india_2003_en.pdf*

Mukherjee, A., A. Gupta and P. Ahuja (2007). "India-U.S. FTA: Prospects for Audiovisual Services", *Working Paper* No. 192, ICRIER.

Mukherjee, A., S. Ray and D. Rai (2010). "Trade in Services", *India-Turkey FTA Report*, ICRIER.

Mukherjee, A. and S. Miglanib (2010). "Non-tariff Barriers in the Transport and Logistics Sectors: India", *Research Report*, European Business and Technology Centre.

Mukhopadhyay, S. (2002). "Globalisation and Indian Services Sector", *Economic and Political Weekly* 37(40): 4097-8.

NASSCOM (2010). *Strategic Review 2010*.

———. (2012a). "The IT-BPO Sector in India", *Strategic Review 2012*, India.

———. (n.d.) "Indian Animation Market", Fact Sheet.

———. (2013) . "The IT-BPO Sector in India", *Strategic Review 2013*. India.

National Information Society Agency (n.d.). *Global IT Initiatives of Korea*. Republic of Korea.

———. (2010). *Yearbook of Information Society Statistics*, Republic of Korea.

National Information Technology Promotions Agency (2010). *IT Industry Annual Report—2012*, available at *http://www.nipa.kr/eng/boardView.it?boardNo=110&contentNo=1&page=2*, last accessed on November 4, 2012.

Organisation for Economic Cooperation and Development (2000). "Regulatory Reform in Korea", available at *http://www.oecd.org/gov/regulatory-policy/oecdreviewofregulatoryreformkorea.htm*

Park, K. and Y. Kim (2011). *Korea's International Comparative Legal Guide to: Telecommunication Laws and Regulations 2011*. Global Legal Group, Chapter 16, pp.109-15.

Price Waterhouse Coopers (2010). "India Entertainment and Media Outlook 2010", available at *http://www.pwc.com/gx/en/entertainment-media/pdf/PwC_India_EM_Outlook_2010.pdf*

Raipuria, K. (2001). "Service Exports: 'Knowledge Bowl' yet to Yield Major Gains", *Economic and Political Weekly* 36(35): 3351-2.

Rausas, M., J. Manyika, E. Hazan, J. Bughin, M. Chui and R. Sai (2011). *Internet Matters: The Net's Sweeping Impact on Growth, Jobs, and Prosperity*. McKinsey Global Institute.

Rim, K. (2011). "30 Korean Software Worthy of Global Recognition in 2012", *Korea IT Times*, available at *http://www.koreaittimes.com/story/15607/30-korean-software-worthy-global-recognition-2012*

Roche, E. (2012). "India Seeks S Korean Funding for Clean Energy, Infrastructure", *Live Mint*. March 26.

Satija, D. and A. Mukherjee (2013). "Movement of IT Professionals between India and the EU: Issues and the Way Forward", *Working Paper* No. 391, Indian Institute of Management Bangalore.

Sinha, A. (2011). "Banking on Technology", *Reserve Bank of India Bulletin* LXV (6).

Sungeun, S. (2008). "Behind the Korean Broadcasting Boom", *NHK Broadcasting Studies*, Number 6.

Taneja, N., A. Mukherjee, S. Jayanetti and T. Jayawardane (2004). "India-Sri Lanka Trade in Services: FTA II and Beyond", *ICRIER Working Paper* No. 145.

Telecom Regulatory Authority of India (TRAI) (2009-10). *Annual Report*.

Thomas, P. (2003). "GATS and Trade in Audio-Visuals: Culture, Politics and Empire", *Economic and Political Weekly* 38(33): 3485-93.

Trade Policy Report (August 10, 2011), submitted to WTO by Secretariat of India.

Trade Policy Review (August 10, 2011), submitted to WTO by Secretariat of India (WT/TPR/S/249).

UNESCAP "National Policies and Strategies for Infrastructure Development", Chapter III, *Country Infrastructure Reports.*

United States Trade Representative Report, South Korea.

Vaidyanathan, G. (February 2007). "Current Status of Logistics in India", *PIANC Magazine.*

Veluree, M. (n.d.) "Key Success Factors of Korean TV Industry Structure that Leads to the Popularity of Korean TV Dramas in a Global Market", *Journal of East Asian Studies,* available at *http://www.asia.tu.ac.th/journal/EA_Journal2_50/B5.pdf*

Wickramasinghe, U. (2000), "Services Trade as a New Frontier in South Asia: Is Optimism Warranted"? *South Asia Economic Journal*, New Delhi: Sage Publications.

World Bank (2002). "Global Economic Prospects 2002: Making Trade Work for the World's Poor", Washington, DC: The World Bank, available at *http://econ.worldbank.org/external/default/main?pagePK=64165259&piPK=64165421&theSitePK=469382&menuPK=64216926&entityID=000094946_0202020411334*

———. (2012). *World Development Indicators*. Washington DC.

World Trade Organization (2010). "Measuring Trade in Services", *Training Manual*, WTO/OMC.

———. (2011). *World Trade Report 2011.*

———. *(2012). International Trade Statistics. Geneva.*

Websites:

Korea Software Industry Association *(http://www.sw.or.kr/) last accessed on February 2, 2013.*

Electronics and Telecommunications Research Institute, Korea, *http://www.etri.re.kr/eng/,* last accessed on November 14, 2012.

http://dipp.gov.in/English/Investor/Korea_Desk/Resource.aspx, last accessed on June 5, 2013.

http://www.kotra.in/index.jsp

http://www.indembassy.or.kr/BilateralTrade.aspx?Cul=en-US, last accessed on October 20, 2012.

http://www.mofat.go.kr/english/regions/intorganization/wto/index.jsp, last accessed on September 2, 2012.

http://www.ficci.com/PressRelease/755/press-21mar-entertainment.pdf, last accessed on December 17, 2012.

http://www.bok.or.kr/contents/total/eng/boardView.action?boardBean.brdid=10782&boardBean.rnum=1&menuNaviId=744&boardBean.menuid=744&boardBean.cPage=1&boardBean.categorycd=0&boardBean.sdt=&boardBean.edt=&boardBean.searchColumn=&boardBean.searchValue=

http://www.kpmg.com/Global/en/IssuesAndInsights/ArticlesPublications/Documents/Logistics-in-India-Part-2.pdf

http://www.kpmg.com/Global/en/IssuesAndInsights/ArticlesPublications/Documents/Logistics-in-India-Part-3.pdf

11 Past, Present and Prospects of Korean Studies in India

Kim Do-Young

Introduction

The development of Korean studies in India has progressed considerably in the field of academia and culture. Indeed, there has been marked development but there are certain issues that have to be confronted in order to direct meaningful change such as an increase in the numbers of researchers, the need to ensure outstanding quality in terms of area studies, etc. As the Korea-India relationship intensifies, there has been an unprecedented increase in the demand for scholars specialising in the field of Korean studies. The supply of scholars falls well short of demand. In 2013, only 10 institutes under 7 universities in India offered Korean language courses and only 2 major universities out of 567 universities offer courses in the field of Korean studies.

Backdrop for the Development of Korean Studies

In India, the universities offering Korean language course include Jawaharlal Nehru University (JNU), University of Delhi (DU), Magadha University, English and Foreign Language University (EFLU), Manipur University, Central University of Jharkand, Hyderabad University, and three colleges of Delhi University: Daulat Ram College, Delhi College of Arts and Commerce, and Khalsa College, besides one college under Magadha University. The Korean language programme began with a one-year certificate course in 1973 in one university. Today, two institutes offer bachelor's courses, three institutes offer master's courses, one institute offers a post-graduate full-time course, six institutes offer a certificate course, and two institutes have MPhil/PhD programmes.

The Korean studies programme came to be visualised after consulate relations between the two countries was established. Korean studies in India started in the late 1960s when a few Indian students visited Korea to learn the language. Mr R.R. Krishnan and Mr Vipan Chandra, who had studied Chinese studies at the University of Delhi, were among the first scholars to be selected and supported with a three year Korean Government scholarship in 1968. In 1972, Ms Alka Gupta was selected as a scholarship student with support from JNU.

The first faculty appointment in the Korean studies programme at Jawaharlal Nehru University was that of Mr. R.R. Krishnan after the first Vice Chancellor Prof G. Parthasarthy initiated the one-year pre-degree course in the newly established School of Foreign Languages. Internal problems at the university in the early 1980s led to the pre-degree courses being reduced to certificate courses, and consequently, the Korean language programme was downgraded to a certificate course. The course, however, did not attract many students, and in 1989, it was again made into a certificate course. Some time later, it was made into an advanced certificate course.

In 1995, significant development was made possible through the active sponsorship of the Korea Foundation, which donated US$ 45,000 to JNU to employ faculty members. The Korea Foundation also facilitated the appointment of a visiting professor at the department.The Korean language programme was upgraded to a degree programme, accepting 25 students in July 1995. The first batch of 22 students graduated in May 1998. In spite of a crippling national economic crisis in Korea, a master's course in the Korean language was started with support from Prof Kapil Kapoor, the then Dean, and Dr Kim Do-young the same year. Nine students finished their postgraduation two years later, the first in the history of Korean studies in India. These students went on to highly successful careers.

In 2013, the Centre for Korean Studies was made independent of the Centre for Japanese, Korean and North East Asian Studies at the School of Languages at JNU. Currently, the Korean language department with 140 students, five Indian faculty, one Korea Foundation visiting faculty and three Korean guest lecturers is quite large.

Besides, the School of International Studies at JNU also offers Korean studies to students of international relations as part of the area studies programme. The school has awarded 3 PhD and 43 MPhil degree in Korean studies since the programme was first introduced in 1983. The research focus of the programme includes the modern history of Korea, the Korean Peninsula in International Affairs Since 1945, and political and economic development in Korea.

At the Department of Chinese and Japanese Studies in the University of Delhi, a programme to include Korean language and area studies was initiated in 2001 under the guidance of the Department Head, Professor Sreemati Chakrabarti. In 2003, the Korea Foundation concluded a Memorandum of Understanding (MoU) with the university to offer a part-time Korean language course and Visiting Professor Dr Kim Do-young was transferred from JNU to the Univesity of Delhi. Subsequently, the department was renamed the Department of East Asian Studies, with the inclusion of a Korean language certificate course, diploma and advanced diploma in 2004. It offers postgraduate advanced diploma and postgraduate intensive advanced diploma (2 years postgraduate full-time course), MPhil/PhD and a postgraduate course in the Korean language from 2011. The department has approximately 140 students. Three colleges under the University of Delhi—Daulat Ram College, Khalsa College and DCAC—offer certificate, diploma and advanced diploma courses in the Korean language.

In 2010, the University of Delhi also started its MPhil programme in Korean Studies that included Korean language and literature. Five students have enrolled for the course. A two-year full-time master's programme in East Asian Studies has been started to promote comparative as well as area-specific studies of themes and issues that fall within the purview of the various branches of social sciences. Thus far, no other university offers courses in Korean studies in India except JNU and DU.

The basic thrust of the East Asian Studies programme at DU is to equip students with the fundamentals of East Asian civilisation and its dynamics as it unfolded in the ancient, medieval, pre-modern, modern and contemporary periods in order to enable them to pursue and undertake meaningful research on the countries that constitute this region. The focus of Korean studies as part of the master's programme in East Asian Studies is on pre-modern Korea, Korea under Japanese Colonial Rule (1910-1945), political developments in South Korea (1953 to the present), political developments in North Korea (1953 to the present), foreign policy of South Korea (1953 to the present), foreign policy of North Korea (1953 to the present), international economic relations of the two Koreas (1953 to the

Table 11.1

Korean Language Institutes in India

	Programme	*Faculty*	*Total Students*	*Students per Course*
Centre for Korean Studies, JNU, New Delhi	BA (3 years) MA (2 years) MPhil/PhD (7 years)	1 Professor 4 Asst Professor 1 Visiting Professor 3 Guest Faculty	140	BA:98 MA:38 MPhil: 14
Department of East Asian Studies, Delhi University	Korean Postgraduate full-time course (2 years) Certificate (1 year) Diploma (1 year) Advanced Diploma (1 year)	1 Visiting Professor 1 Asst Professor 2 *Ad hoc* Lecturers 4 Guest Lecturers	142	Korean Full-time: 36 Certificate: 60 Diploma: 40 Advanced Diploma: 6
Department of Chinese, Japanese and Korean Studies, English and Foreign Languages University, Hyderabad	Certificate (1 year) Diploma (1 year)	1 Asst Professor	46	Certificate: 36 Diploma: 10
Department of Foreign Language, Manipur University	Certificate (1 year) Diploma (1 year)	1 Asst Professor	30	Certificate: 20 Diploma: 10
Center for Far East Languages, Central University of Jharkhand	BA (3 years) MA (2 years) Certificate (6 months) Diploma (1 year)	2 Asst Professor 1 Guest Lecturer	29	BA: 19 Certificate: 7 Diploma: 3
Centre for Study of Foreign Languages, University of Hyderabad	Certificate (1 year)	1 Guest Faculty	6	Certificate: 6
Centre for Study of Foreign Languages, Magadha University	Certificate (1 year) Diploma (1 year)	1 Guest Lecture	35	Certificate: 20 Diploma: 15

Table 11.2

Korean Study Institutes in India

	Programme	*Faculty*	*Total Students*	*Students per Course*
Centre for East Asian Studies, School of International Studies, JNU, New Delhi	MPhil in Korean Studies PhD in Korean Studies	1 Asst Professor (Political Economy)	15	MPhil: 7 PhD: 8
Department of East Asian Studies, Delhi University	MPhil in East Asian Studies PhD in East Asian Studies	1 Asst Professor (Political Science)	5	MPhil: 5

present), development experience of South Korea (1953 to the present) and development experience of North Korea (1953 to the present).

The Korean language programme started expanding to other regions outside Delhi from the late 2000s. In Bodh Gaya, Magadha Unversity began a one-year certificate and diploma course in Korean studies in 2008. In Hyderabad, the EFLU was the first university in southern India to start certificate and diploma courses in 2009 in the Department of Chinese, Japanese and Korean Studies of the School of Asian Studies. Another central university, Manipur University, began its one-year certificate course (batch of 20 students) and one-year diploma course (batch of 10 students) in 2011 at the Department of Foreign Languages. The Centre for Far East Languages at the Central University of Jharkand offers a six-month certificate course and a one-year diploma course as well as a five-year integrated master's programme. The latest development has been the decision of the Centre for Study of Foreign Languages at the University of Hyderabad to offer a course in Korean studies.

Emergence of Korean Studies Associations

A noteworthy development in the field of Korean studies in India is related to the academic activities of two associations formed in 2007: the Association of Korean Language Educators in India (AKLEI) and Research Association of Study on Korea (RASK).

The AKLEI comprises Korean language specialists from JNU, DU, EFLU, Manipur University, Central University of Jharkhand, etc. Twenty odd Korean language educators of various institutes participate in the AKLEI. This association holds a seminar every year with the help of the Korea Foundation, to contribute to the academic debate on Korean language teaching in India to improve the quality of education and to promote unity among Korean language educators. It has been holding seminars for the last seven years, inviting eminent scholars from Korea and published a collection of papers 'Korean Language in India' in 2008.

Most members of the RASK are from a range of social science fields such as political science, economics, history, sociology, etc., mostly from north Indian universities: JNU, DU, Indian Institute of Technology (IIT), Banaras Hindu University (BHU), Jamia Millia Islamia (JMI), Lucknow University, Central University of Jharkhand, etc. It has been organising seminars for the last seven years with the help of the Korea Foundation. The RASK published a collection of papers by budding researchers, 'Korea in Search of a Global Role,' in 2008. This has helped create a group of scholars who support deeper and stronger Korea-India relations. It will produce another publication titled, 'Deepening India-Korea Relations: Towards a Sustainable Future' in 2014.

Summing up, one can say that in the period between the early 1970s and the early 1980s, there was an initial effort to set up some kind of framework for Korean studies and languages in India. This was also the time when the idea of area studies and language courses in general came to be more defined. It was, however, during the 1990s that there was conspicuous progress in terms of increasing the number of both bachelor's and master's courses in Korean Studies as well as enhancing of the quality of these courses. The new millennium thus started with a good foundation. and subsequently, there has been noticeable structural development in terms of setting up of higher degree programmes and formation of academic associations. The MPhil/PhD in Korean Languges was introduced at the DU and JNU, and five more universities opened various Korean language courses. The AKLEI and RASK were established.

Issues

There are three major issues related to Korean studies in India: the overall academic quality which requires the setting up of a faculty of Korean studies in various universities, improvement in the academic capability of the Korean language faculty and the need for more visiting faculty from Korea.

In the case of Korean area studies, the problem with regard to the availability of faculty is particularly acute. Most universities lack qualified candidates to teach Korean studies. For example, it is a technically impossible feat for one assistant professor to cover all aspects of area studies, which is the case in JNU. Besides, it is also necessary to delink Korean studies from Chinese and Japanese studies. There is also the issue of migration of students who have finished their master's in the Korean language to join Korean studies in the School of International Studies in JNU. There needs to be more stringent eligibility criteria for students wanting to pursue higher courses in social sciences. Further, most visiting faculty sent through various educational institutions in Korea are predominantly language teachers. There is need for a more balanced approach and focus on area studies as well.

For the last 40 years, there has been growth and change in the area of Korean studies in India. However, the presence of only two faculty members for Korean area studies in the entire sub-continent after four decades is woefully inadequate. Given the shortage of qualified faculty in Korean studies, academic quality is bound to suffer. Although the Korean Government has provided scholarships for 40 years, only one Korean study faculty member is available in JNU and another in DU. This points to the dearth of faculty members as well as facilities for language course at the MPhil and PhD levels, making it impossible to nurture professional academicians. The university also points out that currently there is no scholarship available for Korean studies *per se*. In the case of the National Institute for International Education (NIIED) scholarship, area studies students have to compete Korean language students. Therefore, those who are focused on area study face difficulty, whereas Korean languge students enjoy advantages. This results in deterioration in the field of area studies in the long run because of the perception of limited avenues for advancement in comparison to language courses. This might be one of the reasons why there are fewer applicants for area studies.

Secondly, Korean language proficiency as a criterion for teaching cannot be overemphasised. However, Korean language teaching does not require the National Eligibility Test (NET) for becoming a lecturer in India since it is considered a relatively new field. In the absence of clear eligibility conditions, lack of academic capability and linguistic knowledge among those who are not specialised in Korean language is observed. Classes for postgraduate courses are conducted by teachers without a master's in the Korean language. The language programmes need to formalise higher eligibility criteria for the recruitment of teachers possessing a level of language proficiency that can cover the demands of the level of the class that they teach.

Thirdly, native Korean faculty should be allocated and utilised for appropriate positions. There have been multiple occurrences when the existing faculty is not able to cover core courses, which are then passed on to visiting professors. The Korean faculty members have been inadvertently reduced to filling in because Indian faculty often lack the ability to teach the language. It is necessary that the Korean faculty are used to improve the proficiency of the Indian faculty and not just to fill in for them. This is not only a ratio matter but a matter of quality. The faculty may not be able to cover core courses, avoiding them and inevitably leaving it to visiting faculty to handle. Because of the lack of qualified teachers to teach the Korean language, there is little difference in the roles delegated to visiting professors, who are officially sent by the Korea Foundation and other Korean guest lecturers employed on a rolling basis by Indian universities. The role of visiting professors should be channelised into more constructive development of Korean studies by setting up language programmes, improving curricula, guiding higher research courses as well as supporting new academic institutions related to Korea.

To develop the Korean language course as a specialised stream of study, it is necessary to change the institutional structure within which the course is offered. For instance, in DU, the Faculty of Social Sciences, which has academic goals and curricular practice that are vastly different from that needed for a language course, conducts the Korean language course.

Consequently, the language programme tends to get reduced to a subsidiary course in social science studies.

As far as the associations are concerned, neither has yet been registered as a society in India.

Tasks Ahead

First of all, the faculty and researchers for area study should be enhanced. Korean support agencies should be focused on area study development. More visiting faculty should be made available for the programmes, and more scholarships provided to higher studies in the field of area studies. Students from social sciences background may be encouraged to go in for higher area studies, while students from the language programme should be encouraged to undertake a deeper study of linguistic practice and research.

Secondly, faculty holding a master's in the Korean language should be encouraged to study one term in Korea to clear at least Test of Proficiency in Korean (TOPIK) level 5 as a basic prerequisite for teaching.

Third, full fledged university programmes may be maintained with guest lecturers if their roles do not differ in any way from those of the Korean visiting professors and Korean visiting faculty should be assigned to training missions for the long run. Overall, the quality of academic work should be given a higher weight rather than expansion in terms of numbers.

Conclusion

The field of Korean studies in India has developed and expanded over the last four decades. This gradual and positive development may be continued, focusing on improving the quality of the education. Compared to Chinese and Japanese studies in India, Korean studies is still at a relatively nascent stage. Therefore, more universities should be encouraged to open Korean study programmes and faculty members should be encouraged to undertake more research work. While there is great demand for Korean studies, the quality of education provided is less than satisfactory. If more research activity is undertaken and course content is improved considerably, it will help improve quality. Along with this development and transition, it is anticipated that more educational and research institutes in India may set up Korean study programmes and Indian understanding on Korea may be expanded and deepened.

References

Information Brochure 2010-2011, Department of East Asian Studies, University of Delhi.

Office Records, Center for East Asian Studies, Jawaharlal Nehru University.

Office Records. Center for Japanese, Korean and North East Asian Studies, Jawaharlal Nehru University.

The Committee for Commemoration of the 30th Anniversary of Korea-India Diplomatic Relations (2003). *30 Years of Korea-India Relations*. Shingu Publishing Co.

Interview:

Jittendra Uttam, Asst Professor, School of International Relations, Centre for East Asian Studies, Jawaharlal Nehru University.

Kaushal, Asst Professor, Jawaharlal Nehru University.

Lee Hyunkyung, Visiting Professor, Jawaharlal Nehru University.

Neerja Singh, Asst Professor, Jawaharlal Nehru University.

Ravikesh Mishra, Asst Professor, Jawaharlal Nehru University.

Shash Mishra, Asst Professor, Central University of Jharkhand.

Vyjanti Raghavan, Professor, Jawaharlal Nehru University.

12

Looking East: Motivations and Experiences of Indian Students in Korea

Ali Mehdi and Divya Chaudhry

Introduction

One of the most notable aspects of our globalising world is the increasing internationalisation of higher education. According to the UNESCO Institute for Statistics (UIS), the number of international students at the tertiary level has increased by 78 per cent, from 2 million in the year 2000 to 3.6 million in 2010.[1] The United States (US), with 19 per cent of international students, remains the most preferred destination, followed by the United Kingdom (UK) (11%) and Australia (8%). China tops the list of source countries, sending out nearly 16 per cent of international students, followed by India (6%) and the Republic of Korea (4%).

The historical flow of international students, however, has been undergoing a gradual transformation with changing international economic realities and the emerging power dynamics within the structures of global governance. For instance, given its status as the world's fastest growing economy, China is being promoted both by the American and British governments as a study abroad destination among their higher education student populations. The US announced its 100,000 Strong Initiative, under which the US Department of State would raise the number of American students in China to 100,000 by 2014 (IIE, 2013). The British government launched the Generation UK project to encourage and support

1. According to *Project Atlas* (Institute of International Education or IIE), their numbers have risen from 2.1 to 4.1 million during this period. However, the difference in numbers is 'mainly due to differences in definition and coverage of international student data' (UNESCO Institute for Statistics or UIS). All numbers, unless stated otherwise, are from UIS for the year 2010, for tertiary-level international students only.

British students gain educational experience in China so as to enhance their employability among British businesses interested in China as well as in international markets and institutions. Targeting other non-traditional educational destinations like India, Brazil, Turkey, Thailand and Indonesia, the IIE, with the support of the US Department of State, launched an initiative to boost the potential of these countries to host more American students (IIE, 2011).

With the emergence of higher education hubs in East Asia and the Pacific—most noticeably in Singapore, Japan, Hong Kong, the Republic of Korea (ROK) and China—countries in the region have not only been trying to stem the traditional brain-drain to North America and Western Europe in order to retain/develop their competitive edge in the global arena, they have also been undertaking a host of measures to make their higher educational institutions (HEIs) attractive to local students, and for those aspiring to study abroad from within Asia and elsewhere. While the US and other Western countries—especially the English-speaking ones—continue to remain preferred destinations for most international students from Asia, given stricter visa regimes in these countries after 9/11, the limited availability of scholarships, discrimination faced by non-Western students, and other issues, many of them are exploring options within Asia itself. There are already 45,757 Chinese students in Korea, and 25,660 Korean students in Japan, for instance.

Indian students are still an important exception. Figure 12.1 shows that 86 per cent still go to the top five traditional study abroad destinations, while only 1,152 of them were in Malaysia (or 0.6% of the total), 576 in Japan, 486 in the ROK,[2] 357 in Thailand and 46 in Hong Kong in 2010. Given the quality of education/instruction, course structure, international student fee, infrastructure, etc., at HEIs in India, there are fewer students from Asia studying in them. The top five source countries include Iran (1,258), Nepal (1,252), UAE (1,110), Kenya (508) and Saudi Arabia (506). As far as East and Southeast Asia are concerned, the country hosted 309

2. In an email communication, the Press Information Division of the Indian Embassy in Seoul indicated that there are around 1500 Indian students enrolled in Korean universities (June 5, 2013). This difference in numbers could either be due to definitional issues or due to increase in the number of Indian students between 2010 and 2013, or both.

students from Thailand, 305 from China, 263 from Vietnam, 192 from Malaysia, 168 from North Korea, 113 from the ROK, 91 from Singapore, 65 from Japan and 11 from Hong Kong.

Figure 12.1

Percentage of International Indian Students in Top Five Educational Destinations

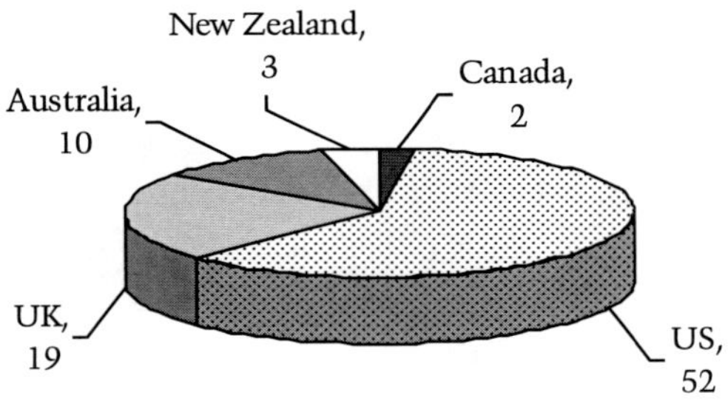

International students bring several benefits to host institutions, societies and governments. Among other things, they bring diversity to local student populations, new knowledge, skills and perspectives into the classrooms and a better understanding of other countries and cultures. They also carry the potential to strengthen diplomatic relations between countries and confer future foreign policy benefits if they go on to assume critical positions in home countries (Lee and Rice, 2007). Given the widening and deepening of relations between India and Korea during the past four decades, educational exchange between them cannot be left out of the ambit. Clearly, present engagement is minimal and several issues would have to be addressed on both sides to enhance the exchange. One way of understanding and addressing them would be through the exploration and analysis of the motivations, experiences and concerns of Indian students in the ROK and Korean students in India. The 12th India-Korea Dialogue (October 24-25, 2013, New Delhi) has taken the welcome step of including them as a central component of its proceedings. We are happy to share the findings and analysis of the motivational factors and the varied experiences of Indian students in South Korea, based on an online survey that we conducted with them over a period of two weeks in July 2013. The issues and concerns of Korean students in India will be addressed in another forthcoming paper.

Internationalisation of Higher Education in Korea

Despite its tiny population *vis-à-vis* China and India, Korea is the third largest source country for internationally mobile students. The country is understandably worried about its brain-drain and has taken a host of measures to internationalise its higher education system to retain its own flock and attract international students, researchers and faculty. Relaxing of visa regulations is the first of such measures. The country has also opened its doors for local campuses of reputed foreign universities: the State University of New York (SUNY) opened its campus in Songdo in 2012, while George Mason (USA) and Ghent (Belgium) universities are planning theirs by 2014. Massive funding is available for research-oriented programmes, and institutes like the Institute for Basic Science in Daejeon are being encouraged to compete with their counterparts in Japan, Germany and elsewhere. Funds are also being allocated under the World Class University project to universities to invite renowned academics from around the world.

The Korean government as well as a number of foundations and corporations offer numerous scholarships to foreign students.[3] For instance, the Ministry of Education, Science and Technology has instituted the Korean Government Scholarship Program for graduate and undergraduate students from countries having diplomatic ties with the ROK. The National Institute for International Education (NIIED) provides Global Korea Scholarships (GKS) to self-financed foreign students, apart from various other scholarships. It also offers support services to exchange students for up to 6 months or a year. Earlier this year, it invited graduates and undergraduates from IIT Chennai in a bid to strengthen diplomatic relations between India and Korea. The Korea Foundation for Advanced Studies offers International Scholar Exchange Fellowships to university professors and researchers from Asia in social sciences, energy, telecommunications and other fields. Steel manufacturing giant POSCO

3. For Korean scholarships: *www.studyinkorea.go.kr/en/sub/overseas_info/korea_edu/edu_scholarship.do* (31/7/2013, 14:28).

is expanding its scholarship programme and has doubled the number of beneficiaries this year onwards. In 2006, POSCO's Indian subsidiary announced scholarships and grants for meritorious Indian students, particularly from leading universities in Odisha to promote research and academic collaboration between the two countries.

Among the several steps that the Korean government has undertaken towards internationalisation of higher education in Korea is special funding for those Korean universities that offer courses in English, under its 'Study in Korea' programme launched in 2004. Such funding has not only resulted in several English courses at these universities, but has also played a central role in boosting the tally of foreign students enrolling in them. Nevertheless, as we shall see later, while English is being promoted at the governmental level, its acceptability even within the educational realm, let alone in broader Korean society, is still rather limited. However, one could add countries like France and Germany here, which are experiencing similar issues and which is one of the major reasons why Indian students continue to predominantly prefer English-speaking countries.

To enhance the quality of education, the Korean Ministry of Education, Science and Technology has been actively supplementing the government's attempts to restructure and improve the higher education sector in Korea. In 2011, 43 private universities in Korea were 'named and shamed' (Kim, 2011) by the ministry on the basis of an evaluation of 346 private institutions in terms of such indicators as 'the employment rate of recent graduates, the student retention rate and the quality of faculty.' Such blacklisted universities are no longer eligible for state subsidy. In its latest measure to crack down on sub-standard higher educational institutions, the ministry has named 11 institutions that will be banned from admitting foreign students this year. An additional 19 institutions have been ordered to improve their policies on management of international students. Such stringent checks on quality of higher education have paid off—Korean universities rank high in the Asia as well as the world university rankings (see Table 12.1), even as no Indian institute of higher education does.

Table 12.1

Korean Universities in Top 100 World and Top 20 Asia Rankings of Universities

University	*World Rank*	*Asia Rank*
Pohang University of Science & Technology	50	5
Seoul National University	59	8
Korea Advanced Institute of Science & Technology	68	10
Yonsei University	183	20

Source: The Times University Rankings 2013.

Survey Analysis

Since we did not come across any survey of Indian students in Korea,[4] we conducted our own online, with the support of the Indian Students Association of Korea (ISA Korea) and the Office of International Affairs, Seoul National University, Seoul.[5] The questionnaire was adapted from the Survey of International Students (Ministry of Education, New Zealand, 2004) and the International Student Survey (City of Melbourne, Australia, 2010). It generated 48 responses from Indians pursuing higher education in Korea within two weeks (July 8-21, 2013).

Background Characteristics of Survey Participants

While such a sample size will not allow us to undertake a complex analysis of responses, it does provide broad insights into the experiences and concerns of Indian students in Korea, given that the respondents

4. To the best of our knowledge, there is no survey with any group of international students in Korea, a finding which was confirmed by International Graduate Insight (i-graduate), an agency that specialises in surveys with international students.

5. Our special thanks are due to the Founder of ISA Korea, Dr Satyanshu Srivastava, currently Assistant Professor, Centre for Japanese, Korean and North East Asian Studies at Jawaharlal Nehru University in New Delhi as well as Ms Hyunjin Jo, who is Student Ambassador, Office of International Affairs at the Seoul National University for encouraging students to fill out the survey. Other Korean universities we contacted did not respond to our repeated requests.

come from 16 Indian states,[6] are studying in 16 Korean cities,[7] are a mix of age-groups (Figure A-12.1), marital and living status (Figures A-12.3 and A-12.4), though not gender (Figure A-12.2).[8] Two-third are pursuing their doctoral research in Korea (Figure A-12.19), and so we can take their responses more seriously and make recommendations on improving their educational and living experiences as well as enhancing educational exchange as far as Indian students are concerned.

Apart from the basic demographic characteristics pointed out above, it is important to note that 90 per cent of survey respondents never studied abroad before coming to Korea (Figure A-12.5), and 71 per cent of them are pursuing their first Korean degrees (Figure A-12.6). Couple this with the facts that two-third of them did not take any Korean classes before starting their studies in Korea (Figure A-12.7) and are pursuing their courses primarily in English (Figure A-12.8), and it becomes easier to identify where part of the cultural adjustment problems—which we shall discuss later—emanates from (i.e., limited exposure to the outside world and lack of familiarity with the language of host society).

Choosing Korea

Figures A-12.9 to A-12.16 highlight some of the major factors that did—and those that did not—motivate these Indian students in choosing Korea as their destination abroad for higher study. The efforts of the Korean

6. Ten respondents are from Tamil Nadu; six each from Andhra Pradesh, Maharashtra and Uttar Pradesh; three each from Delhi and Jammu & Kashmir; two each from Assam, Bihar and Odisha; and one each from Haryana, Himachal Pradesh, Jharkhand, Karnataka, Madhya Pradesh, Rajasthan and West Bengal.

7. Twenty-three in Seoul; three each in Busan, Gyeongsan and Suwon; two each in Cheongju, Daegu and Yongin; and one each in Changwon, Daejeon, Gwangju, Jeonju, Pohang, Sejong, Ulsan, Wonju and Yeosu.

8. According to UNESCO's *Global Education Digest 2010*, females constituted 27 per cent of internationally mobile students from India in Australia, Canada, France, South Africa and United Kingdom in the year 2008. In the absence of figures for South Korea, one can safely assume that female representation is not going to be better than in these five countries, and hence the participation of six female respondents in our survey is not that bad. Two of them were from Delhi, one each from Jharkhand, Tamil Nadu, Uttar Pradesh and West Bengal. All but one was in the age group of 26-30 years. Two were married, the rest were single. Three were Hindus, one Christian, one Muslim. Four of them were doing their PhD and two their Master's. One was financially supported by her husband; the rest were on scholarships. Three were studying engineering while 1 each was in natural sciences, humanities and the 'other' category.

Government towards providing scholarships and improving the quality of education seem to have borne fruit inasmuch as these two emerge as very important factors in choosing Korea for higher education. These factors are particularly significant for doctoral students; it is no wonder, therefore, that two-third of survey respondents are there for their doctoral degrees.

Another significant motivational factor is the desire to gain international experience (Figure A-12.10), which also received a high rating in the survey among Indian students in Europe, conducted by Mukherjee and Chanda (2012). However, we know from interactions with some Indian students that some of them just want to go abroad (for international experience/higher education/both), and the choice of country and institution is only a secondary one. From a policy perspective, the Korean government and HEIs may want prospective international students to view Korea and Korean institutions as their first preference, not as backup options, as seems to be the case at the moment as far as Indian students are concerned (Figures A-12.17 and A-12.18).

Related to this is the fact that most Indian students do not wish to go abroad, not because they consider higher education in India as lacking quality, but because they consider international exposure for the sake of better employment chances and for its own sake as desirable. In India, there is a prevalent perception that many of those who go abroad—with the exception of those who go to Oxbridge-league institutions—are those who are unable to get admissions in prestigious institutions within India, where seats are limited and competition is overwhelming. The point here is that just because India is the second largest source country for internationally mobile students does not imply that its HEIs lack quality, although this is an issue as far as inflow of international students is concerned. Paradoxically though, in a country where large swathes of population still lack access to basic education, tertiary education has been given preference by the Indian Government *vis-à-vis* primary/secondary education. However, the government has been making efforts to redress this imbalance.

What should be of concern here to the relevant departments of the Korean Government and HEIs is the fact that information dissemination from their side does not play a major role in choosing Korea. One could argue that this could be one of the major reasons for the limited number of international students in the country. On the other hand, the British and the French Governments, for instance, organise huge dissemination events across major Indian cities through their relevant agencies. In India, Korea is popularly known for its technological products, and not for its higher education. So, this is one area that Korean agencies working towards the promotion of international education really need to look into.

The perception of the Korean government that international students would choose Korea due to lower costs does not appear to hold true in our case. Tuition fee at HEIs in both the US and UK are huge, but they still remain the preferred destinations for Indian students. In fact, many of them go there on massive bank loans, and so the idea of lower costs is not something which would attract many Indian students. In the lower cost segment, Korea—or, for that matter, other non-Western nations—would have to compete with European countries like France and Germany, where education is subsidised, and there exist well-established and renowned institutions, together with all the glamour that comes with living and studying in a European country. Studying in Europe has even greater appeal when one takes into consideration the fact that it also offers the prospect of being able to travel freely in several European countries in the Schengen region.

It is noteworthy that 73 per cent of survey respondents did not consider the opportunity to live in Korea permanently later as a motivational factor 'at all' in choosing Korea for higher education. Even when given a real choice, 71 per cent would prefer to live in India, 15 per cent in Korea and roughly around the same elsewhere (Figure A-12.56). This may not seem very surprising, if at all it does, if we consider the results from Mukherjee and Chanda (Ibid.)—only 12 per cent of survey respondents in the UK, which has historically been one of the most preferred destinations for Indian students and others, selected 'migration overseas' as a reason for studying outside India. Job prospects for the foreign-educated have been brighter in India and they have only improved since liberalisation. A fair number of survey respondents think that their chances of a job with Korean companies 'in India' get enhanced after studying in Korea (Figure A-12.16).

Figures A-12.17 to A-12.22, viewed together, seem to indicate that while Korea is not seen by the majority of Indian students there as their first choice for higher studies—largely due to the language factor—it could improve upon its competitive advantage in the technical sciences at the research level to project itself as a country for mature international researchers in such sciences. And this could be an area where it can increase scholarship support—both in terms of number of scholarships and the amount of scholarship given to each researcher so that they do not have to work at all and can instead focus on their research. Language is not so much an issue for them. Germany, for one, has developed its competitive advantage in these sciences and is well-known internationally. Competing with traditional destinations like the US and the UK in social sciences would not be easy for a variety of historical and sociopolitical reasons, which we do not have the space here to go into.

Issues at Korean HEIs

Here, we are largely going to raise those issues that are of concern and need attention either of the HEIs or Korean policy makers or both.

Faculty

A significant number of respondents find it difficult to understand lectures. They say that classes are not always in English and, even when they are, the pace of teaching is quite fast and it is difficult to understand the accent. Some students also said that 'Korean professors are not well-trained' (Figure A-12.23), although they are well-qualified. Another issue is the workload (Figure A-12.24). According to some respondents, teachers "don't allow to work freely and asked the students to work like factory workers", "they want outsiders also to work like Koreans and work under pressure … put unnecessary stress on students. Koreans are habitual of working for 13-15 hours a day. They expect same from us also." Others also complained about lack of 'free environment for research', 'platform to express talents' or 'space to explore … creativity.' They feel that research life is extremely mechanised, and teachers expect machine-like outputs without use of much 'analytical skills'.

As one student framed it, "education is not like factory working. Sixteen hours of work may produce 160 cars but it's difficult to come [up with] 160 different ideas." Another related issue is that teachers don't really appreciate that students ask questions in class. Producing papers is another issue, where intellectual property rights are a concern too. "Professors ask foreign students who are writing research articles for publication to include the name of Koreans who have not even contributed and sometimes professors just take the article and publish in their name." It seems that even otherwise, respondents did not have a very good impression of teachers. Many said that they neither empathise with foreign students—with the exception of American students, whom many respondents said are unduly favoured due to their ethnicity and national background—nor do they try to understand their problems or make special efforts to help them (Figures A-12.31 and A-12.32). Nevertheless, most respondents are quite appreciative of the quality of instructors, assessment procedures, course content as well as its utility for future studies or job (Figures A-12.27 to A-12.30).

Institutional services

Services provided by the international students' office are rated highly by two-thirds of respondents. However, relations between national and international students is something which needs attention, as highlighted by one respondent. This is also reflected in the fact that respondents found it difficult to work on group projects (Figure A-12.25). The missing social aspect is also reflected in the relatively poor ratings of international student associations, friendship programmes, and clubs and societies in the sphere of institutions services (Figures A-12.34, A-12.37 and A-12.39). Counselling and learning support are other areas of concern (Figures A-12.35 and A-12.36), and these are particularly relevant given the problems students face with respect to the faculty, teaching speed, workload, lack of personal leisure, etc., so are sports and recreation, which again are areas where some attention seems to be required (Figure A-12.38). Nevertheless, nearly two-third of the respondents rated the institutional services highly in terms of overall quality and most were satisfied with the support they received (Figures A-12.40 and A-12.41).

Support Systems

While most were satisfied with support from their educational institutions, the Indian embassy/consulates ranked lowest in this regard (Figure A-12.43), although admittedly there isn't much they have to do with them. Support from Korean public offices or society was not very satisfactory either, and these are areas policy makers should definitely look into. However, most respondents felt very safe living in Korea, which is especially a serious concern and consideration for girls as well as their parents. In fact, many Indian parents do not wish to send their daughters abroad due to safety issues and the high safety perception of Korea is something that could be advertised by Korean agencies to attract students, especially female students, from countries like India, which can also be another competitive advantage for the country.

Lack of fluency in the Korean language is an issue not only at the academic level—though to a lesser degree—but also in interactions with Korean students and members of wider society, which is one important reason why most Indian students fall back upon fellow Indian students for support. However, a vast majority did acknowledge receiving support from fellow Korean students where language was an issue. In fact, Korean students also emerge as a critical source of support where educational issues, local registrations and life in Korea are concerned. Given the problems that arise at multiple levels due to lack of fluency in the Korean language, language classes should be made compulsory at least up to a level that ensures that international students can interact with fellow Korean students and can carry out their day-to-day activities outside the campus.

Part of the discrimination issue also probably arises from this deficiency. Most respondents claim that they have experienced discrimination and have complained about it in qualitative sections of the survey, some of them in very strong terms, and in most cases, they have pointed fingers at the faculty, sometimes at Korean students, society and the media. However, it is surprising to see, in Figure A-12.48, that a majority of them said that they never experienced unfair or negative treatment at the hands of teachers due to their racial/cultural/national background. One respondent even said that "the teachers are very kind and they try their best to help you even outside the class." It seems that intercultural understanding and expectations are a serious issue as far as teaching and teachers are concerned, something that both the Korean HEIs and policy makers could evaluate. Nevertheless, it must be added here that discrimination is a much bigger issue in Western nations, and with certain checks and balances, it can probably be taken care of here and projected as a point of comparative advantage *vis-à-vis* the traditional destinations.

Postscript

Issues related to faculty, language, food, accommodation (Figures A-12.51 and A-12.52) and overall adjustment seem to have taken a toll on general impressions about the country and its educational system, if Figures A-12.53 to A-12.56 are appropriate indications. Only half of them think that education in Korea is good value for money, and even fewer would recommend family members or friends to study in Korea. This is definitely not good for the promotion of Korea as an attractive destination for study among prospective students in India, and for the overall future of educational exchange between the two countries. A vast majority wants to return to India because they are either: 'fed up with the attitudes' of Koreans, 'Korea is not a good society for multicultural values,' 'discrimination towards foreigners,' 'working environment [is] very bad' and 'stressful,' and 'bad experience' in general on the negative side. On the positive side, they want to return to India because 'India is the best country with lots of relationships, friends, etc.,' 'have responsibilities in India,' 'want to serve my country,' etc. However, given women's safety issues that have come to the limelight due to recent events and media coverage in India, it is interesting to read what one female respondent had to say:

> I like the safety I get to feel as a girl in Korea, and which is completely absent in India. Also in Korea, people keep to their own business and do not interfere with others' matters. Another aspect of Korean society that I do respect a lot is the discipline and punctuality that is evident in all spheres of their daily lives. But yes, I do want to spend the rest of my life in my motherland, close to my family. So am still not sure about the final plans.

Conclusions and Recommendations

The overall conclusion that one could draw from the survey responses is that there are a number of cultural issues that negatively affect the experience of Indian students in Korea: language, undoubtedly the first one; then, limited intercultural understanding between teachers and students; limited exchange between Indian and Korean students and society; limited personal time and leisure, etc. International education is not just about education, it is also about international experience, and this is something that seems quite limited at the moment, although that has emerged as one of the most important motivational factors for deciding to study abroad. One of us has been part of the Next Generation Leaders Program in 2008, which was organised by the Korea Foundation for people from various walks of life, and we were given a fabulous and memorable exposure to Korean society, culture, arts, industry, etc.

And this brings us to a set of recommendations that could be considered by relevant Korean policy makers and institutions to enhance educational exchange and the experience of international, especially Indian, students in Korea.

(1) Life in Korea for international students could start with these three programmes if it is not at present:

   a. A general orientation to Korean society, culture, educational system and its expectations.

   b. A week-long tour to provide exposure to Korean geography, culture, arts, society, etc.

   c. An intensive Korean language course, to begin with, then at least 1-2 classes per week to keep them in touch with the language.

(2) Faculty, university staff and local students should also be made to undergo an orientation programme to sensitise them to the needs of foreign students who come to study in Korean institutions. It is also necessary to provide platforms or events by means of which regular interaction between local and foreign students, on and off the campus, is ensured.

(3) Korean policy makers and institutions should consider the idea of developing their competitive advantage in technical sciences at the research level, which could be buttressed through better and more scholarships for doctoral aspirants.

(4) Among their distinct features, relevant Korean agencies and HEIs could further highlight as well as develop (a) quality education, (b) more scholarships, (c) safety for women, (d) Asian connection and (e) enhanced job prospects in Korean companies that have already made a name in countries like India.

(5) Educational institutions could try to improve counselling, sports, recreation, leisure, interactional and other extra-curricular activities to make the experience enjoyable for international students.

(6) They also have to focus more on information dissemination abroad to attract more international students. They could take a cue from the British Council, for instance.

(7) As far as work pressure and the creative spirit are concerned, Korean HEIs have to develop a more flexible system, which is seen as enabling rather than debilitating by international students. They could also be consulted in the design of certain programmes towards this end, and so can universities in the Western world and elsewhere.

(8) The use of English could be improved within the campuses to attract and sustain more international students, especially Indians who are still heavily inclined towards English-speaking countries. The experience of France and Germany, for instance, can be considered in this regard.

(9) International students should be treated on par with local students, at least institutionally—there is not much that can be done about general social or local student attitudes in this regard. Discrimination should be strictly checked so that international students from developing countries like India feel welcome.

(10) International student satisfaction surveys should be regularly conducted by Korean HEIs as well as independently by relevant government institutions to get to know and address the issues they face.

References

IIE (2011). *Expanding U.S. Study Abroad to India: A Guide for Institutions*. New York: Institute of International Education.

———. (2013). *US Students in China: Meeting the Goals of the 100,000 Strong Initiative*. New York: Institute of International Education.

Kim, Han-Suk (2011). "South Korea: Private Institutions 'named and shamed'", *University World News*, Issue 188. September 11.

Lee, Jenny J. and Charles Rice (2007). "Welcome to America? International Student Perceptions of Discrimination", *Higher Education* 53(3): 381-409.

Mukherjee, Shahana and Rupa Chanda (2012). "Indian Student Mobility to Selected European Countries: An Overview". *IIMB Working Paper* No. 365. Indian Institute of Management, Bangalore.

Annexure

Selected Graphs from the Survey

Figure A-12.1: Age

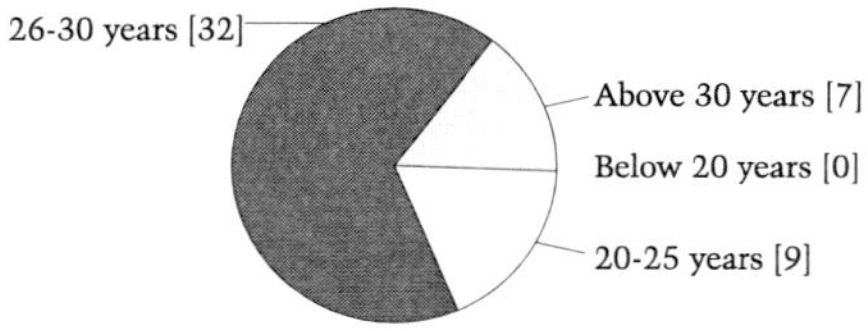

Figure A-12.2: Gender

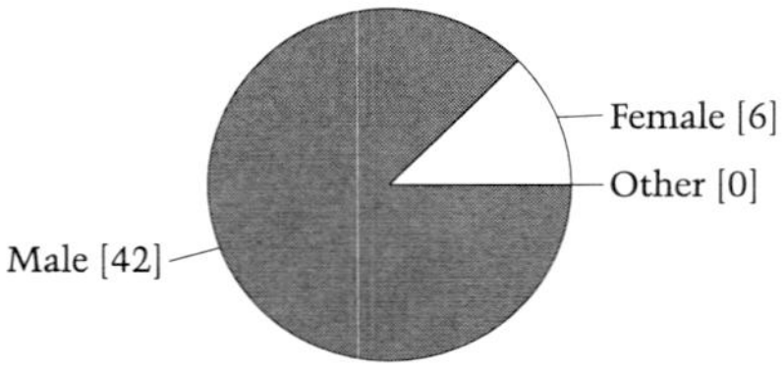

Figure A-12.3: Marital Status

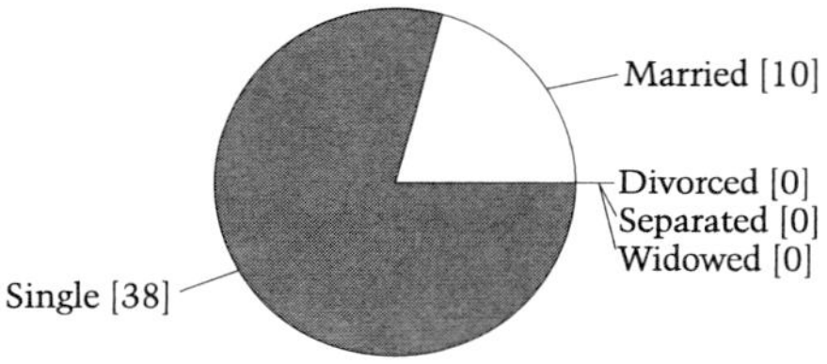

Figure A-12.4: Living with Family

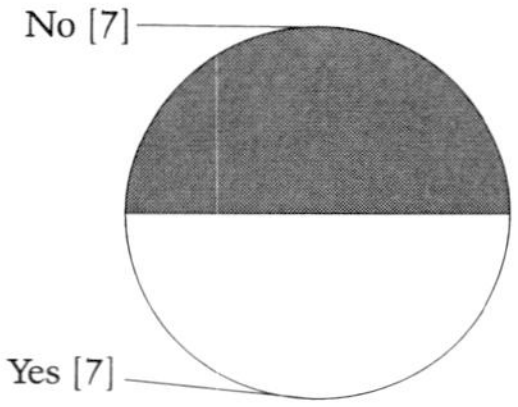

Figure A-12.5: Studied Abroad before Coming to Korea

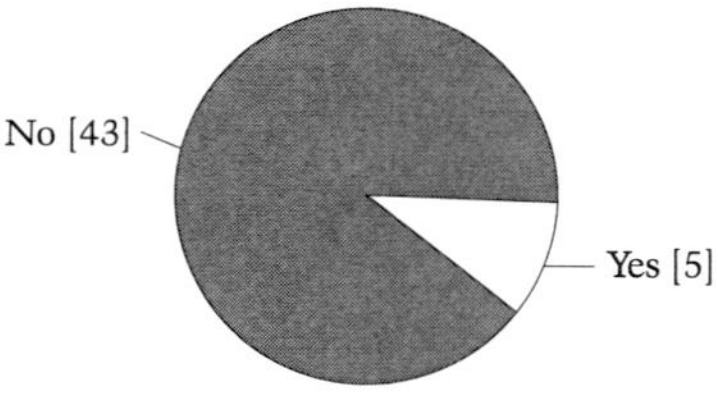

Figure A-12.6: Studied at another Korean Institution before

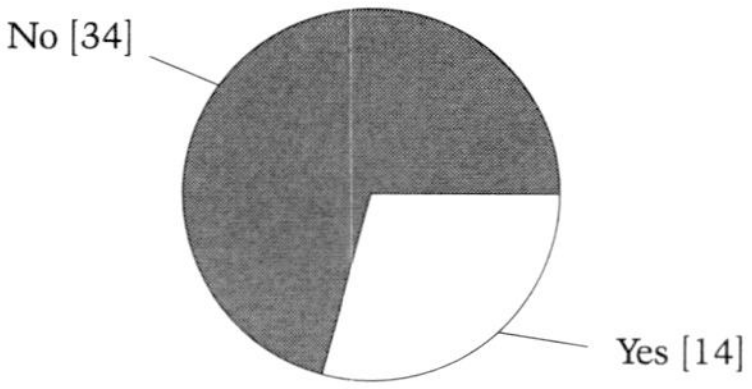

Figure A-12.7: Korean Language Classes before Starting Studies

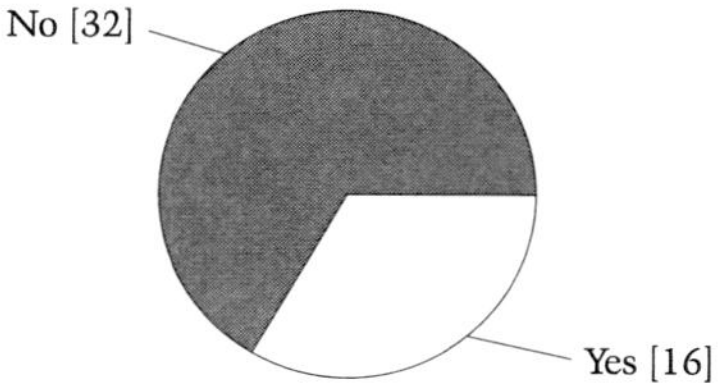

Figure A-12.8: Primary Medium of Education in Korea

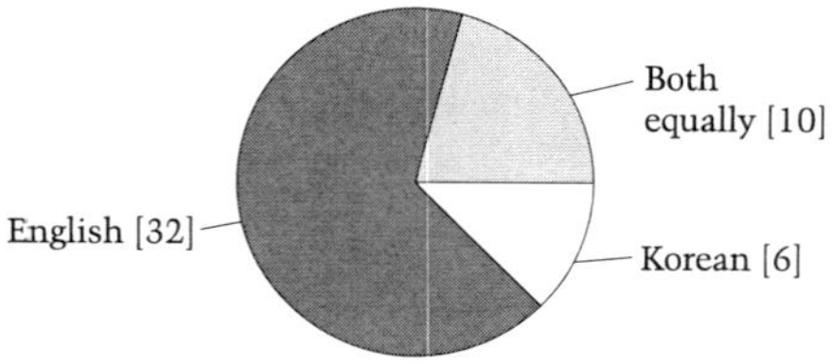

Figure A-12.9: Choosing Korea: Korean Scholarship

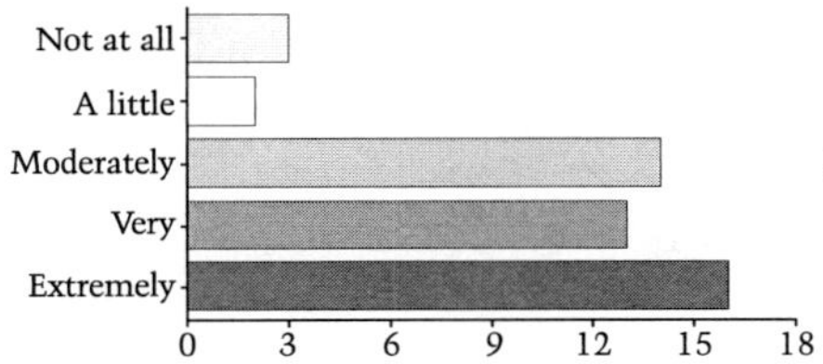

Figure A-12.10: Choosing Korea: International Experience

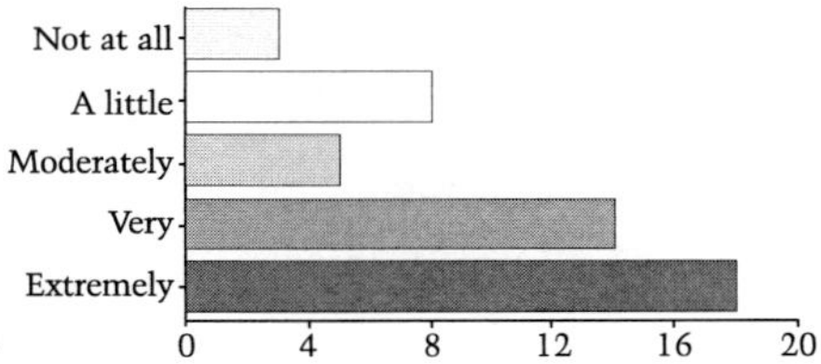

Figure A-12.11: Choosing Korea: Lack of Quality Education in Home State/India

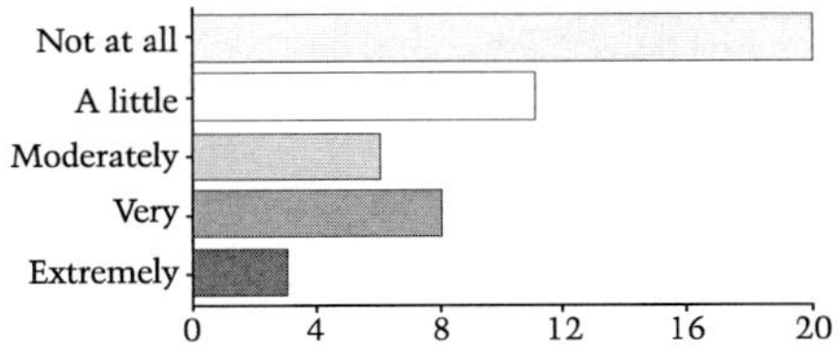

Figure A-12.12: Choosing Korea: Quality of Korean Education

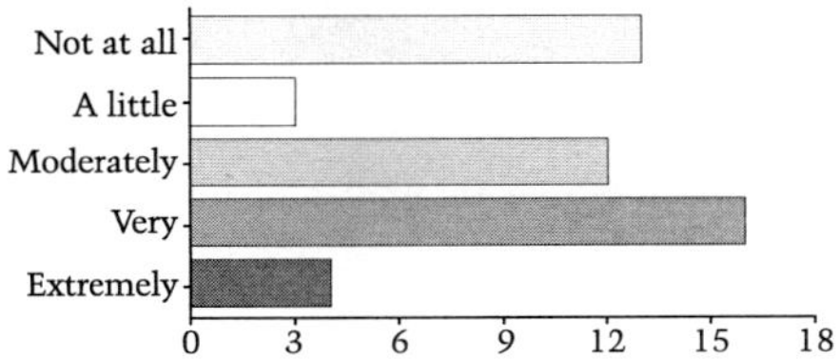

Figure A-12.13: Choosing Korea: Information from Korean Agencies or Institutions

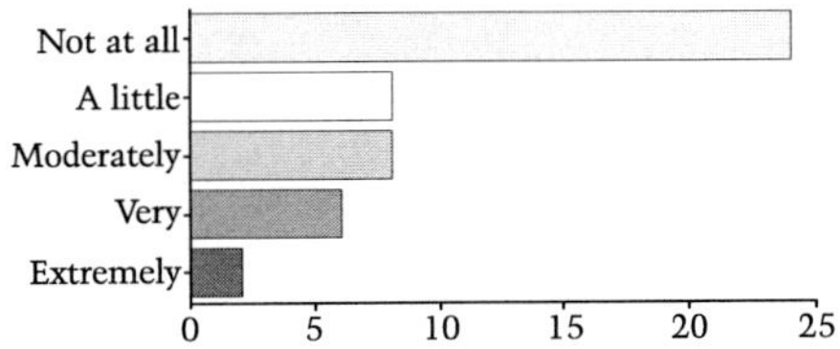

Figure A-12.14: Choosing Korea: Lower Costs

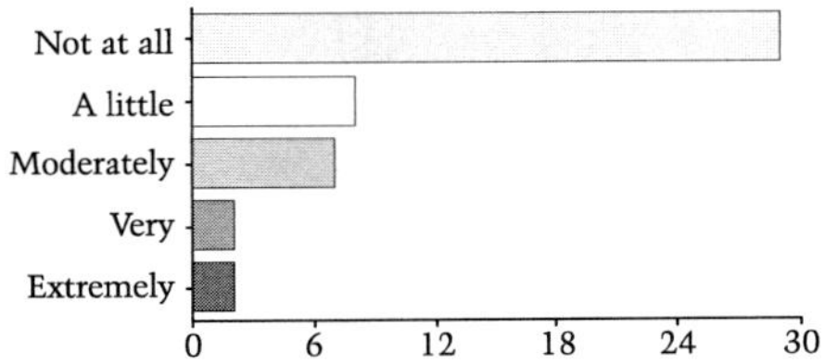

Figure A-12.15: Choosing Korea: Permanently Settle Later

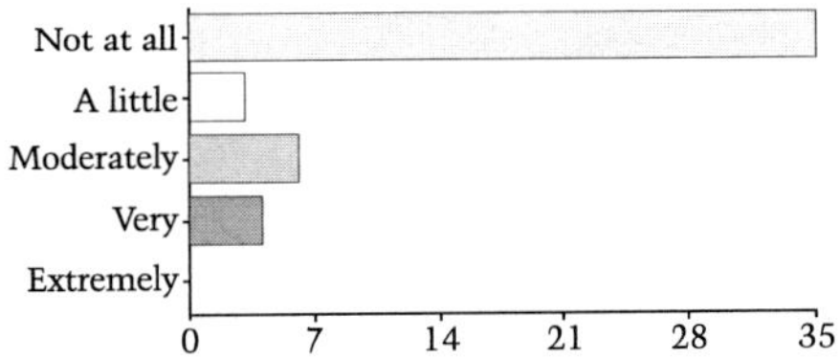

Figure A-12.16: Choosing Korea: Job Chances with Korean Companies in India

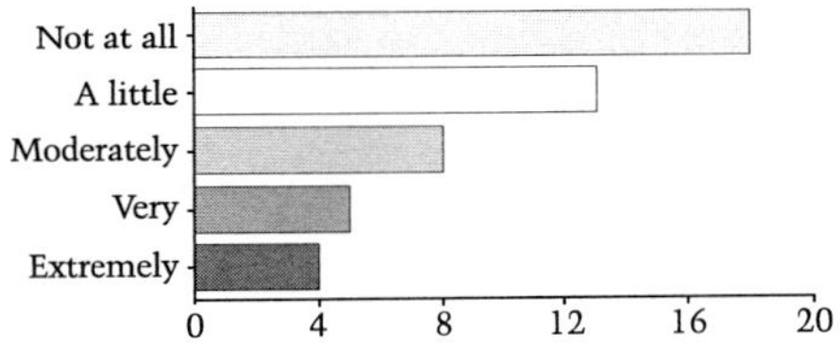

Figure A-12.17: Korea as the First Choice for Higher Studies

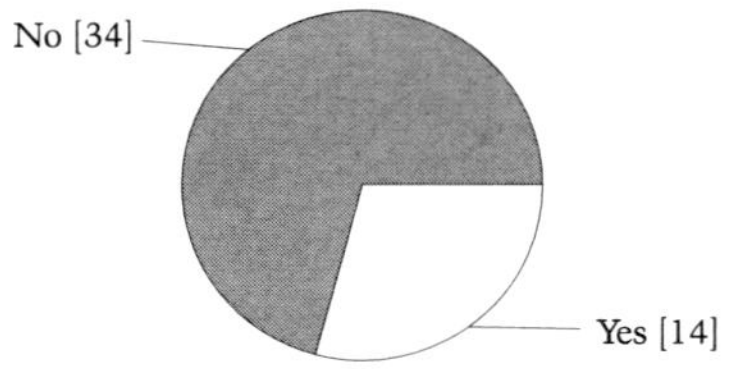

Figure A-12.18: Prefer to Study in an English-speaking Country

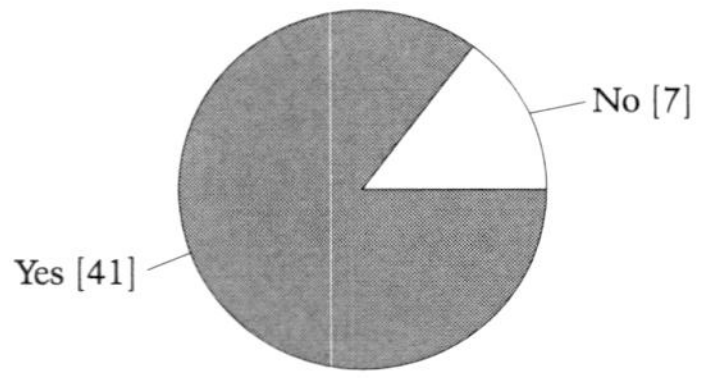

Figure A-12.19: Qualification Pursuing

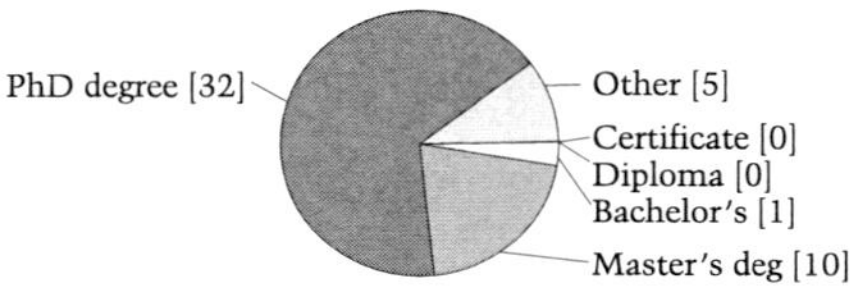

Figure A-12.20: Main Area of Study

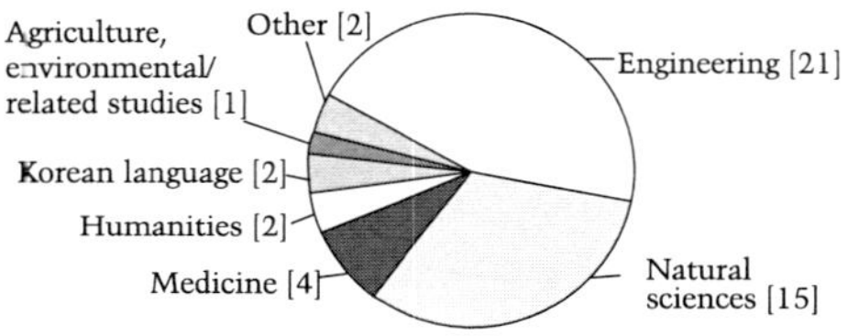

Figure A-12.21: Primary Source of Funding

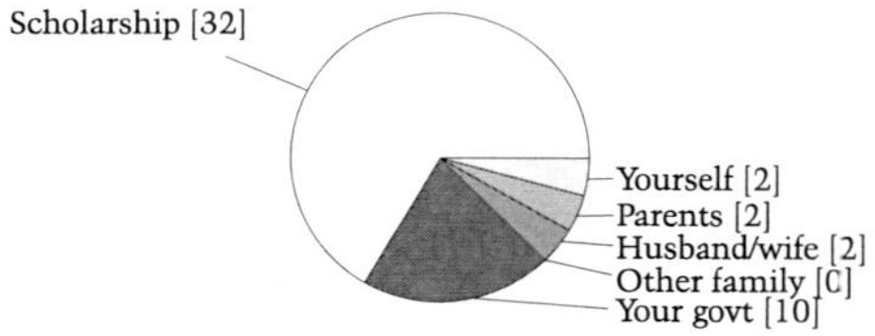

Figure A-12.22: Work of Support Education/Living in Korea

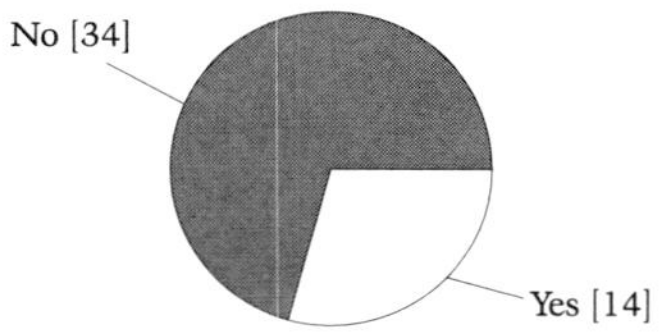

Figure A-12.23: Educational Difficulty: Understanding Lectures

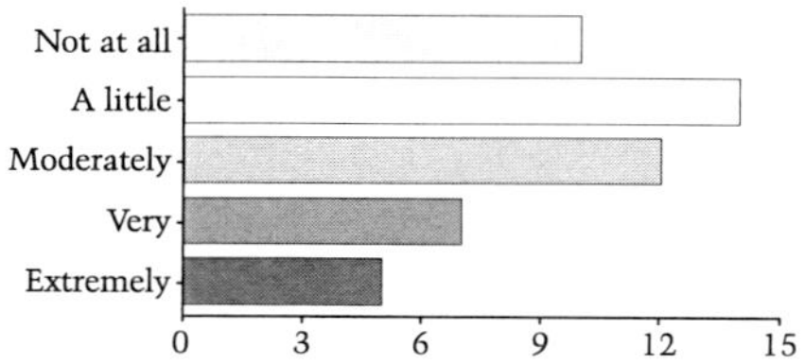

Figure A-12.24: Educational Difficulty: Managing Study Workload

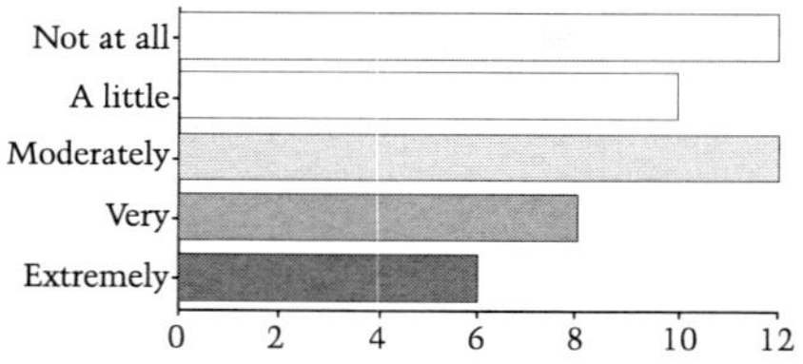

Figure A-12.25: Educational Difficulty: Working on Group Projects

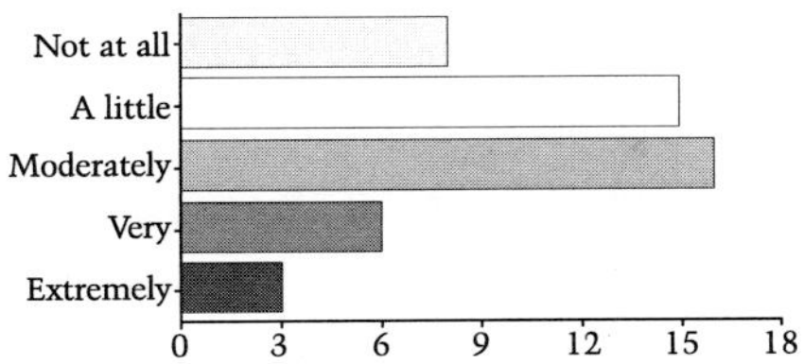

Figure A-12.26: Educational Difficulty: Asking Questions in Class

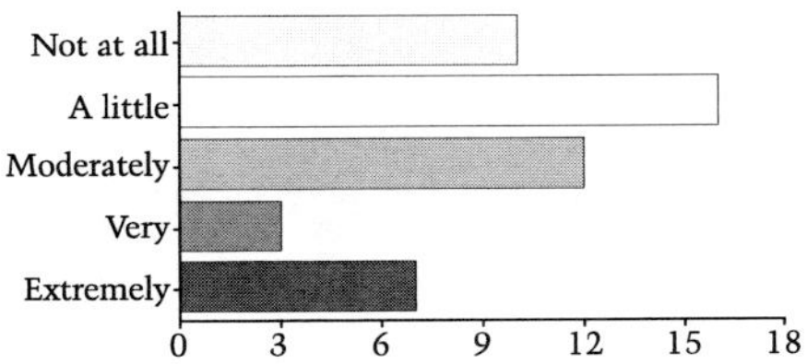

Figure A-12.27: Educational Quality: Course Content

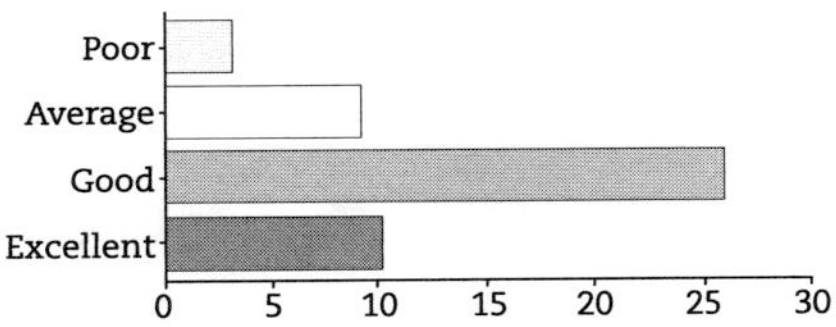

Figure A-12.28: Educational Quality: Instructors

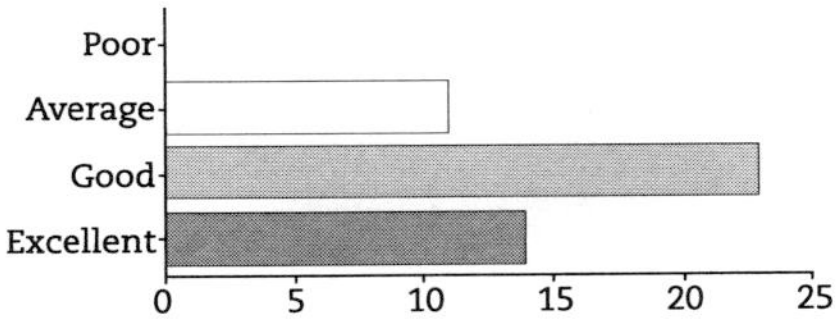

Figure A-12.29: Educational Quality: Assessment Procedures

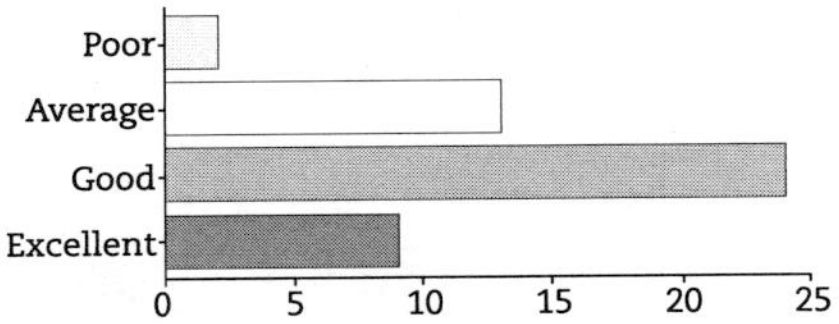

Figure A-12.30: Usefulness of Courses for Future Study/Job

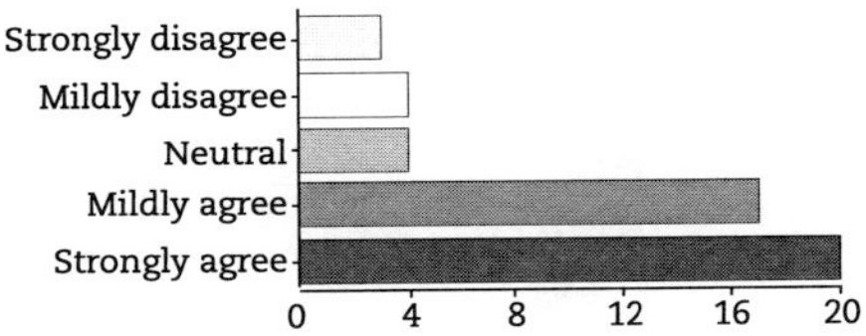

Figure A-12.31: Lecturers Understand Problems of Int'l Students

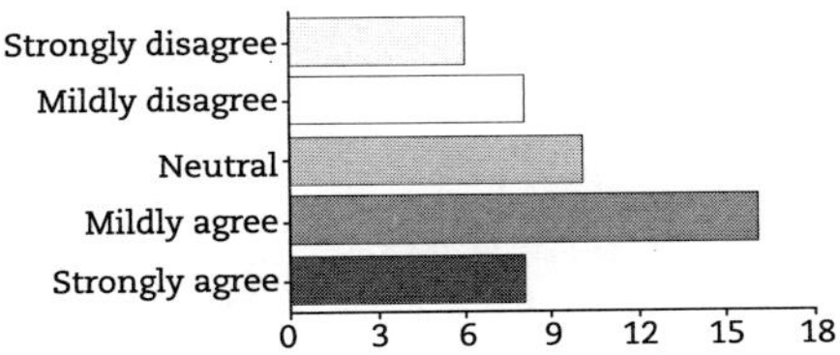

Figure A-12.32: Lecturers Provide Special Support to Int'l Students

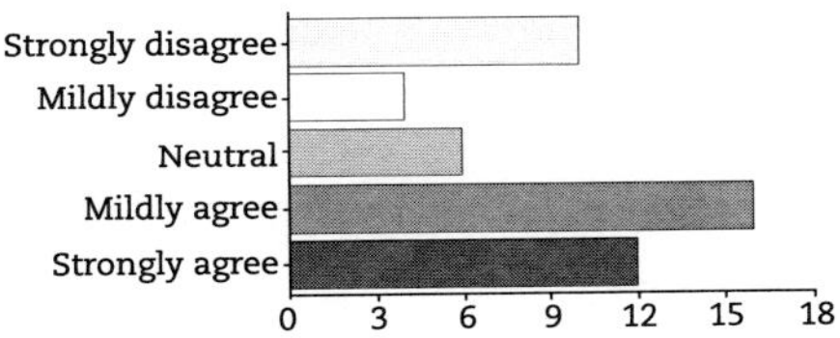

Figure A-12.33: Institutional Services: International Student Office

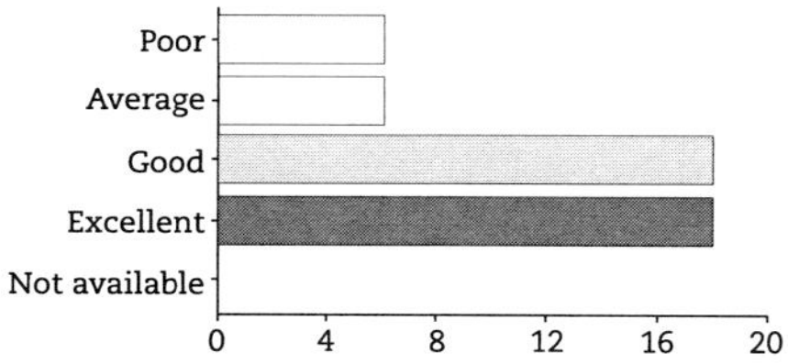

Figure A-12.34: Institutional Services: Int'l Student Associations

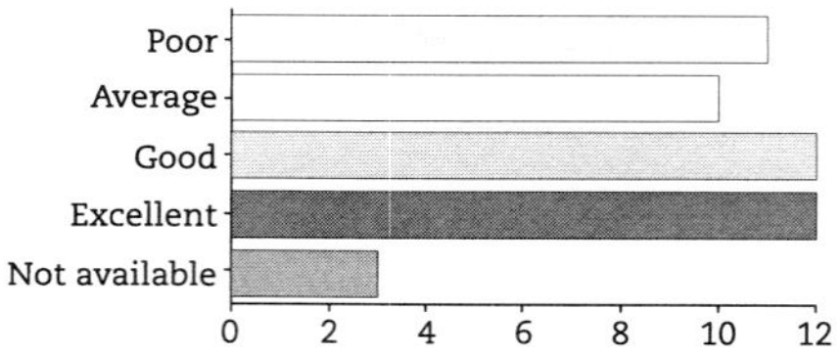

Figure A-12.35: Institutional Services: Counselling

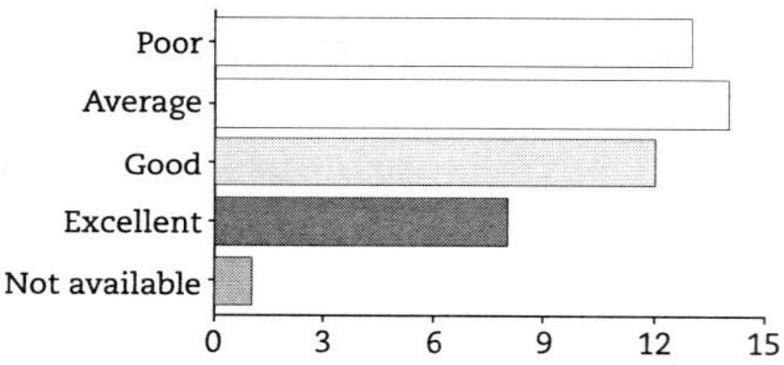

Figure A-12.36: Institutional Services: Learning Support

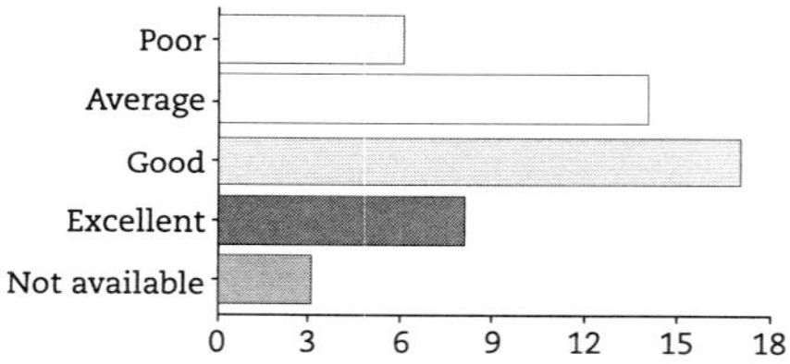

Figure A-12.37: Institutional Services: Friendship Programmes

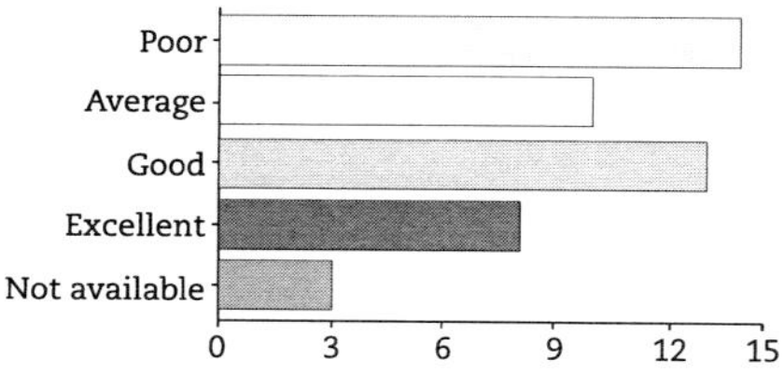

Figure A-12.38: Institutional Services: Sports and Recreation

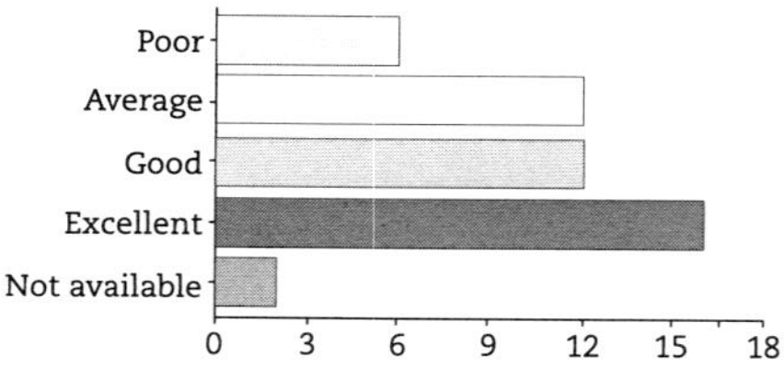

Figure A-12.39: Institutional Services: Clubs and Societies

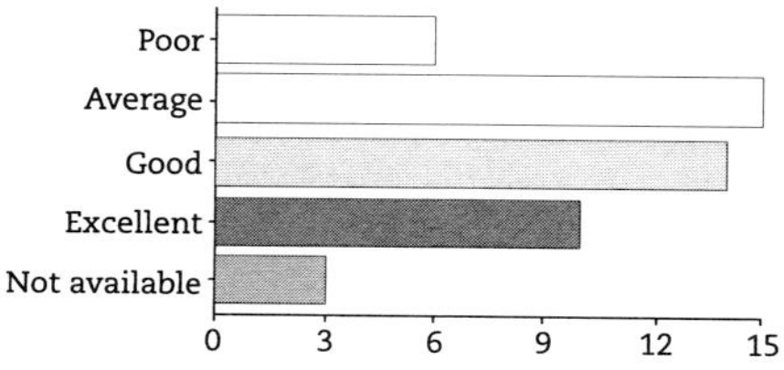

Figure A-12.40: Institutional Services: Overall Quality

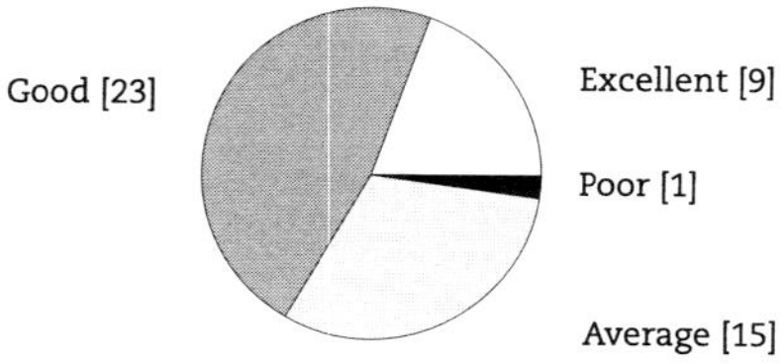

Figure A-12.41: Satisfied with Support: Educational Institution

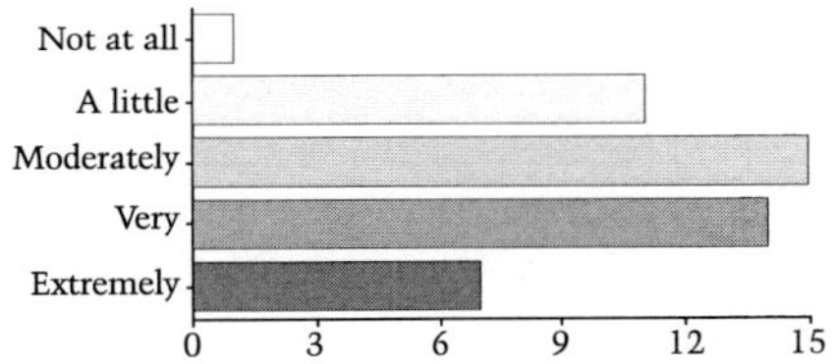

Figure A-12.42: Satisfied with Support: Korean Public Offices

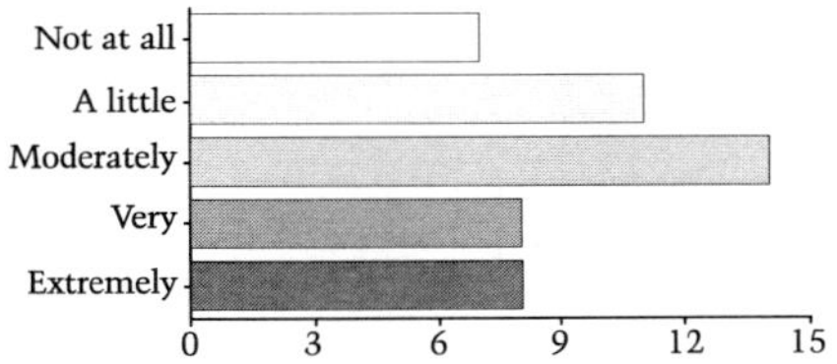

Figure A-12.43: Satisfied with Support: Indian Embassy/Consulate

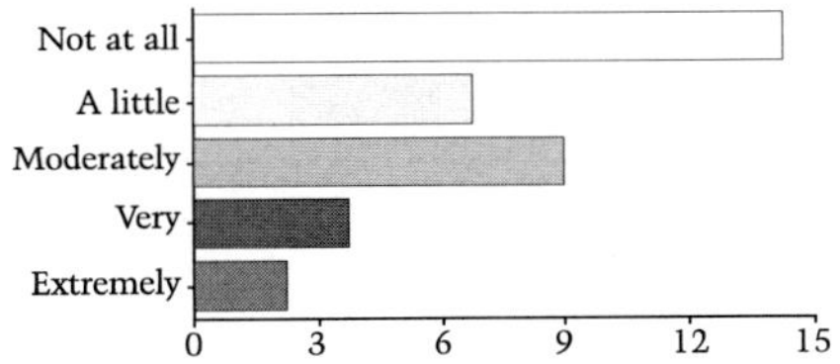

Figure A-12.44: Satisfied with Support: Host Society

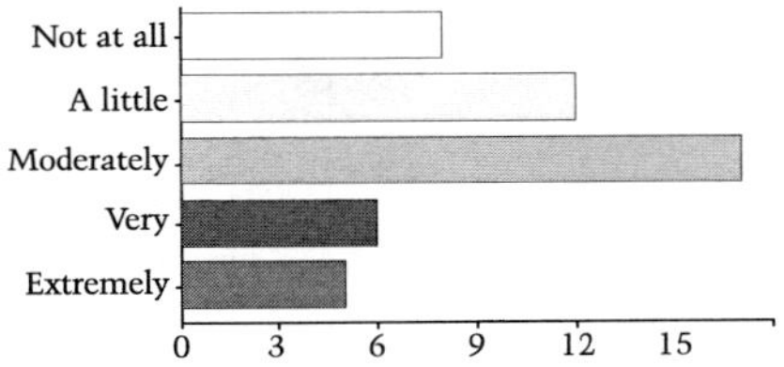

Figure A-12.45: How Safe do You Feel Living in Korea?

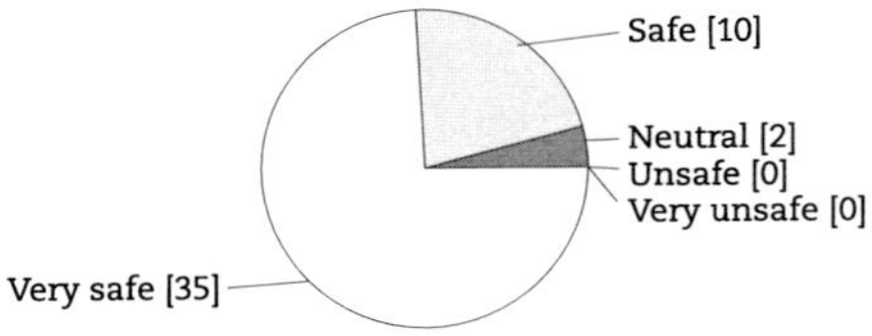

Figure A-12.46: Indian Students often Experience Discrimination

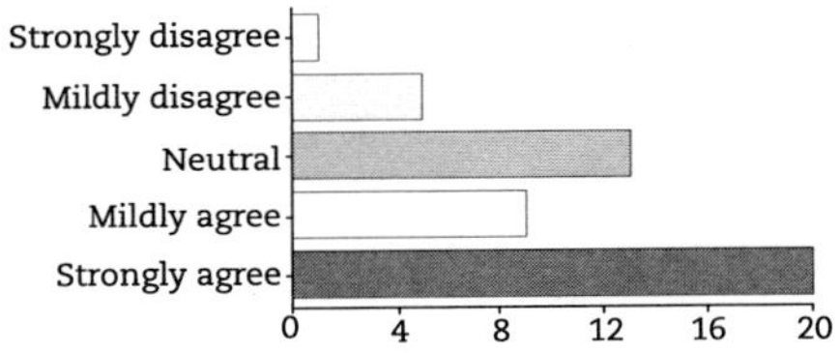

Figure A-12.47: Source of Discrimination: Korean Students

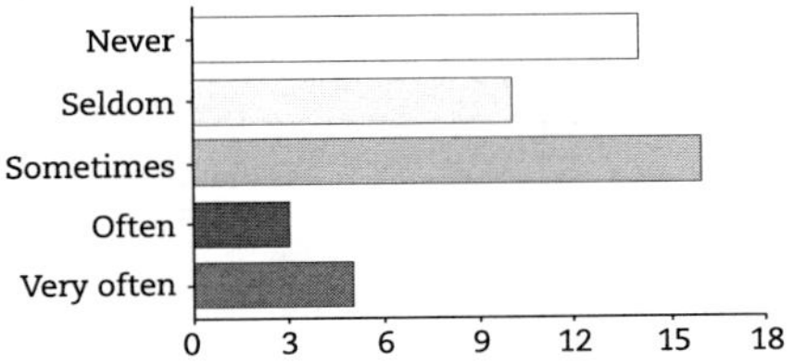

Figure A-12.48: Source of Discrimination: Teachers

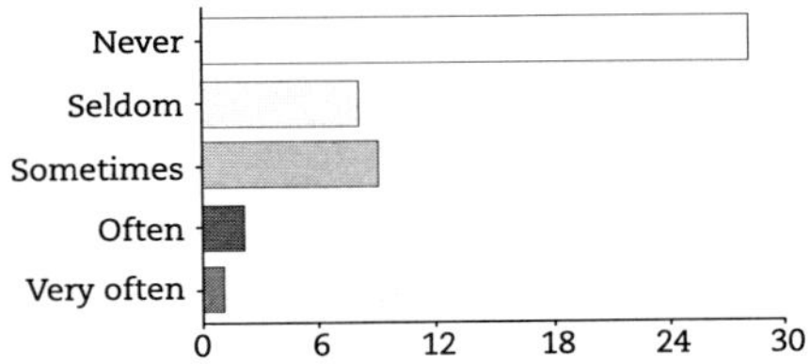

Figure A-12.49: Source of Discrimination: Institutional Staff

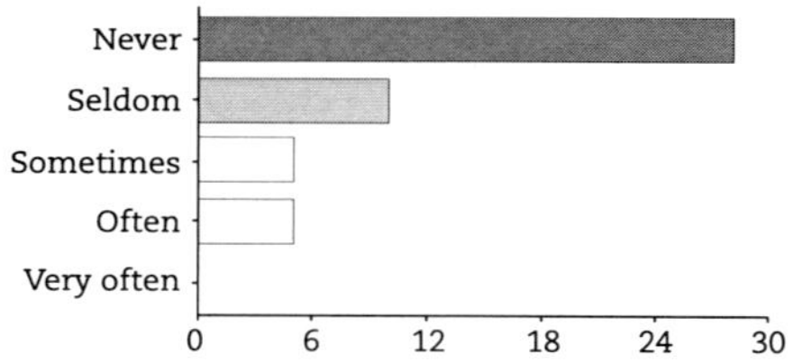

Figure A-12.50: Source of Discrimination: Wider Community

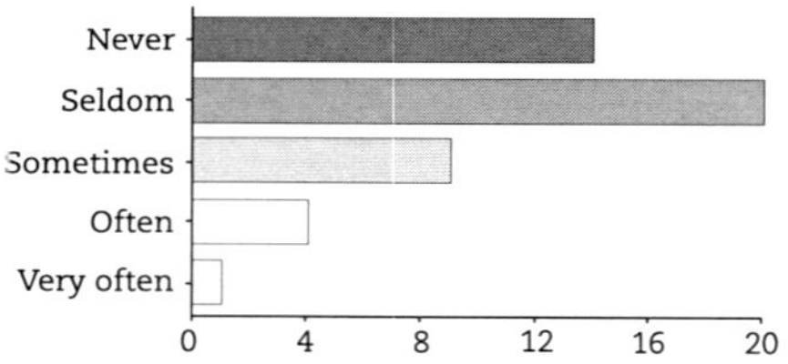

Figure A-12.51: Where do You Live?

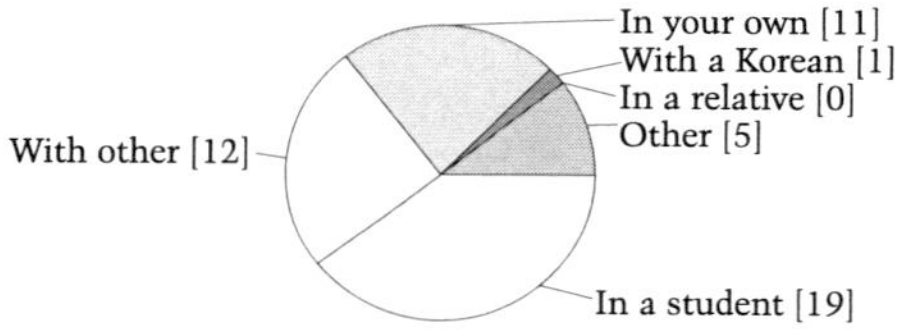

Figure A-12.52: How Satisfied are You with Your Accommodation?

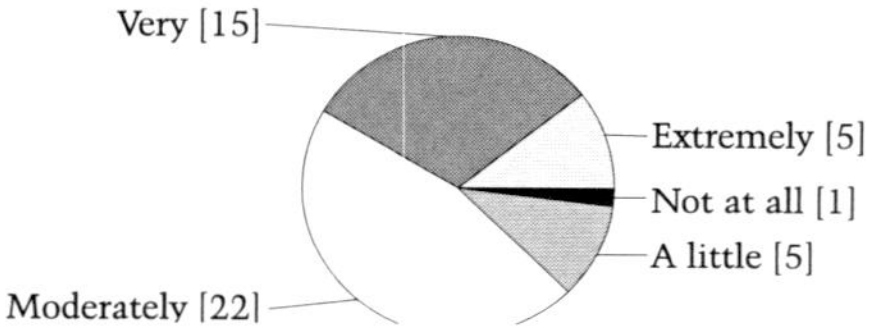

Figure A-12.53: Is Education in Korea Good Value of Money?

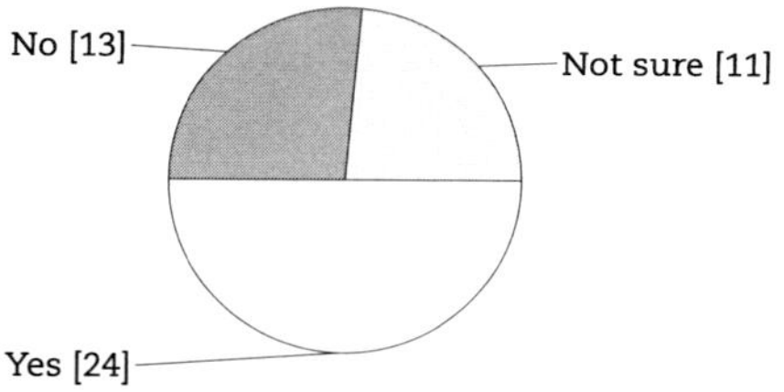

Figure A-12.54: Recommend Family or Friends to Study in Korea

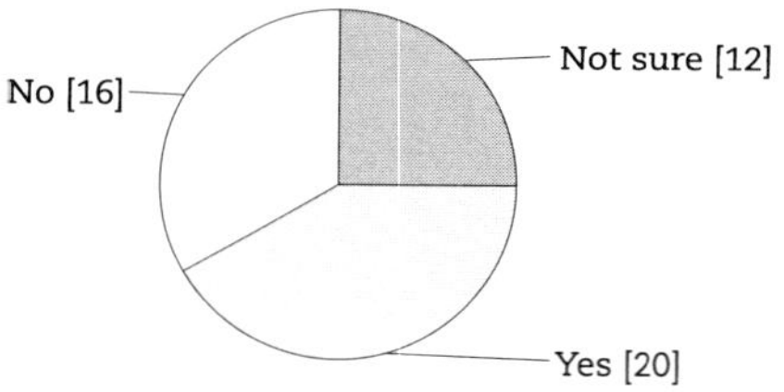

Figure A-12.55: After Studies, What do You Plan to do?

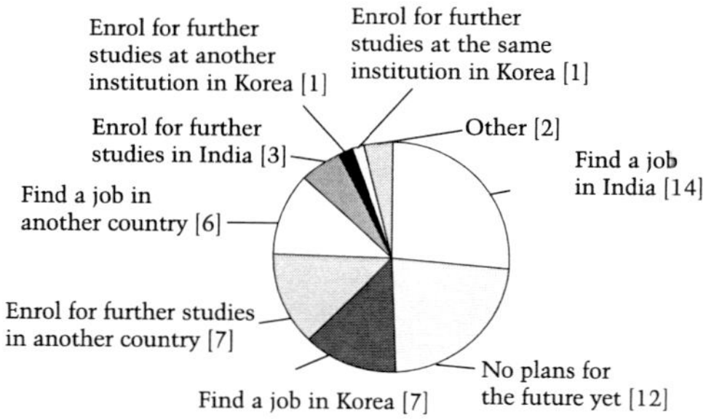

Figure A-12.56: After Studies, Where would You Prefer to Live?

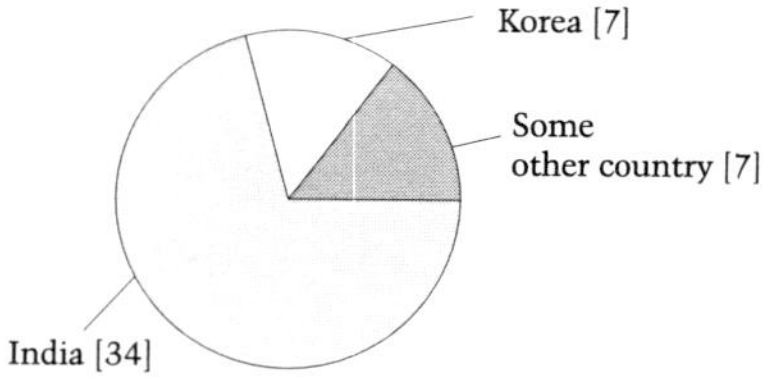

13 Cultural Aspects of India-Korea Relations

Vyjayanti Raghavan

Introduction

Korea and India have had formal diplomatic relations since 1973. But informal relations have existed for several centuries. One of the early interactions that have come to light is one that took place about 2,000 years ago when a princess from Ayutha (apparently Ayodhya) went to Korea and married King Kim Suro of Gaya Kingdom.

In modern times, however, for the first 20 years after formal diplomatic relations were established, the level of interest in each other remained at a very low key. This was despite the fact that the two governments had signed a few agreements of cultural and economic exchange during this period, and the Korean firms had started to explore the Indian market from the early 1980s.

India started a process of economic reform in 1991 that had foreign direct investment (FDI) as one of its main components. That has led to a sea-change in interaction between the two countries. In 1993, Prime Minister Narasimha Rao visited Korea as part of his 'Look East' Policy (LEP) and signed an agreement of cooperation. Korea swiftly grasped the opportunity that the vast Indian market could provide, and the next few years saw a massive upsurge in Korean investment in India. This surge led the two governments to sign the Comprehensive Economic Partnership Agreement (CEPA) in 2010. Today, Korean firms have become household names in India and they account for significant markets shares in every market in which they are present. However, it has also been found that while there was a steady increase in Korean investments in India until 2002, there has hardly been any significant increase since then. Korea was the 5th largest investor in India even until 2006 but has now slipped to the 12th or 13th position. There have been a number of factors that have contributed to this such as the political, economic and global environment but, cultural factors have also played a significant role.

This paper attempts to understand, analyse and explain these cultural factors with the objective of bridging some of the gap that exists in the perception of the people of the two countries. The paper is divided into two major sections. The first has two sub-parts. The first sub-part deals briefly with the larger cultural differences that Koreans encounter in India and the second sub-part is a shorter section in which I have tried to identify some core non-verbal cultural concepts of Korean society, which would be useful for Indians to imbibe while interacting with Koreans. The second major section is an effort to understand the cultural differences that Indians working in Korean firms experience. This has been done with the help of a survey conducted online.

I

Cultural Differences Encountered by Koreans in India

Koreans are known for their adaptability to situations, but despite this, the difficulties faced by Koreans living in India in adapting to the local living and work environment are endless. The impediments are due to internal factors as well as external factors. The internal factors like personal taste or tolerance to heat, etc., are resolved through their own effort but it is the external factors that try their patience and which could become important determinants for their developing a liking or dislike for India.

Culture and Politics in India

The political issues that the Koreans come face to face with in India often tend to bemuse them. To begin with, India, unlike Korea, is a country divided by a number of minority groups. As a result, it has never been as easy to mobilise people for a common cause as in Korea. In Korea, the entire nation comes together, be it to fight the communists or to adopt austerity measures to overcome a financial crisis, or for that matter to cheer the home team, etc. It surely happens elsewhere too, but certainly not on the scale, or to the extent to which, it does in Korea. There are certainly no social cleavages due to the caste system in Korea. The only divide in society is in the hierarchical status of people. The seemingly endless divisions in Indian society and the lack of consensus that this generates is a source of constant wonderment to Koreans. Most of them simply cannot comprehend what is going on.

Another issue relates to property rights. For example, when Korean firms invest in building factories in India, they need land. But because 60 per cent of India's people still depend on agriculture, acquiring land for industrialisation means displacing hundreds of thousands of people. While in China, this creates only an economic and management problem, in India, which is a multi-party, federal democracy, it creates a political problem as well. Political parties worry about losing votes and, therefore, tend to oppose efforts by organisations to acquire land, be it for building factories, or for special economic zones (SEZ), mining, or for that matter even for diversion of water from reservoirs, etc. Often political parties and even some NGOs with a political agenda use these opportunities to play on the caste and communal sentiments of the population to inflame one against the other. South Korea's POSCO steel plant's investment in Orissa is facing such problems in its land acquisition effort, with the rallyists constantly launching state-wide agitation. However, such agitations do not have merely a political agenda, they have an economic dimension as well because the livelihoods of the displaced persons vanish and they need to be compensated. Korea does not face such a problem as large parts of Korea are mountainous where no large-scale farming is possible. This means that it is relatively easier to acquire uninhabited land for various projects—industrial, housing or infrastructure.

The other economic aspect relates to opposition by incumbent firms, whether Indian or foreign, to allowing new firms to enter their business as they do not want more competition. This is true of not only foreign firms but also of large Indian business houses. For instance, a few years ago one of India's big business houses, Reliance launched its new business venture of setting up a chain of retail stores for fresh fruits and vegetables in all Indian cities. Even though the middle class consumers were pleased with the bargains they were getting, there was very stiff resistance by small vegetable vendors, and in many places, they resorted to vandalising Reliance outlets. In fact, in some states which are headed by left wing governments, the leaders themselves warn the central government not to set them up in their state. Resistance to the Walmart chain of stores entering India's retail market is the latest example. This kind of covert protectionism is absent in Korea and therefore, Korean firms find it hard to comprehend.

Another aspect is the Confucian practice of vesting the patriarch in a family with the fullest authority to take decisions. Although Korean firms tend to view themselves as a large family and therefore observe the Confucian ethic, in India, this does not happen because India has a different philosophical value system in which no single authority enjoys powers that cannot be questioned. For instance, when Korean firms strike a deal and have done what it takes to get the deal, they rightly expect the leaders with whom they have negotiated to take care of the hurdles or resistance that may arise from other quarters. But, in India, every person heading a small department or section within the purview of the deal is a kingpin in his own right and either exercises his power by raising objections or expects to be compensated separately. Unlike in Korea where the hierarchical power works to their advantage and prevents the lower downs from raising their head, in India each section officer is a king in his fiefdom. Therefore, when Navin Patnaik, the Chief Minister of Odisha, gave the go ahead signal to POSCO, the Koreans thought that they had won all battles. The agitators who were egged on by NGOs accused Navin Patnaik and the IAS officers with him of having accepted bribes. Thus, in a vastly pluralistic democracy like India, industrialisation cannot but be slow. India, being large and diverse, is like a big ship that can turn only slowly. This appears to Koreans as a lack of urgency and they get frustrated.

Culture and Society

Again, at places of work, misunderstandings arise because of the communication gap resulting from cultural differences in the manner of working or nuances of words or expressions. A very simple example might illustrate the point. When a Korean points to a table that has things scattered on it and says to his junior colleague 'Ch'iweora' meaning, 'clear it', as a Korean he expects the table to be not only cleared of the things on it but also those things to be put back in their places, the table to be wiped/dusted and set right. If it is an Indian who receives the instruction to clear it, he would only go to the extent of clearing away the things on it and will do nothing more. This is more because of the conditioning of the Indian mind, than due to laziness. Most Indians will confine themselves to doing only exactly what they have been instructed to do because doing anything more might result in intruding into another's domain. The deeply ingrained caste system strongly demarcates spheres of work.

In Korea, if any senior colleague admonishes a junior colleague for any work not done properly, there is no question of the junior passing on the blame to anyone else. As the person next in the line of authority, he takes full responsibility for it. He then might pull up the person immediately under him and this might go on. Indians hate taking the blame for something they think is not exactly their fault. Standing quiet even in front of authority, to an Indian mind, is like admitting to having made the mistake and therefore, he feels the need to save his face and clear his name by explaining the situation or passing the blame. This is seen as being argumentative by the Koreans and results in enraging the senior colleague, who then feels he has lost face. He then in a typically Korean style goes red in the face with anger and starts to shout. The tempo of his voice keeps rising as the Indian keeps arguing. Indians are used to being ticked off but are not used to public demonstration of fury and fire spitting. Such situations very often result in the Indian quitting his job or in some such unhappy turn of events.

Another dimension comprises the way Indians and Koreans view foreigners. As an ancient society with an extremely strong philosophical and cultural tradition, which makes the system of social beliefs very resilient, Indians do not particularly care what others think about them. In sharp contrast, the Koreans place a very high value on the way they and their country are perceived by foreigners. They thus view the Indian attitude as arrogance. The most important consequence of this difference in approach is reflected in professionalism and pride in work. Koreans are unable to understand Indians lack both these virtues, whereas Indians think that the Koreans are needlessly fussy. Overall Indians resist rapid change, which the Koreans regard as being essential to survival and prosperity.

Some Non-verbal Korean Cultural Concepts that Indians Need to be Sensitive to

(1) The concept of *punigi*. *Punigi* has been translated as 'external environment' by some western scholars. In any situation, Koreans are very particular about creating the right *punigi* or environment to achieve an objective. Therefore, I would say that the environment is more a 'created' one than an 'external' one, as defined by some westerners. It is an environment that needs intervention by the organiser or initiator of the event or occasion. Depending on what the occasion is, a befitting environment is created to elicit the right response, objective or result. In other words, it is like 'setting the stage' for the event. Although tangible things have to be got ready to create the *punigi* for any event, the non-tangible things are equally important. For instance, if it is a seminar that is being organised, then it will be necessary to ensure the right kind of room, equipments, audience will all be necessary for creating the *punigi*; however, besides these, it is ensured by the organiser, if he/she is a Korean, that the chairs are filled up as far as possible and the speaker feels encouraged. In cultural events, even the responses by the audience are to a large extent tailored or conditioned to give the right effect. Active participation is involved in creating the right *punigi*. Such effort has been seen to end in a positive result, regardless of what the situation or event is. However, for this to happen effectively, there is another element that is important called *kibun*.

(2) The concept of *kibun*. *Kibun* has been translated by some western scholars as 'good feeling' but refers more to the frame of mind. The positive aspect of it would be 'good feeling.' It is invariably used to mean creating a comfortable state of mind. In the above instance, when the environment created is favourable, then the chances of developing a good *kibun* is bright. But, on the other hand, if it is unfavourable, for instance, if the room is quite empty during a presentation or cultural event, or responses not encouraging or the equipment is not functioning, then the speaker's *kibun* is affected and his/her performance will also be

adversely affected. In other words, *punigi* and *kibun* go hand in hand for the success of any event. In the context of a negotiation or business, it is very important to ensure that good *kibun* is maintained by avoiding loss of face for either party or bearing in mind one's *che'myeon* (another cultural value in Korea that is very important and has been dealt with briefly later in the paper). Adversarial damage to *kibun* could affect not only one's mental but also physical well-being. Therefore, in Korea, one would also hear people saying *"kibun-i unchoayo"* when they are not feeling physically well. Damage to *kibun* could be caused by failure, loss of face, rudeness or disrespect, betrayal, humiliation or any such unfavourable situation. Therefore, care needs to be taken not to hurt any of these sentiments when desiring to create the right *punigi* or hoping for a positive result.

(3) The concept of *Che'myeon*. *Che'myeon* means saving face or maintaining face and refers to safeguarding one's self-esteem. This concept is of great importance to people of all cultures but it is of utmost importance in the countries of East Asia. In any situation, the aggrieved party needs to be given space to be able to manoeuvre or wriggle to save their face. In any kind of negotiation, there is some amount of give-and-take, and therefore, they need to be conducted in a manner, which leaves some space for manoeuvre for the other party to help it maintain its public face. Any compromise that needs to be made by a party could be seen as face-losing if not handled properly by the counterpart, which could be seen as gaining something in the process. Being conscious of this aspect is beneficial and would yield quite pleasant and satisfactory results during heated discussions or arguments.

(4) The concept of *nunch'i. Nuch'i Ch'aeda, or just nunch'i* for short, means the shrewdness to sense or assess the situation. Literally the expression means 'eye measure.' In any situation, the Koreans, with their *nunch'I*, are able to sense or have an inkling of either the situation or, in the case of a business deal or negotiation, the opponent's or counter-part's intention or motive. The Koreans are very sensitive to or aware of the subtleties in communication

and non-verbal cues, and through this they are able to assess the situation far better than from verbal communication. Since Korean society is a highly hierarchical one, the codes of behaviour are deeply ingrained in people, so much so that they are able to gauge what is expected of them from the non-verbal cues like body language or facial expressions and also often from the intonation or pitch of voice. Those dealing with Koreans need to be made aware of being sensitive to the situation or occasion and act accordingly. They sometimes become so engrossed in proving their point that they lose sight of what they ought to do to turn things around, and end up losing the opportunity to benefit themselves.

Besides these, there are many other cultural concepts in Korea like *jeong*, *han* etc., but I have limited myself to some concepts relevant to Indians in their place of work.

II

Cultural Differences Encountered by Indians in Korean Firms

During my current stay in Korea under the Fellowship Program of the Academy of Korean Studies (AKS), I conducted an online survey of Indians working in Korean firms here to assess the cultural differences perceived by Indians working in Korean firms and its effect on them. The study revealed a set of interesting facts.

The survey method adopted was as follows:

(1) The survey questions included multiple choice questions, rating scale questions as well as open-ended questions.

(2) Those who were invited to participate were Indians working in Korean firms in Korea.

(3) The respondents were given three week's time to send their response. They were also sent follow-up reminders.

(4) Response was received from 36 people. The analysis has been based on their response.

5. The sample included both men and women. It included workers at various levels like senior management, middle management, supervisors and employees. It also included those on a permanent appointment basis and those on temporary, contractual basis. The graphic representation of the respondents' pool is as follows:

Figure 13.1

Responses of the Participants on Some of the Questions (Sample Size: 36)

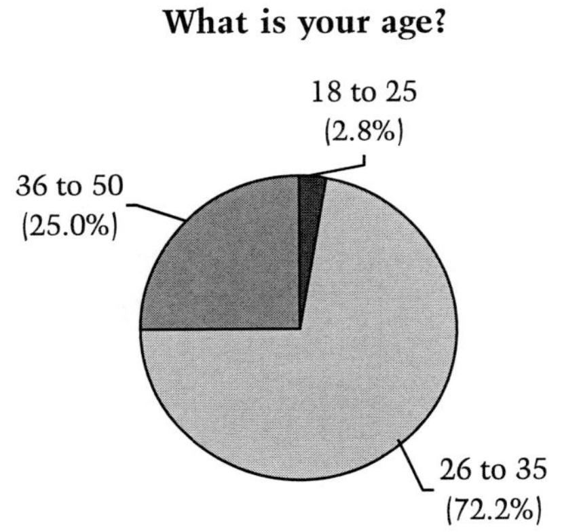

(a)

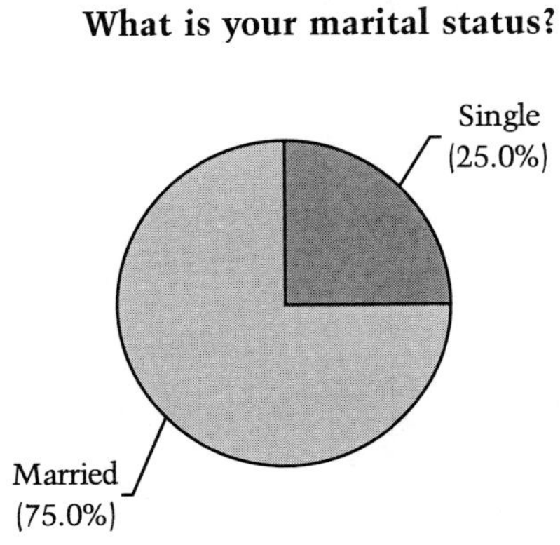

(b)

What is your gender?

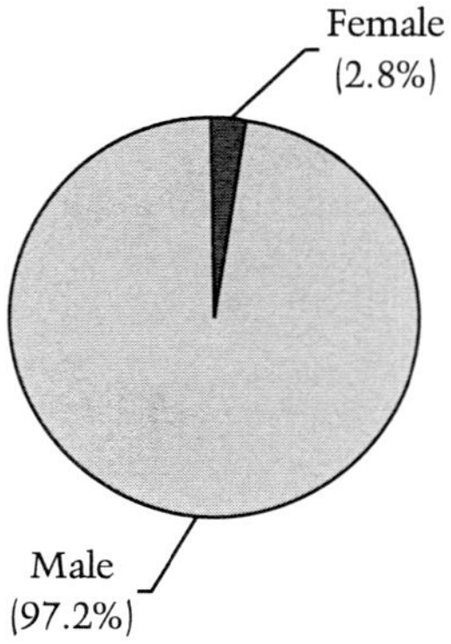

(c)

How many jobs have you held before this one?

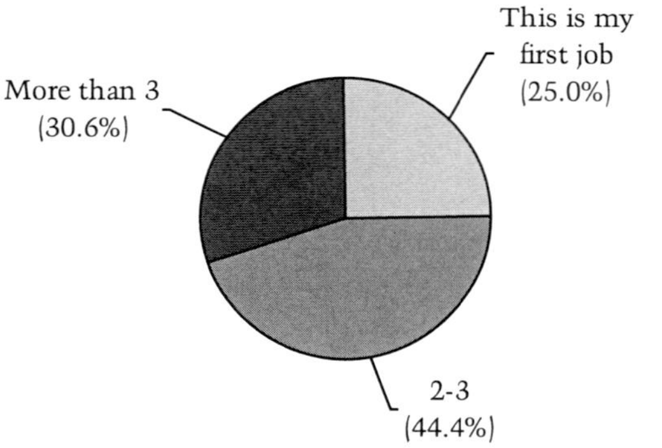

(d)

Which of the following best describes your job?

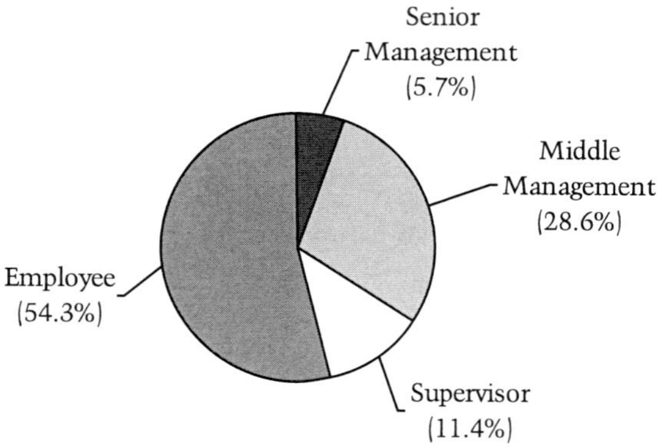

(e)

First, I present the graphic representation of the responses to some of the main questions and key issues and then a consolidated analysis.

The responses to various questions regarding attitudes to work were as follows:

Figure 13.2

Responses to Questions regarding Attitudes

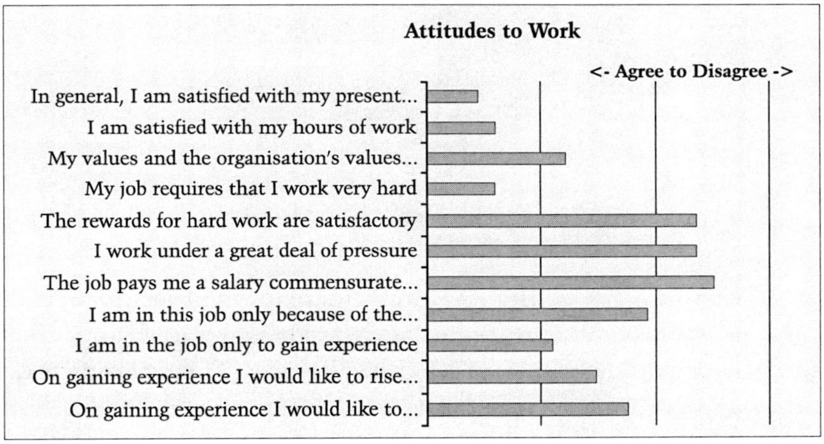

The responses reveal that by and large the respondents are happy in their present job even though the job requires them to work very hard. But, they are not happy with the rewards for hard work and feel that the salary is not commensurate with the amount of work they do. That, I suppose, would be the response of most of the people all over the world, regardless of where they work. What is most revealing is the fact that they do not feel that they are working under great pressure. It is on this aspect that their responses are different from those working in India in Korean firms as revealed in another survey conducted among Indian workers working in Korean firms in India. The responses there showed that as many as 90 per cent of them felt that they were working under a great deal of pressure. The respondents in India also showed high percentage of dissatisfaction with the hours of work, which is not the case here.

Various questions were asked to study the role of cultural differences at the place of work. Their representative response to one such question is shown in Figure 13.3.

Figure 13.3

The Instructions Given to Me at My Job are not Clear Because

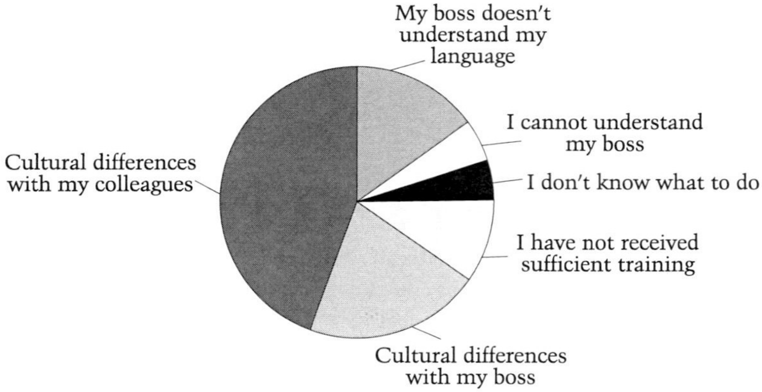

It has been found that cultural differences between people, and a lack of understanding of these, often produce unsatisfactory results, especially during the course of business dealings. This happens because both verbal and non-verbal forms of communication have a certain amount of culture-specific element, the lack of awareness of which leads to misunderstandings, delays, missed opportunities and unsatisfactory results. It must also be added that it often takes more than mere awareness to communicate effectively and arrive at satisfactory results.

The dissatisfaction or frustration, if any, for foreigners at the place of work has been usually found to be largely due to cultural differences. Although the above question does not assess the nature of the cultural differences, it nevertheless does reveal that it is because of mainly cultural differences with either the boss or colleagues that instructions are not clear to Indian workers. The other factors like language, training, etc., also play some role but the cultural factor plays the dominant role.

The next set of questions was to assess this difference in work culture. There were many multiple choice questions and some open-ended ones. I present below the response to one open-ended question which corrobarates the responses received for the multiple choice questions. The open-ended question below was to see what the respondents had learnt about Korean work culture. Their response is presented in Figure 13.4.

Figure 13.4

What I have Learnt about Korean Work Culture Includes

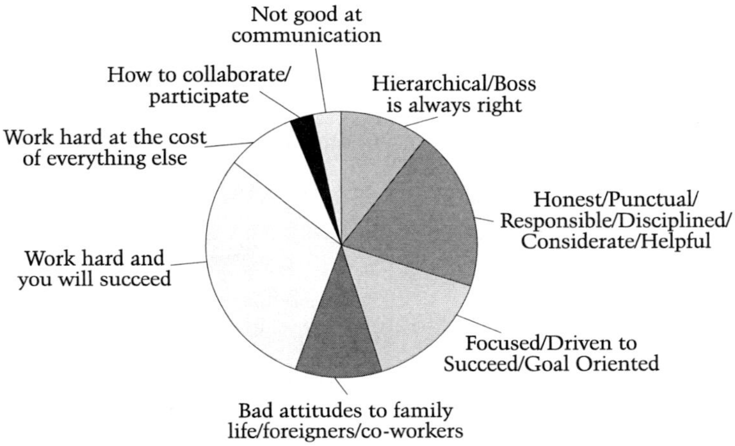

The responses reveal the following things that Indians have learnt while working here:

(1) Work precedes everything else or in other words work is supreme.

(2) They are driven to succeed and therefore focused and goal oriented, and working hard is very important to succeed.

(3) Koreans are honest workers, punctual, responsible, disciplined, considerate and helpful. They collaborate and work well as a group. However, there seems some reservation about consideration shown to family life, their attitude towards foreigners and co-workers.

(4) They are hierarchical and the boss has to be followed and can rarely be questioned.

Even though the nature of the cultural difference felt by Indians working in Korea may be different from the nature of the cultural differences felt by Indian workers in India, I would assume that this difference between the two sets of respondents would not be great as they belong to the same cultural stock.

Therefore, I use 'simple regression analysis' to determine what factors might have led to this outcome. If one were to analyse the results against the broad cultural differences observed between Indians and Koreans that manifest in the place of work, they can be categorised broadly as following.

Work Culture in Korea

(1) Formal and hierarchical. Hierarchy is sacrosanct.

(2) Result and target oriented and therefore:

  (a) working hours could extend beyond the normal hours fixed at the time of appointment;

  (b) there is no place for non-performance or non-delivery;

  (c) they appear inconsiderate and lacking in softness as there is no place for any other consideration, only head rules;

  (d) they are punctual and time conscious and meetings are held on time;

  (e) hold regular meetings and rely on regular feedbacks, reviewing, reflecting and revising are normal ways of functioning;

  (f) critical assessment has now found a place at work places in Korea.

(3) Koreans prefer working in groups. Therefore, collective responsibility taken.

(4) They prefer sticking to rules, format and norms. Therefore, there is standardisation and very little scope for deviation and at the same time, very little space for originality.

(5) They are quick at adapting to changing situations and making necessary changes. This often bemuses foreigners and gives a feeling of a constant state of flux.

Work Culture in India

(1) Comparatively less formal and less hierarchical. Or simply, hierarchy can at times be challenged. It is also not essential for juniors to stay at work until the boss leaves.

(2) More process oriented than target oriented and therefore less professional. Therefore:

(a) normally stick to working hours specified at the time of appointment;

(b) a lot of adjustments are made for non-performance and non-delivery, intention plays a major role;

(c) all other considerations too find space at the work place, both head and heart rule;

(d) a very flexible concept of time therefore no major tensions;

(e) meetings are usually treated as get-togethers for a cup of tea, feedback meetings are rarely held;

(f) criticism is often avoided or either left unsaid or is garbed to lessen the impact.

3. Quite individualistic but hate taking blame, and hate taking responsibility. Find extraneous reasons as excuses.

4. Very contextual rules that can be bent to make adjustments; a lot of scope for intuitive working.

5. By and large like to stick to well-trodden ways of doing things, maybe with minor modifications at times.

However, because of the advent of globalisation and because of employees working across borders, work culture all over the world has become quite uniform. Even so, each country has its own values and beliefs, which affect people's behaviour. Although India and Korea both belong to the Orient and have a lot of cultural similarities, their work cultures show some marked differences as seen above. These could be explained in the following way.

Korea being an export-oriented country has had to meet deadlines and global standards. These demands have required the Koreans to become a more professional, time-oriented and rule-based society. The presentation of products is also professional. On the other hand, Confucianism is still so deeply ingrained in society that they remain hierarchical and prefer working as a group or collectively. Any form of questioning by juniors is misconstrued as insolence. Korea, therefore, shows some social cultural values that are oriental but has had to adopt a western work culture to be able to compete in the global market. One observes a mix of both in their work culture.

On the other hand, export is only a small percentage of the Indian market. Indians are, therefore, still quite laid back about deadlines or targets. There is little standardisation of products because these are produced by a very large number of small- and medium-scale enterprises. They lack professionalism. As mentioned earlier, Indians do not seem particularly concerned about what the world thinks of them. They would rather concern themselves with ethics, morality, intentions, etc., or on immediate gains. Indians are also individualistic and, therefore, questioning is a natural part of their nature. However, one must add that there is a section in India that has to deal with the global market and is, therefore, changing fast.

The reason why the ratings of 'feeling the pressure of work' or 'feeling the pressure of long-hours of work' of Indians working in Korean firms in India and those working in Korea are different can be explained as follows. The workers anywhere have to comply with the pressures of the society they are working in. For instance, Indians working in Korean firms in India are caught in the pressures of Indian society, even though at the place of work they have to comply with the Korean ways of functioning, timing, etc. In India, private life often co-exists with official life and could make some demands on a working person, which is unthinkable in a Korean working environment. In India, family life also plays a crucial role and spouses/ families do not like work time intruding into family time. So those Indians who are working in Korean firms in India are caught in the crossfire. Indians working in Korea do not face such pressures because society itself is geared towards working long hours. The families are also attuned to this and are more understanding because this is the norm. The Indians in Korea can also function without their private lives intruding into their office hours.

I conclude with a quote by a Korean scholar who had said it in a different context but which seems to fit perfectly in the context of India and Korea: "Koreans are very good at pursuing and accomplishing conspicuous and tangible projects, rather than setting up long-term goals that are uncertain and nebulous."